CYBERBULLYING

What Counselors Need to Know

D1258731

• Sheri Bauman •

AMERICAN
COUNSELING ASSOCIATION
5999 Stevenson Avenue
Alexandria, VA 22304
www.counseling.org

CYBERBULLYING
What Counselors Need to Know

10   9   8   7   6   5   4   3   2   1

American Counseling Association
5999 Stevenson Avenue
Alexandria, VA 22304

Director of Publications Carolyn C. Baker

Production Manager Bonny E. Gaston

Editorial Assistant Catherine A. Brumley

Copy Editor Kimberly W. Kinne

Text and cover design by Bonny E. Gaston

Library of Congress Cataloging-in-Publication Data
Bauman, Sheri.
    Cyberbullying : what counselors need to know/Sheri Bauman.
        p. cm.
    Includes bibliographical references.
    ISBN 978-1-55620-294-0 (alk. paper)
    1. Cyberbullying. 2. Cyberbullying—Case studies. 3. Bullying.
I. Title.
    HV6773.B38 2010
    371.5'8—dc22   2010015303

DEDICATION

This book is dedicated to my husband, Bob, whose love and support make all things possible.

• • •

Just as steel can be used to build hospitals or machine guns, or nuclear power can either energize a city or destroy it, modern information networks and the technologies they support can be harnessed for good or for ill.

—Hillary Clinton, January 21, 2010

CONTENTS

Contents

PREFACE

I wrote this book to share with counselors and others in the helping professions what I have learned and experienced in my efforts to understand cyberbullying and its effects on individuals and groups. I hope that counselors in all settings recognize the importance of communication via technology and the potential for harm that accompanies the recent reliance on these forms of communication. In this book, I provide background information and practical recommendations so that counselors may be more effective in combating the problems that result from cyberbullying. Many counselors use technological communication in their work and personal lives; the ways in which these same tools are used by cyberbullies to cause harm may not be as well known. Counselors are likely to see clients whose lives are lived in a technological context; my purpose in this book is to equip counselors with knowledge and options to be most effective in their work.

Although counselors are the primary audience, psychologists, social workers, teachers, and parents will also benefit from the information and suggestions I provide. It is important that all helpers be familiar with cyberbullying and have strategies both to combat the problem and to assist individuals who are involved or concerned.

In recent years, I have been repeatedly horrified and alarmed by the examples of cyberbullying I have read about or heard about from my students, clients, and audiences; new incidents seem to arise daily. Although schools are familiar with bullying in general and are becoming more informed about cyberbullying, too many adults assume this is a problem that affects only adolescents. Adults who are victimized may be completely blindsided and uncertain about how or where to get help and support.

The damage inflicted by a cyberbully can be devastating. Thus, it is important for counselors to know enough about cyberbullying to have meaningful conversations with clients and to know how to provide appropriate support and treatment when necessary. In a focus group I held with a group of high school students, the participants (juniors and seniors) told me they would never tell an adult if they were cyberbullied because they believe that adults would not even know what they were talking about. They shared many examples of how ill-informed and unaware adults are about their technological world, which they all found quite amusing. The purpose of this book is to ensure that adults in the counseling profession are not among those benignly ignorant adults who do not speak the language of technology.

I include examples throughout the book. Those cases that have received media attention are presented with real names of participants, as these are available in the public record. Other examples that are drawn either from my own personal experience or from others who have shared those experiences with me are well-disguised to protect the privacy of those individuals. Although I have altered anything that might lead to revealing the identity of the source, I have made sure that the cyberbullying actions are described in a way that is faithful to the original incident. I also provide visual illustrations. Some of these illustrations have been created for the purpose of this book because using actual examples would compromise the privacy of other people. Others have come directly from the Internet. I have been careful to distinguish the "real" images from those that were created for the book.

There are many excellent books on conventional bullying that cover bullying in schools and bullying in the workplace. I do not repeat that information here. However, because cyberbullying is such a new phenomenon and information about conventional bullying may inform and have implications for cyberbullying, I refer to that body of knowledge to enrich the discussion.

Counselors, by virtue of their role in both the prevention and remediation of problems, are in a unique position to have an impact on preventing and reducing the harm from cyberbullying. I have written this book to provide essential information for counselors so they may be more effective in their work with adults and youths who are affected by cyberbullying. I also hope that the book will inspire counselors to take a more active role in prevention and advocacy to encourage institutions and society to take bolder steps to limit the harmful consequences of the misuse of technology.

Overview of the Book

Each chapter in the book focuses on a specific aspect of cyberbullying, and each concludes with a summary of the major points covered. The book begins with an introductory chapter that sets the stage by providing background and historical information and giving examples to illustrate the kinds of situations that have occurred. I then review what is known about the prevalence of cyberbullying and summarize the research that has been conducted so far. This research review presents what is known about cyberbullying in general terms. A more extensive summary of research is given in the Appendix for readers who are interested in more detail about the empirical studies.

In Chapter 2, I provide background information about conventional bullying and discuss the ways in which cyberbullying is different. There are many similarities between both forms of bullying, but there are also ways in which cyberbullying is unique—ways in which harm may be amplified.

Chapter 3 reviews cyberenvironments, that is, the various electronic or technological contexts in which cyberbullying takes place. Many of these contexts may be familiar to readers, but others will be less so. Understanding where and how cyberbullying occurs provides strategic information for counselors when considering how to intervene. I then describe, in Chapter 4, the types of cyberbullying. Just as conventional bullying can be perpetrated in more than one way (physical, verbal, and social), so cyberbullying can take various forms, and each form has particular features that are appropriated by cyberbullies.

Because both bullying and cyberbullying are types of aggressive behavior, Chapter 5 provides an overview of the most prominent theories of aggressive behavior. These theories provide a framework for thinking about all forms of bullying and are important when considering how to prevent or intervene in these behaviors. In Chapter 6, I examine the ways cyberbullying manifests and affects individuals at different developmental ages and life stages. I point out developmental characteristics that may be related to how cyberbullying impacts particular age groups. In Chapter 7, I outline several general strategies to reduce cyberbullying, including the use of technology to prevent, rather than to inflict, cyberbullying.

In Chapter 8, I describe various types of responses to cyberbullying, including both technological remedies and legislation that has been enacted and proposed to curb it. There are also ways that one can apply the very technology used in cyberbullying as a way to respond to cyberbullying; I discuss such techniques in this chapter.

Chapter 9 provides information about a variety of counseling approaches that are useful in dealing with incidents of cyberbullying. Counselors already may be familiar with many of these approaches, but their application to bullying and cyberbullying is not as widely known. Several of these strategies are commonly used in other countries but are less familiar to a U.S. audience. Having a choice of approaches allows the counselor to tailor the response to the particular situation.

Chapter 10 looks more closely at cyberbullying among adults. Although the focus in much of the book is on children and adolescents, cyberbullying also happens among adults and in the workplace. Adults may not recognize their experience as cyberbullying; sensitive counselors can help them understand their experience and assist them in deciding on the most appropriate response.

Chapter 11 focuses on the broader roles of counselors: being an advocate, training and consulting, and counseling victims of cyberbullying as well as counseling the cyberbully. In this chapter, I also review some ethical dilemmas that counselors may face when working in the area of cyberbullying. Although cyberbullying is a recent phenomenon and there are no specific ethical guidelines to follow, the ethical codes of our profession do provide standards that can be applied to cyberbullying and the use of communications technology.

In Chapter 12, I describe numerous resources that are available to counselors for additional or more specific information. Many of the websites are constantly updated with current information, so they are important sources of new and accurate material. The Appendix lists all research published or available at the time of this writing, with information about the sample, most important findings, and limitations.

I hope that counselors find this book to be a valuable resource. There is every sign that communications technology will continue to be ubiquitous in the future, which means that cyberbullying is likely to increase with time. As new technological innovations provide new weapons for cyberbullies' arsenals, cyberbullying is likely to endure. Counselors have such crucial roles to play in reducing the harm from this problem, and I want to raise awareness, impart information, and recommend a variety of tools and strategies to increase counselors' efficacy in this domain.

ACKNOWLEDGMENTS

I wish to acknowledge the many individuals who have shared their stories with me and helped me become technologically literate. I owe special thanks to Jason Sample, who several years ago introduced me to the world of social networking via MySpace and to texting. Lindsay Holbrook keeps me informed and frequently sends me current information that I might miss otherwise. I appreciate Tanisha Tatum's research work on young children's websites and her help constructing visual examples to illustrate some concepts for the book. I am indebted to my husband, Bob, for his patience and support, and I thank him especially for his feedback on an earlier draft of this book. I am grateful to Drs. Jina Yoon and Justin Patchin for their very helpful reviews of a previous draft of the manuscript. Finally, I appreciate Carolyn Baker and the Publications Department at the American Counseling Association (ACA) for supporting this effort.

ABOUT THE AUTHOR

Dr. Sheri Bauman is an associate professor and director of the School Counseling master's degree program at the University of Arizona. Prior to earning her doctorate in 1999, Dr. Bauman worked in public schools for 30 years, 18 of those as a school counselor. She is a licensed psychologist, and until recently she maintained a small private practice in Las Cruces, New Mexico.

Dr. Bauman teaches in the master's program and conducts research on bullying and cyberbullying, professional issues in school counseling, and group work. In July 2007, she became editor of the *Journal for Specialists in Group Work*. She is a member of the editorial board for *Professional School Counseling* and is an ad hoc reviewer for a number of scholarly journals. She writes a quarterly column for *Counseling Today* called "Spotlight on Journals."

Dr. Bauman is involved in many professional organizations, with current memberships in the American Counseling Association, American School Counselor Association, Association for Multicultural Counseling and Development, Association for Specialists in Group Work, Society for Research on Adolescence, and Society for Research on Child Development. She has given presentations on topics related to bullying at state, national, and international conferences, including a presentation on cyberbullying at the National Coalition Against Bullying conference in Melbourne, Australia, in November 2007. Her book *Current Topics for Helping Professionals* was published in August 2007. Her vita lists numerous publications in peer-reviewed journals.

Dr. Bauman lives in Las Cruces, New Mexico, with her husband and two spoiled golden retrievers. She travels to Tucson every week to her office at the University of Arizona.

CHAPTER 1

Introduction

Access to technological communication in the United States is widespread and growing. Different sources have slightly different data, but the lowest rate I found is that almost 75% of the U.S. population used the Internet as of June 30, 2009 ("Internet World Stats," 2009). The United States is also one of nine countries in which there is Internet access in 100% of schools. Currently, Internet usage declines as age increases, but 40% of Americans age 66 and older go online (Annenberg School of Communication, 2009). In fact, the greatest increase in Internet use from 2005 to 2009 was in the 70- to 75-year-old age group: In 2005, 26% were online, and in 2009, 45% were (Jones & Fox, 2009). The Center for the Digital Future also reported that the average Internet user now spends 17 hours per week online, with heavy users averaging 42 hours per week (Annenberg School of Communication, 2009). Twenty-four percent of U.S. households have three or more computers. As of the end of 2008, approximately 84% of the U.S. population had cell phone service (Reardon, 2008), with some industry experts predicting 100% access by 2013 (Malik, 2007). In addition, 20% of households now rely on cell phones exclusively ("Wireless Quick Facts," 2009). With the increase in the use of smart phones, the distinction between Internet and cell phone activities is disappearing.

The popular media has raised public awareness of the dangers of these technological communication tools by publicizing sensational examples and extreme cases with tragic outcomes. Although these cases illustrate many aspects of cyberbullying, which is an increasing and serious problem, it is important to keep in mind that there are many positive aspects of technological communication. My focus in this book is on cyberbullying—clearly a negative element—but I caution readers not to assume that I am discouraging the use of digital communication tools. I am an enthusiastic user of technology. The purpose of the book is to inform counselors about cyberbullying so that they will be in the best position both to assist clients who experience this behavior and to proactively educate their communities about strategies to ensure that these exciting technological tools are used in the most productive manner.

Definition

The term *cyberbullying* has yet to be included in a dictionary, but people often hear (and use) the term. According to Bill Belsey, the developer of the website www.cyberbullying.ca, which was launched in 2003, he was the first to use and define this term. Belsey said (personal communication, November 6, 2009) that he was moderating a website dedicated to bullying prevention; on this website, youths were describing being bullied online. To describe this behavior, Belsey coined the term *cyberbullying*, which was based on the term *cyberspace* (a term Belsey indicated was coined by Canadian science fiction author William Gibson). Belsey is credited in many articles (e.g., Aricak et al., 2008; Campbell, 2005; Li, 2007a) as the originator of the term. However, according to the new word team at the *Oxford English Dictionary*, the first use of the term was by Christopher Bantick in an article in the *Canberra (Australia) Times* on November 18, 1998 (M. Charlton, personal communication, October 27, 2009). Bantick (personal communication, November 8, 2009) indicated that in his article, he was describing research in which the term had been used, but he was unable to locate his notes about the study in question. Thanks to able library sleuths at my university, the earliest use of the term was revealed to be in a 1995 *New York Times* article on cyberaddiction (O'Neill, 1995). Although there may be other, earlier uses that haven't yet been detected, it is safe to assume the term was "created" spontaneously by several users, and the emergence of numerous *cyber-* compounds in the lexicon meant the meaning was obvious from the context.

Belsey (2008) defined the term *cyberbullying* this way: "Cyberbullying involves the use of information and communication technologies to support deliberate, repeated, and hostile behaviour by an individual or group that is intended to harm others" (para. 1). A concise definition was also provided by Patchin and Hinduja (2006), who described it as "willful and repeated harm inflicted through the medium of electronic text" (p. 152), but that definition omits images and video, which have become popular means by which to cyberbully. A revised definition presented in a later paper added "through the use of computers, cell phones, and other electronic devices" to the definition (Burgess-Proctor, Hinduja, & Patchin, 2009, p. 1). Stutsky (2006) offered this definition: "Cyberbullying is the use of modern communication technologies to embarrass, humiliate, threaten, or intimidate an individual in the attempt to gain power and control over them" (para. 1).

Burgess-Proctor et al. (2009) made a distinction between cyberbullying and online harassment, which they described as "less insidious" (p. 1). In their study of 3,141 females who responded to a survey advertised through websites, Burgess-Proctor et al. found that the two behaviors most often reported were being ignored and being disrespected (45.8% and 42.9%, respectively). The authors described these experiences as "mild" and labeled them "online harassment," in contrast to cyberbullying, a label they reserved to describe the experience of being threatened (11.2%). I respectfully disagree with this distinction for several reasons. First, the term *harassment* has legal implications and is inappropriately used. (I discuss this topic in more detail later in this chapter.) Second, with all bullying behaviors, there is a range of severity from mild to severe, and I think it is a matter of degree of severity rather than nomenclature. Furthermore, it is challenging to determine the severity level of a particular incident without considering the victim's perception and reaction. What seems mild to an observer might be otherwise to the recipient of the behavior. This difference in perception is important for counselors to consider when working with those who are involved in cyberbullying; that is, the response of the victim is the determinant of severity and impact. A perpetrator may justify his or her actions by thinking they are trivial or humorous, but if the recipient is hurt, that is the measure of impact that matters.

A definition of cyberbullying that more closely parallels the standard definition of conventional bullying was proposed by Smith, Mahdavi, Carvalho, and Tippett (2006): "Cyberbullying therefore can be defined as an aggressive, intentional act, carried out by a group or individual, using electronic forms of contact, repeatedly and over time, against a victim who cannot easily defend him or herself" (p. 6).

The term *cyberbullying* implies that these behaviors are a variation on, or extension of, the conventional types of bullying: physical, verbal, and social–relational bullying. I am not convinced that the term is the best one to describe the actions included under this umbrella term (e.g., cruel text messages, forwarding electronic mail [e-mails] or photos without permission, creating websites for the purpose of collecting negative comments about an individual). The defining characteristics of face-to-face bullying are (a) that it is intentionally harmful aggressive behavior, (b) that it is repeated, and (c) that it is directed toward a target who is unable to defend against the aggression. So, bullying implies intention. What if someone accidentally sends information intended for an individual to a group (such as an electronic mailing list) by inadvertently clicking on *Reply All* instead of *Reply* in an e-mail message? The information that was intended to be private is now known to a sometimes large group of people, and that information can be embarrassing or harmful. Would this be called cyberbullying even though it was not intentional? What about two peers (friends or coworkers) who engage in an online spat using one of the technological methods available— e-mail, instant messaging (IM), a blog, social networking? Assume that each one is sending mean or cruel messages that are reciprocated by the other, occurring several times over the duration of the conflict. Is this cyberbullying, even though the imbalance of power is not present? And what about a single incident, which does not meet the criterion of repetition? What about posting a humiliating photo on a webpage? The act of posting the photo is singular, but the number of viewers is potentially enormous. Does this qualify as cyberbullying? I believe we have yet to define this term with any precision, but it is used so widely that creating a different term for this book does not seem prudent.

Many measures of cyberbullying list specific behaviors (e.g., "I received mean text messages" or "Someone posted an embarrassing photo of me online without my permission") that, taken out of context, might mislabel a behavior as cyberbullying. I recently posted a photo of myself and a long-time friend that was taken when we were both gawky preteenagers. I did not request the friend's permission. The photo could be construed as embarrassing, so I suppose that my behavior could be categorized as cyberbullying, but I don't think most readers would categorize it as such. In addition, some restrict the definition of cyberbullying to children (e.g., Kerkhof, 2009), whereas others extend the meaning to include adults

I suspect that scholars will eventually refine the definition or change the terminology so that it is more precise and clear. In this book, I use the term *cyberbullying* to refer to actions using information and communication technology to harm another person. Thus, I include both actions that may not have been deliberate but that cause harm nevertheless and individual incidents that can reach a wide audience; I do not take into consideration the power differential between the bully and the target. It is certainly true that much of cyberbullying is perpetrated by more powerful individuals against those with lower status, but that is not necessarily a defining attribute as it is in conventional bullying.

An important distinction must be made between bullying (including cyberbullying) and harassment. Bullying is the abuse of power as described above. *Harassment* is a legal term that describes hostile behavior toward someone with legally protected status, such as religion, age, gender, race, or disability (e.g., see Appel, 2009). Stein (2003) discussed the danger of subsuming harassment under the broad category of bullying; harassment is against federal law, whereas bullying is generally a violation of school policy (see Chapter 8 for more detailed discussion of this distinction). Both harassment and bullying can be perpetrated via electronic communication methods, but the key distinction is the basis for the mistreatment. If the action is directed toward a person in a legally protected category, then harassment is the more accurate—and actionable—label.

Well-Known Cases

Several incidents of cyberbullying have become public knowledge because of broad coverage by the popular media. They are illustrative of the types of cyberbullying that have occurred—and the potential devastation that can result—and also provide information regarding possible legal ramifications. Although some of these incidents received notoriety because they ultimately led to the suicide of the victim, I want to be clear that the decision to take one's life is not the result of a single event; rather, an event may overwhelm a vulnerable individual who generally has other risk factors for suicidal behavior.

The Star Wars Kid

The first case of cyberbullying to gain widespread attention occurred in 2002. An overweight teenage boy from Quebec, Canada, made a 2-minute video of himself practicing Star Wars–like moves with a "light saber" (actually, a golf ball retriever). Gyslain Raza's private video, which was made in his high school studio, was found by another student and then uploaded to the website Kazaa without Gyslain's knowledge or permission ("Star Wars Kid Files Lawsuit," 2003). The video was eventually viewed more than 900 million times and was the single most widely viewed online video of 2003 (BBC News, 2006); Gyslain became known as the "Star Wars Kid." After the initial video was posted, edited versions (with music, lights, and other effects) were also posted, and the number of mocking comments the videos generated was enormous. The taunting about the video that he received at school was so extreme that Gyslain eventually dropped out of school and received psychiatric care. His parents eventually sued the families of four classmates who were responsible for posting the original video, claiming that the ongoing harassment caused severe psychological harm. The case was settled out of court. Because the case was not heard in a court of law, one is left to wonder how a jury or judge might have ruled. The offense in this case was "harassment." This case highlights how easily material can be disseminated to infinite audiences. Once the offenders in this case obtained the video, it was an easy task to upload it (and alter it with so-called enhancements to further humiliate the victim), making it available to the world. The importance of keeping one's data and material private cannot be overstated.

Megan Meier

Arguably the best known case of cyberbullying in the United States is that of Megan Meier, a 13-year-old girl in Missouri. Megan had been bullied throughout her school career. With the reluctant approval of her mother, Megan joined MySpace, a popular social networking site, presumably to meet and interact with other youths. It is important to note that MySpace restricts membership to persons over the age of 14, but age is determined by the birth date provided by the user. Megan formed an online friendship—soon romance—with a boy named Josh Evans, whose attentions delighted Megan. After about 6 months of pleasant exchanges, Josh sent hurtful and mean comments to Megan (including the oft-quoted, "The world would be better off without you"), and as Megan became increasingly upset, her mother, sitting with her by the computer, insisted she sign off. When Megan did not, her mother was irritated and scolded Megan for ignoring her instructions. Megan rushed upstairs to her room, where her mother later found Megan hanging by a belt in her closet. Attempts to save her failed, and Megan died the next day. Her parents, distraught by the suicide, eventually attempted to locate Josh Evans to tell him of the damage he had done. However, Josh Evans's MySpace page had been removed. The Meiers discovered that Josh Evans was not a real individual but a fictitious persona created by a neighbor who was the mother of one of Megan's sometime friends. The mother, Lori Drew, apparently thought the fictitious Josh's page (created by a 19-year-old family friend, Ashley Grills, and Lori's own daughter) would be a way to find out what Megan was saying about the Drew daughter. When the interaction became tedious, the nasty exchange was, according to Ashley Grills, an attempt to anger Megan so that she would no longer want to communicate with Josh and they could end the charade. During court proceedings, the prosecutor revealed that Megan's response to the "better off without you" comment was "you are the kind of boy a girl would kill herself over" (San Miguel, 2008). This case might never have achieved the notoriety that has surrounded it had Megan reacted differently. Her parents attempted to use the legal system to respond to Lori, but they soon learned that there were no laws in their community that applied. They eventually filed in California (where MySpace headquarters are), with the prosecutor using a law—the Computer Fraud and Abuse Act of 1986—that was designed to apply to hackers. Rather than the felonies she was originally charged with, Lori Drew was eventually convicted of a misdemeanor, based on her violation of the Terms of Service Agreement with MySpace. The agreement that one must endorse in order to set up a MySpace account includes a prohibition against content that "harasses or advocates harassment of another person." Sentencing was scheduled for May 2009, but the judge delayed that phase of the proceedings in order to study the legal basis for the case more closely. On August 31, 2009, the judge dismissed all charges against Lori Drew. Judge Wu commented that prosecuting anyone who violated a website's terms of service would be unconstitutional and noted that his ruling referred to the misapplication of the legislation. Federal prosecutors have decided not to appeal the judge's ruling. Readers interested in accessing the legal documents in this case will find a wealth of additional details at *United States v. Drew* (2008).

It is important that counselors keep in mind that however thoughtless Lori Drew's actions may have been, a suicide is not "caused" by one event. First, Megan responded to what she thought was a rejection by an age-appropriate suitor. This rejection could have happened as she believed, or it could have occurred in a face-to-face relationship. Relationships are often ended by one party to the chagrin of the other. Although some rejected persons may contemplate (or commit) suicide, those individuals bring other vulnerabilities to the situation; many who are spurned grieve the loss and go on with their lives. In Megan's case, she had been bullied for many years, and she lacked confidence and self-esteem. She had also joined MySpace (with her mother's knowledge) by falsifying her age. The more salient issue here is that all users need to know that people met online may or may not be who they claim to be, and extreme caution should be the norm in such encounters.

Aaron White

Another Internet prank gone awry is the 2006 case of Aaron White, a 19-year-old African American man (Chun, n.d.). The available information is based on Aaron White's testimony. A threatening message that ostensibly came from Aaron White's MySpace page was received by a girl, who told her friend Daniel Cicciaro, age 17, about the message. After the tragic events unfolded, a friend of Aaron's, Michael Longo, confessed that he had gotten into Aaron's MySpace page and sent the message (which threatened to rape the girl) as a joke. At a party attended by Daniel and the girl in addition to Aaron White, Daniel became angry and asked Aaron to leave the party. After Aaron left, Daniel and another male friend of his phoned Aaron on his cell phone, demanding that he return to the party and using a racial epithet. Aaron said that the threatening calls continued and included a statement that Daniel and his friends were coming to Aaron's house to kill him. Aaron then woke his father, who got a handgun. Daniel and four other males (none apparently armed) arrived at Aaron's house at about 11:00 p.m. Aaron and his father, both armed, were waiting, and an angry verbal exchange occurred. Aaron's father, John White, told the boys to leave, and then, according to police, John White shot and killed Daniel at close range.

John White's attorneys argued in court that Mr. White believed that the boys were there to commit the racially motivated murder of his son. The Cicciaros contended that Mr. White did not call 9-1-1 and had not called the police between the time he was informed of the threat and the arrival of the boys at his home. John White was convicted of second-degree manslaughter and was sentenced to 2 to 4 years in prison.

This case is an example of the many risks involved in electronic communication. First, a friend sent the message to the girl using Aaron's account. Sharing passwords with friends is a common practice among youths—and a very foolish one. Whether a person's intent is malicious or otherwise, once that person has access to your accounts, you no longer have personal control. Second, the absence of nonverbal clues makes it difficult to know when someone is joking. Misinterpretation of such communication is not unusual; care in using what is intended to be sarcasm or a joke must be exercised at all times.

Ryan Halligan

Ryan Halligan's story is told by his parents in a moving video (*Remembering Ryan Halligan video*, 2009), and the details of this boy's experience are also recounted elsewhere ("Cyberbullying: The Ryan Halligan Story," 2009). This case illustrates how face-to-face and technological bullying can be combined to torment a young boy. His parents describe Ryan as having a great personality, although he did not excel in academics or sports and received special education services until fifth grade. The Halligans say that he had been bullied at school starting in about fifth grade. He told his parents, who obtained professional counseling for Ryan and also taught Ryan some self-defense. Although the bullying was intermittent for the next few years, Ryan seemed to be managing better. In seventh grade, Ryan told his parents he hated his school and asked to move or be home schooled. His parents later learned that he was receiving cruel e-mails accusing him of being gay, and a rumor to that effect was spread technologically around the school, where additional taunting occurred. Ryan was miserable. Then Ryan began chatting online with a girl at school that he liked, and he was very encouraged. He hoped that she would become his girlfriend and that would dispel the rumor about homosexuality. Apparently, after many chats online, Ryan approached the girl at school, and in front of a group of her friends she told him he was a loser and their friendly chats were all a joke. Within a month, on October 7, 2003, Ryan had hanged himself in his room. His father has since dedicated himself to being an activist against bullying and cyberbullying in Ryan's memory.

Ryan's case is an example of the vulnerability of youths with any disabilities. Ryan's learning disabilities may have increased his risk for being targeted. In this case, although Ryan knew the girl in person, he did not detect her malicious intent in engaging him in encouraging online chats. The online conversation then triggered an in-person interaction that increased Ryan's humiliation and exceeded his ability to cope with his social ostracism.

Sexting and Cyberbullying

Jesse Logan

Jesse Logan's case involved the increasingly common practice of *sexting*, sending nude or provocative photos via cell phone or the Internet. Eighteen-year-old Jesse had sent nude pictures of herself to her boyfriend, who sent them by e-mail to other girls at their high school after he and Jesse broke up (Celizic, 2009). The girls reportedly called Jesse a "slut" and "whore," harassed her verbally, and even threw objects at her. Jesse's mother learned from the school that Jesse was skipping school but did not know the cause. Jesse's mother notified the school of the problem, but according to Ms. Logan, their response was inadequate. Ms. Logan suggested that she and Jesse contact the parents of the girls involved, but Jesse feared being ridiculed even more should she take that step. She finally decided that the best strategy was to go public with her story. Jesse told her story on a Cincinnati television interview to alert other young girls to the dangers of this practice. But 2 months later, she hanged herself in her room. Ms. Logan is attempting to hold school officials responsible, but at the time of this writing, she has not been successful. No charges were filed against Jesse's 19-year-old boyfriend, who had sent the photo.

Hope Witsell

Another case more recently became the second known suicide related to sexting. Hope Witsell, a 13-year-old seventh grader, hanged herself after a topless photo she sent to a boy was intercepted and circulated around the school (Inbar, 2009). She was taunted repeatedly at school, and at the end of the year, school officials informed Hope and her parents that she would be suspended for the first week of the next school year because of the disturbance the photo created. Unfortunately, Hope sent another photo of her breasts to boys at a summer convention of Future Farmers of America (FFA). At school in the fall, Hope was told she could no longer serve as an FFA advisor. She hanged herself on September 12, 2009.

Phillip Alpert

The other side of the sexting problem is illustrated by the case of Phillip Alpert, who was 18 years old at the time the events that changed his life took place (Feyerick & Steffen, 2009). After an argument with his 16-year-old girlfriend, Phillip forwarded nude photos of her (which she had sent him) to her family and friends. Phillip was charged and convicted of sending child pornography, a felony. He pleaded no contest but was convicted as charged and received a sentence of 5 years probation—and is required to register as a sex offender until he is 43 years old. This case, among others, has fueled a heated debate about whether this conviction served justice and protected society. It is likely that people will read much more about this form of cyberbullying, because a January 2009 report revealed that 20% of teens participating in a national survey said they engaged in sexting; that survey also found that 11% of girls ages 13 to 16 said they had done so (National Campaign to Prevent Teen and Unplanned Pregnancy, 2009).

Sexting is an increasingly widespread behavior among teens and young adults. One survey reported that about a quarter of teenagers and a third of young adults indicated they had engaged in this practice (Associated Press, 2009). Despite efforts by adults to discourage this behavior, it continues to proliferate. The thinking of those who engage in this practice may be influenced by an adolescent sense of invulnerability. They know there is some risk, but they tell themselves, "That will never happen to me."

Two Unpublicized Examples

Examples are provided throughout the book to illustrate types of cyberbullying, but the two examples that follow are examples of actual incidents that illustrate common cyberbullying strategies. An overweight high school student was advised by a friend to check out a particular website. On it, she found a photo of a hippopotamus with her face. The pranksters (cyberbullies?) had used the popular software Photoshop to alter a photo by superimposing the student's face on the hippo's body. Before the victim saw the photo, many other students at the school had viewed it. This particular incident illustrates the ways in which technology can be used not only to make private images public but also to alter images for nefarious purposes. What is interesting about this case is the response of the victim. When she saw the website with the photo, she laughed and made some observations about the flaws in the technique used to superimpose the photo. The bullies were deprived of the reaction they expected (shock, distress), and the interest in the website rapidly waned.

In another case, a website was created with a very insulting (some would say obscene) title using the target's nickname. The nickname was not a friendly one or one used by friends; rather, it was a derogatory insult that a group of students used to taunt the victim. On the site, many viewers made disparaging comments about the target. Again, after a period of time during which the cruel comments accumulated, the target received an e-mail suggesting he might want to look at the site. This incident reminds me of the slam book of my adolescence (a notebook in which each page was headed with someone's name and on which everyone wrote derogatory comments), but the number of views and comments is vastly increased by the electronic format. As in the previous case, the victim in this case said he was not interested in the comments and actions of such mean-spirited people and did not otherwise react. He emphasized that he did not continually revisit the site (as have many victims) because it was not in his best interest to do so.

The Digital Divide

At one time, the term *generation gap* was commonly used to describe the divisions between young people and their parents' generation. Although differences among generations have likely always existed, modern generations have experienced more rapid cultural shifts, and so these differences are magnified—and deserving of a term to describe it. The term *digital divide* can refer to the differences in access to the Internet and other technology between socioeconomic groups and countries, and it has also been used to describe the differences in the way technology is used by so-called digital natives versus so-called digital immigrants (Prensky, 2001). Digital natives are those persons through college age who have always had technology available and who speak the language of technology fluently. Most digital immigrants use technology as a tool; digital natives live in a technological world. Their social lives are conducted technologically; they are always connected. Most middle-aged and older adults are digital immigrants: They have learned to use technology later in life, and most do not become fluent in this new language. Some are reluctant immigrants: Forced by workplace expectations or even their own children, they adopt some elements of technology but do so awkwardly and use it only when unavoidable. A dramatic example of the difference in technological expertise between adults and young people occurred in Australia. The federal government spent $84 million to create a free pornography filter to protect youths from reaching online porn sites. Within 30 minutes of the filter's launch, a 16-year-old was able to disable and circumvent it (Treyvaud, 2007). This phenomenon contributes to the difficulty many adult clinicians have in understanding the world of clients whose problems either occur in the universe of technology or are exacerbated by technology. Although one cannot magically turn digital immigrants into digital natives, I hope that this book will encourage more counselors to engage in the digital world in which so many of their clients exist.

Terminology

I use the terms *Internet* and *online* to refer to the use of the World Wide Web, however it is accessed (computer, cell phone, or other digital device). I use the terms *perpetrator* and *cyberbully* interchangeably to denote the person who initiates the harmful action, and I use *target* or *victim* to refer to the person to whom the actions are addressed. I use both *bystander* and *witness* for persons who are aware of the cyberbullying activity through first-hand experience (e.g., seeing a website, receiving a forwarded text) but are neither the bully nor the target. I use the term *social networking site* to describe any website whose purpose is to create a community online, usually by allowing users to create a profile, identify friends, and view the sites of and exchange information with friends within the site.

Prevalence

One challenge related to prevalence numbers is that they are almost immediately out of date. Surveys must be completed, data analyzed, reports written, and results submitted for publication then reviewed and revised and so forth; hence, by the time the results appear in print, the data are generally several years old. Given the rapidity with which cyberbullying devices (e.g., cameras on cell phones) are enhanced and availability extended (e.g., more high-speed lines added), surveys often do not include items of current interest or reflect the current state of technology. In addition, different surveys use different methods to determine what is considered cyberbullying. One method is to count any reports of having been harmed via technology (e.g., receiving a nasty e-mail), whereas another is to count only those cases that report more than one incident. Surveys typically ask about experiences within a specific time frame (e.g., previous 3 months, this school term, this year, ever), and different rates will be found for different time frames. The reader is cautioned to keep these reservations in mind when thinking about reported prevalence figures.

Surveys to determine the extent of cyberbullying among youths have produced wide ranges of prevalence figures, so it is difficult to pinpoint the extent to which this problem occurs. Kraft (2006) reviewed the prevalence studies that had been conducted so far worldwide and reported that in the United States, prevalence rates varied from 6% to 42%, depending on the study. Kowalski, Limber, and Agatston (2008) located 14 studies worldwide on cyberbullying since 2000 and found that rates of students reporting victimization ranged from 4% to 53%, and rates of students who acknowledged perpetrating cyberbullying ranged from 3% to 23%. Findings from two surveys, one of 92 students from 14 U.K. schools and another of 533 students in five schools (Smith et al., 2008) found rates of cyberbullying of 22.2% in the first group; a focus group of students believed prevalence is underreported. In the second study, 17.3% indicated that they had been cyberbullied. In both cases, rates of traditional bullying were considerably higher than those for cyberbullying. Lenhart (2009) put the prevalence of cyberbullying at somewhere between 9% and 33% for youths. She cited figures from the Pew Internet survey in 2007, which found that of teens ages 12–17 who are online, 32% had experienced at least one of the following: having something they considered private forwarded without their permission, receiving threatening messages, having rumors spread about them, or having an embarrassing photo posted without their consent. Additional prevalence data are based on a nationally representative sample of U.S. adolescents (Wang, Iannotti, & Nansel, 2009); in this study, the authors found that 13.6% of participants in Grades 6–10 indicated they had been cyberbullied in the 2 months prior to the survey. The authors found that 20.8% of participants reported being bullied physically, 53.6% said they had experienced verbal bullying, and 51.4% acknowledged being socially bullied. These estimates are based on participants' indicating that such incidents had happened to them at least once; again, the reader is left to decide whether or not this constitutes cyberbullying. Canadian middle school students surveyed in 2007 indicated that cyberbullying was a greater problem at the time of the survey than it had been a year before (Cassidy, Jackson, & Brown, 2009).

Survey information on workplace cyberbullying is sparse, and the little available data are from other countries. Nevertheless, they provide some evidence of the extent of the problem. A survey in the United Kingdom of 1,072 workers found that 20% had been cyberbullied at work via e-mail and 6% by text messages (Daniloff, 2009). A study of 1,700 workers in Australia revealed that 41% of participants had experienced cyberbullying from bosses and/or management; half of all incidents of the cyberbullying were perpetrated by coworkers (CQR Consulting, n.d.). A survey of Australian men employed in manufacturing jobs found that almost 11% had been victimized by technological means (Privitera & Campbell, 2009). Although this study had several important limitations (a very low response rate, a sample composed of men only, and a sample from an industry where constant access to technological communication is likely to be less than in many other occupations), the fact that cyberbullying was detected at all is informative. Although it is a stretch to draw any conclusions about U.S. workers from these data, there is ample anecdotal evidence that the problem exists in the United States as well.

Research So Far

Research articles on cyberbullying have begun to appear in the scholarly journals in recent years, but the extant literature is best described as preliminary and exploratory. Because studies vary in methodology and definitions, results cannot be generalized across studies. For example, if participants in surveys are recruited via particular websites, are those participants representative of Internet users in general? Do survey questions include items about cyberbullying by cell phone, which is a widely used device in cyberbullying? How are cyberbullies and cybervictims identified? Are they identified by their answer to a single question? If so, is a definition provided? What is the number of behaviors or frequency of experiences used to classify a participant as a cyberbully? Given all these differences across studies, it is premature to say the research has provided initial understanding of this topic.

The studies reported to date have focused on several basic questions: Why do people cyberbully others? How prevalent is cyberbullying and cybervictimization? What gender, racial, or age differences are there in this behavior? What is the relationship between conventional forms of bullying and cyberbullying? What are the consequences of cyberbullying? I will briefly summarize what the research has suggested about these questions, and for the reader interested in more details, the Appendix provides information on the location of these and other studies, including samples, findings, and limitations.

Earlier in this chapter, I reported on the range of findings regarding the prevalence of cyberbullying. Note that there is no U.S. research on cyberbullying in the workplace, although anecdotal reports abound. Thus, I am referring to the literature on cyberbullying among youths.

The reasons for any given incident of cyberbullying are varied and complex, but a survey by the National Crime Prevention Council (2007) found that 81% of 824 middle and high school teens surveyed thought that kids cyberbully others because they think it is funny, 64% thought it happens because the bully just does not like the target, and 45% thought the bully considers the target to be a loser. Fifty-eight percent also reported that they did not think the cyberbully considers the action to be serious.

Gender and age differences have been addressed in several studies. In Patchin and Hinduja's (2006) research, there were some indications that girls are more involved in cyberbullying than boys. Other researchers (Wang et al., 2009) found that boys were more likely to be cyberbullies and girls were more often cybervictims. Higher rates of cyberbullying in boys were also detected by Gradinger, Strohmeier, and Spiel (in press) and by Li (2006), although they found no gender differences in cybervictimization. Gender differences were not found in cyberbullying or cybervictimization in other studies (Slonje & Smith, 2008; Varjas, Henrich, & Meyers, 2009; K. R. Williams & Guerra, 2007). It is safe to say that the question of gender differences has not yet been answered.

Regarding racial or ethnic differences in cyberexperiences, Wang et al. (2009) reported that African American youths of both genders cyberbullied others more than youths of other racial groups, but these African American youths were victimized less often themselves. On the other hand, African Americans and students who self-identified as "Other/Multiracial" experienced more online racial discrimination and harassment than did Whites according to other research (Tynes, Giang, Williams, & Thompson, 2008).

The relationship between cyber- and conventional bullying has been examined in several studies. Findings suggest that cyberbullying involves a different group of students than conventional bullying; 64% of cybervictims were not victimized conventionally (Ybarra, Diener-West, & Leaf, 2007), and 75% of cyberbullies denied that they would bully others via conventional means (Mishna, Saini, & Solomon, 2009). On the other hand, Raskauskas and Stoltz (2007); Werner, Bumpus, and Rock (in press); and Smith et al. (2008) found that cyberbullies and victims in their samples were almost always traditional bullies and victims. None of these studies found evidence that traditional victims used cyberbullying as a way to retaliate. Although a positive correlation between traditional bullying and victimization and cyber-forms was also detected by Steffgen and König (2009), these researchers also found that conventional victims were cyberbullies (17%) more often than those who were not conventional victims (8%). In Werner et al.'s study, online victimization increased the chances of engaging in Internet aggression (the authors' term for cyberbullying) by 1500%. Finally, a study examining relationships among bullying, cyberbullying, and school safety conducted with 427 urban middle school students found that technological bullying was a "unique modality" from physical, verbal, and relational bullying that is "different in fundamental ways" from conventional forms of bullying and victimization (Varjas et al., 2009, p. 170).

Much of the discussion about the consequences of cyberbullying is based on the assumption that the consequences will parallel those of conventional bullying, with some experts (e.g., Campbell, 2005) suggesting that the psychological damage could be more severe for those victimized by cyberbullying. That assumption has not been empirically tested, with few exceptions. Hinduja and Patchin (2007) found that negative emotional consequences (frustration, anger, and sadness) were experienced by many victims, although 35% of respondents indicated they were not bothered by their treatment. Youths who reported online harassment had more problem behaviors at school and were eight times more likely than others to say they had carried a weapon to school in the previous month. Negative emotional states, including fear of going to school, were reported by cybervictimized youths (Raskauskas & Stoltz, 2007). In their study of 364 middle school students, Cassidy et al. (2009) found that of the 7 to 55 students (2% to 15%) who experienced cyberbullying, 19 respondents reported that their experience negatively affected their concentration at school, 20 said it impeded their school friendships, and 14 said they had suicidal thoughts brought on by the cyberbullying.

Although it may seem as though this review of extant research on cyberbullying has covered numerous studies, the number is meager compared with the thousands of articles that have been published on conventional bullying. It is clear that this line of research is early in its development, and much more work needs to be done. What can one glean from these few studies to date? Clearly, many youths are involved in cyberbullying (even in populations where access to technology might be limited), although the rates reported so far are lower than those for conventional bullying. Girls seem more engaged than boys, although this is not absolutely clear, and those youths who are most at risk are those who use technology the most. A key finding—that victims do not tell adults—has implications for prevention and intervention and is discussed later in the book.

Summary

- There is not a consensus on the precise definition of cyberbullying, but most researchers agree that it involves using electronic communication technology to harm another. Data show that the problem is widespread, but prevalence rates vary dramatically from one study to another because of different methods used to gather the data. No data on U.S. workplace cyberbullying have been located, but data from other developed countries suggest the problem exists.
- There have been several cases of cyberbullying leading to death or severe consequences that have been widely covered by popular media. Such cases exemplify the extreme end of the cyberbullying severity continuum, but they illustrate the types of cyberbullying that occur and the consequences that may ensue.
- Because of the recent proliferation of electronic communication technologies, adults tend to be less familiar with devices and their uses than younger people; adults tend to use the technologies as tools, whereas youths live technological lives.
- The research has focused mostly on prevalence rates. Some studies have suggested that prevalence rates vary based on gender, race, and age; however, results have often been conflicting, which leaves the question open. Another question of interest is whether cyberbullies are conventional bullies using new techniques or are a fundamentally different group. The studies to date suggest that many, but not all, cyberbullies also bully conventionally. Some researchers have suggested that conventional victims will use cyberbullying to retaliate in what is seen as a safer way; however, studies have revealed that although some conventional victims do cyberbully others, there are many who do not.
- There are many questions about cyberbullying that researchers will address as this line of inquiry goes forward. Very few studies have examined the cell phone and its role in cyberbullying, although the posting or forwarding of embarrassing photos has been identified by victims as particularly difficult to overcome.

CHAPTER 2

Conventional Bullying Versus Cyberbullying

Is cyberbullying a variation of conventional, face-to-face bullying? The jury is still out, but it is useful to compare both forms. The standard definition of conventional bullying is that it is a subset of aggression characterized by intentional harm, repetition, and power imbalance. Power imbalance is the feature that distinguishes bullying from conflict, and repetition is the aspect that distinguishes bullying from other forms of aggression. I will begin with a very broad overview of what is known about conventional bullying and then move on to cyberbullying and the unique elements of that form of bullying.

Conventional Bullying

A large, nationwide study reported that about 30% of U.S. students in Grades 6–10 were moderately or frequently involved in bullying (Nansel et al., 2001). Seals and Young (2003) surveyed 454 students in Grades 7 and 8 and reported that 24% were involved in bullying, with more boys than girls involved and more seventh graders than eighth graders involved. No differences by ethnicity were detected. Bullying in elementary school has been estimated to be more frequent than at the secondary level (Ross, 1996), so it is reasonable to conclude that many children are affected by bullying. These studies documented the seriousness of bullying in schools. Bullying is more prevalent in school than on trips to and from school, and it occurs most often in areas with limited adult supervision, such as playgrounds, hallways, and restrooms (Payne & Gottfredson, 2004).

Several different types of bullying have been identified. Overt bullying includes physical bullying (hitting, pushing, kicking, and so forth) and verbal bullying (e.g., malicious teasing, threatening, taunting). Indirect bullying is not always immediately apparent to the victim, as when the bully starts a rumor about the victim. Indirect bullying may take the form of social exclusion or the demand for certain behaviors as a condition of inclusion. Indirect bullying is sometimes called *relational bullying,* and the intent is to damage the victim's relationships or social standing. Researchers have found that relational bullying is more predictive of emotional distress than other forms of bullying (Bauman, 2008; Bauman & Summers, 2009; Hawker, 1998), despite some perceptions that it is normative for girls and thus not a matter of concern (Harachi, Catalano, & Hawkins, 1999). There is evidence that social exclusion is the most painful of bullying experiences (Mynard, Joseph, & Alexander, 2000; Sharp, 1995), even leading to experiences of post-traumatic stress disorder (PTSD); unfortunately, relational bullying is difficult for teachers to detect, and they tend to regard this form of bullying as the least serious (Birkinshaw & Eslea, 1998; Jacobsen & Bauman, 2007; Yoon & Kerber, 2003).

In addition to variety in the types of bullying, there are also a variety of roles in bullying situations: Bullies and victims do not account for all actors. Salmivalli (1999) identified the roles that may be present in a given incident: the *bully* is the person who initiates the bullying and may invite others to join; the *assistant* does join in and helps the bullying; the *reinforcer* may not directly participate but will encourage the bully(ies) with verbal support, laughter, and so forth; the *defender* takes the side of the victim, telling the bully to stop, comforting the victim, encouraging the victim to report the offense, and sometimes intervening on behalf of the victim; and finally, the *outsider* does not participate or take sides. Taking into account the individuals in these roles is very important when designing prevention and intervention programming, as effective action can be taken apart from the bully–victim dyad. This notion resulted in research on bystanders, which began to appear in the 1990s.

Craig and Pepler (1997) used observational methods with cameras and microphones and found that peers were present in 85% of bullying incidents at school. Following that important work, P. O'Connell, Pepler, and Craig (1999), using videotaped incidents, found that when peers were present at a bullying incident, they intervened about 25% of the time and encouraged or supported the bully 20% of the time. When peers did intervene, their efforts were effective in 57% of cases (Hawkins, Pepler, & Craig, 2001). The willingness to intervene appears to diminish with age, with older children being less likely to intervene than younger ones (Rigby & Johnson, 2006). In South Australia, Rigby and Johnson conducted a study of 400 students (6–9 years of age) who completed a number of measures after viewing a video of bullying incidents in which bystanders were present. Forty-three percent of participants said they would probably or definitely intervene if they were present, and they were more likely to do so if the bullying was verbal. When asked what they had done in actual situations at their school, 30% of primary and 24% of secondary students said they repeatedly tried to help victims, whereas 20% said they had never done so. Students were also asked what significant adults (parents, teachers) would expect them to do if they observed bullying, and the majority of students (with variation by age, gender, and "type" of significant adult) said the adults would expect them to help the victim. A smaller group believed their friends expected them to support the victim, and 22% of secondary school boys indicated their friends expected them to support the bully. Smith and Shu (2000) conducted a study of bystander behavior in the United Kingdom. Participants were 2,308 students aged 10–14. When asked what they did when they observed incidents of bullying, 47% self-reported that they tried not to get involved, 34% indicated they told the bully to stop, and 18% said they asked an adult to help. Younger students were more likely to ask for adult help. Eleven percent of participants revealed that they enjoyed watching incidents of bullying, and 4% joined in.

Given the various roles involved in bullying, researchers have investigated the relative stability of those roles over time and situations. Are bullies forever bullies, or do they change their behavior over time? How stable are the other involved roles? As Pepler, Jiang, Craig, and Connolly (2008) pointed out, there is reason for concern that those who bully often and continue to do so throughout their school career may be developing an interpersonal style based on power and control of others that will persist beyond adolescence. In their longitudinal study—composed of eight waves of data collection over 10 years, beginning when participants were between 10 and 12 years old—they identified several different bullying trajectories with characteristic individual and familial risk factors. Members of the high-bullying group, who exhibited high levels of bullying across the data collection period, composed 10% of the sample; members of the desist group (13%) showed moderate levels of bullying in early adolescence that practically disappeared by the end of high school; members of the moderate group displayed fairly consistent, but less extreme, levels of bullying over time; and members of the never group (42%) were essentially not involved.

In general, researchers have found that victimization tends to be fairly stable, with children who are bullied in elementary school often continuing in that role through adolescence. Barker and his colleagues (2008) examined the stability of bullying and victimization beginning in preschool and found that peer victimization in preschool was predictive of peer victimization in first grade. Those children who were chronically victimized could be predicted from (a) having high levels of physical aggressiveness at 17 months of age and (b) coming from families with parenting styles characterized by harsh reactive discipline and with insufficient income. These researchers noted that prior research had revealed both that children who were physically aggressive when they started elementary school were likely to be victimized and that children who were depressed and socially withdrawn or hyperactive were likely to be chronically victimized in later childhood. In a longitudinal study of aggression and victimization from kindergarten through fourth grade, Kochenderfer-Ladd (2003) also found that aggressive children were victimized in kindergarten, and the relationship between aggressiveness and victimization was stable throughout the 4-year period. There were no gender differences in this relationship. In addition, she found that high levels of aggression in kindergarten predicted stability of victimization over the 4 years, and low peer acceptance was related to chronic victimization.

Another study, conducted in the Netherlands (Scholte, Engels, Overbeek, de Kemp, & Haselager, 2007), found that 46% of children classified as bullies in childhood were still classified as such by adolescence, whereas 9% had become victims by adolescence. Forty-three percent of victims in childhood remained victims in adolescence. Among children who were uninvolved in childhood bullying, 15% had become bullies by adolescence and 7% had become victims. Boys were more likely than girls to remain classified as a bully from childhood to adolescence (perhaps because the measure referred to overt aggression); however, boys and girls were equally likely to remain victims. An interesting finding was that those who were bullies in childhood but not in adolescence reported more help-seeking behaviors than those who remained bullies. For victims, those who were victims at both times were more likely to be disliked and to use help-seeking behaviors more often than those whose victimization did not persist into adolescence. Stable bullies were more disliked, more disruptive, and more aggressive than the bullies who did not remain bullies in adolescence. They also had fewer friends and did not seek help often.

Salmivalli, Lappalainen, and Lagerspetz (1998) examined the stability of bullying roles from sixth through eighth grade. Among other things, they found that there were fewer victims (but the same amount of bullies and assistants) in eighth grade than sixth grade. Those who were most often victimized in sixth grade remained in that category in eighth grade. Bullying others, as well as assisting and reinforcing the bully, was quite stable among boys from sixth through eighth grade and was moderately stable in girls. The role of defender of the victim was stable for girls but not boys. These researchers also compared the stability of roles between those who changed classes versus those who remained with the same classes over the period of the study. Victimization tended to persist in both situations, but results for other roles were inconclusive because of the small cell sizes of those groups.

Several researchers have focused on school context in relation to stability of roles, theorizing that bullying behavior results from a struggle for dominance, which is generally established by the end of elementary school. However, the transition to middle school, with a different and larger group of students and other environmental changes, results in renewed struggling and increased levels of bullying. Pellegrini (2004) summarized a number of studies and concluded that when students change schools after fifth grade, bullying increases in sixth grade. That trend is not observed when students are in the same school; instead there is a gradual decline in the prevalence of bullying. Carney and Merrell (2001) concluded that the peak period of bullying found in middle schools is due to the structure of schools. They noted that middle school is the peak period for bullying in both American and Japanese schools, which have similar structures. It is at this age that young adolescents are focused on being accepted and included by peers, making this a particularly vulnerable time period. German researchers (Schäfer, Korn, Brodbeck, Wolke, & Schulz, 2003) investigating similar questions, however, found that bullying involvement over a 6-year period extending from primary into secondary school was unstable; the bully role was unstable, but the victim role was stable. In general, most children changed roles toward the neutral status from primary to secondary school.

There is a significant body of evidence that there are negative consequences of bullying for all involved youths. For example, bullies and victims have more social, emotional, behavioral, and academic problems than others who are not involved (Glew, Fan, Katon, Rivara, & Kernic, 2005; Seals & Young, 2003). Victims are more likely to have depression (e.g., Bauman, 2008; Craig, 1998; Fekkes, Pijpers, & Verloove-Vanhorick, 2004; Olweus, 1993; Rigby, 2004), anxiety, low self-esteem, and loneliness, and these consequences are still detected when the victims are adults (Leff, Power, & Goldstein, 2004). Marsh, Parada, Craven, and Finger (2004) found that peer rejection, delinquency, criminality, violence, and suicidal ideation (also see West & Salmon, 2000) were additional outcomes of involvement in bullying. In addition, school attendance issues and low academic performance have been found among both victims (Smith, Talamelli, Cowie, Naylor, & Chuahan, 2004; Smokowski & Kopasz, 2005) and bullies (L. Ma, Phelps, Lerner, & Lerner, 2009).

Researchers have attempted to identify characteristics of bullies, victims, and bully–victims. Bully–victims are those who take the bully role in some incidents and the victim role in others. It is important to note that Olweus (1978) proposed that victims may be passive (insecure, helpless, sensitive, and submissive when attacked) or provocative (displaying hyperactive, irritable, defensive behavior). Veenstra et al. (2005) examined the individual and familial characteristics of 2,230 preadolescents (M age = 11.09 years) classified as bullies, victims, bully–victims, and uninvolved on the basis of peer-report data. Boys were more likely to be classified as bullies and bully–victims than girls, and girls were 1.74 times more likely to be victims (especially passive victims) than boys. Veenstra et al. compared the four groups using both univariate and multivariate analyses. In the univariate analyses, all three involved groups came from homes with a lower socio-economic status (SES) than the uninvolved group. Bully–victims reported the most rejection at home, and uninvolved participants reported the least. Bullies and bully–victims experienced the least emotional warmth at home, whereas members of the uninvolved group and victims found significantly more warmth at home. Bully–victims also scored highest on "familial vulnerability to externalizing disorder" (p. 677), and the uninvolved group scored the lowest. Bully–victims and bullies had the highest scores on aggressiveness—scores that were significantly higher than those of the other two groups. An interesting finding was that the victim group's scores on aggressiveness were significantly higher than those of the uninvolved group. Victims and bully–victims were the most isolated, and uninvolved respondents were the least isolated. Academic performance was highest in the uninvolved group, and victims had significantly better performance than bully–victims. Prosocial behavior was highest among victims and uninvolved participants. Bully–victims were the most disliked of the four groups, and the uninvolved were the least disliked. No difference was found on the degree to which bullies and victims were disliked. The multivariate analysis did not find a significant impact of parenting characteristics once other factors were taken into account, which differed from earlier research that found such parenting variables to be important.

X. Ma (2004) reviewed research on victim characteristics and noted that victims generally have been found to be less intelligent than other students. Victims have also been found to have close relationships with their parents (especially with mothers for boys who are passive victims), in contrast to bullies, who have families that tend to have financial and social difficulties as well as parents who are often authoritarian, hostile, and rejecting. Victims tend to have few friends in school, and they experience social distress. Bullies tend to be fairly popular with peers (although they may not be well liked). Victims tend to have negative self-concepts and high levels of social anxiety, and they often have symptoms of depression. Victims are also likely to have ineffective social problem-solving skills as well as ineffective strategies to cope with victimization. Victims are often physically weaker than other students, which increases their vulnerability. Victims also may not readily initiate prosocial interactions.

Summarizing previous research on victim characteristics, Reid, Monsen, and Rivers (2004) found the following had been reported: "passive, anxious, weak, lacking self-confidence, unpopular, having a low self-esteem" (p. 249). They also noted that special education students, slow developers, minority children, and children who do not conform to gender stereotypes are often targeted by bullies. Children who are victimized often do not behave assertively and are likely to be obviously distressed or anxious in social interactions.

According to Holmes and Holmes-Lonergan (2004), bullying behavior can be viewed as the individual's attempt to gain or keep status by means of degrading others. These researchers suggested that in reaction to a cold emotional climate in the home, authoritarian parenting, inappropriate (including physical) discipline, and other negative family characteristics, the bully resorts to bullying behavior to gain status among peers.

It is generally accepted that bullying and victimization are most problematic at the middle school level, with these behaviors declining in high school (e.g., Dake, Price, Telljohann, & Funk, 2003; Limber, 2002; Marsh et al., 2004; Nansel et al., 2001; Pellegrini & Long, 2002; Smith, Shu, & Madsen, 2001). However, bullying and victimization continue to exist at the high school level, with 25% of U.S. high schools reporting that bullying is a problem (Bauman, 2008; U.S. Department of Justice, 2005), and 54% of students surveyed at one high school reporting that they had been victimized by bullying at school (Holt & Espelage, 2003).

Research on gender differences in bullying and victimization has not been conclusive, but when types of bullying are taken into account, boys experience physical bullying more often than girls. By middle school, rates of relational victimization do not differ by gender. Victimization rates have been found to vary by race–ethnicity in some studies. For example, Nansel et al. (2001) observed that African American youths were victimized the least, and Storch, Nock, Masia-Warner, and Barlas (2003) found that Hispanic children were victimized at higher rates than Whites. Hanish and Guerra (2000) pointed out that race and ethnic differences in bullying and victimization varied by the racial–ethnic composition of the school.

Cyberbullying

If one accepts that cyberbullying qualifies as a form of bullying, then it is necessary to note the characteristics that are unique to cyberbullying. The unique features of cyberbullying magnify the potential for harm such that cyberbullying may be more severe than conventional bullying (Campbell, 2005). The perceived anonymity of cyberbullying is often noted (Hinduja & Patchin, 2009; Kowalski et al., 2008; Slonje & Smith, 2008; Willard, 2007b) as a distinguishing element that increases the appeal of cyberbullying to the perpetrator. However, anonymity may not be as perceived; indeed, one can often find evidence tracing the source of cyberbullying material, and in criminal cases, even more records can be retrieved.

Nevertheless, the illusion of anonymity seems to reduce social inhibitions for some youths and adults. For example, Patchin and Hinduja (2006) reported that 37% of the teens in one survey indicated that they had said things in electronic communications they would not say in person. This finding is consistent with the online disinhibition effect described by Suler (2004). A series of public service announcements (PSAs) produced by the National Crime Prevention Council uses this attribute to great effect. A 30-second video clip shows several teens around a table in the kitchen, with a mother in the background. One girl makes a series of derogatory remarks to another girl at the table (e.g., "You're a tramp and everybody knows it," "That zit is huge, zitface"), and the viewer is typically shocked to hear someone say such cruel things. The clip ends with a keyboard saying, "If you wouldn't say it in person, don't say it online."

A message that appears to be anonymous can add to the level of fear and distrust for the victim. If the source of a message is unknown, the victim is left to wonder who it might be and why it was necessary to conceal the identity. The message could have come from anyone—including one's friends. The feeling of uncertainty can undermine one's trust, because anyone—even a close ally—could be the source.

The power balance that is such an important element of bullying is altered in cyberbullying. The conventional bully's source of power is often physical stature (size or attractiveness) or social standing (popularity, wealth), but neither of these is relevant in cyberbullying. In fact, although there are no data to support the hypothesis at this point, it has been suggested that cyberbullying may be appealing to victims of conventional bullying because it offers a "safe" and anonymous way to retaliate. The source of a cyberbully's power is technological expertise, which is commonplace in contemporary society. The cyberbully does not even need to possess the tools of the trade, so to speak, as many public facilities (e.g., libraries and community centers) have Internet access available at no charge. Using public computers has the advantage of leaving an IP (Internet protocol) trail that cannot be traced to the individual unless the facility keeps a record of who is on each computer at what time. Even when it comes to cell phones, which are owned by such a large majority of Americans, many are not reluctant to borrow a friend's phone in order to deflect responsibility of the behavior onto someone else.

Another important difference between conventional bullying and cyberbullying is that most technological communication is at a distance and without visual cues to the intent of the message. The message in a verbal communication is conveyed by more than the words. The speaker's facial expressions and gestures reveal much about the speaker's intent. A message accompanied by a wink is very different from the same message coming from a scowling visage. In addition to visual cues, the tone of voice, emphasis, pauses, and so forth also add information to the content of the words. Thus, a message conveyed electronically lacks this essential information about the true meaning of the message, so the recipient is left to infer the complete meaning and intent. Some experts believe the absence of nonverbal clues easily leads to misunderstandings, which in turn can lead to escalating hostilities and cyberbullying. Consider the person who receives a message intended to be sarcastic and who interprets the meaning literally. The recipient could be sufficiently insulted to either respond with a hostile retort or forward the message to others as an example of the callous treatment at the hands of the original sender. One attempt to mitigate this problem is the use of emoticons, or symbols that provide the information usually conveyed by nonverbal content. Emoticons may help, but not all users can easily insert these, and they are almost always absent from text messages. If one receives a message that could be interpreted in more than one way, it is helpful to check with the sender.

Without face-to-face contact, the bully does not have to observe the effect of his or her actions on the victim. Some bullies truly believe their behavior is funny, but when they observe the victim's distress, they may realize the harm they have done. The direct observation of the victim has at least the potential to encourage the bully's empathy. The cyberbully is far removed from the victim's suffering and lacks the opportunity to empathize with him or her. It is easy to rationalize that the incident was funny, or did little harm, if one is spared the victim's reaction. On the other hand, some bullies seek evidence of their victims' distress, which serves as a reinforcement of the behavior. In these cases, cyberbullies would seek more indirect evidence of the effect on the victim.

For many victims, the most distressing aspect of cyberbullying is the potentially vast size of the audience. Recall Gyslain Raza's humiliation: His embarrassment was viewed 900 *million* times. Conventional bullies often have witnesses to their actions, but the numbers are limited by time and space. The lunchroom onlookers to one's taunting pale in comparison to that same incident recorded and posted on the Internet or sent electronically to most students at a school. Not only can actual incidents be widely publicized, but images can be edited to add to the entertainment of the audience and to the infamy of the victim. Although incidents like this are relatively rare, the damage done in each is significant.

Finally, the absence of time and space restrictions on cyberbullying makes it very difficult to escape. No longer can the victim retreat to the safe haven of the home to feel protected from the aggression. E-mails and texts can arrive at any time, and Internet postings can be viewed around the clock. It is often suggested that the victim simply turn off these devices to avoid the harassment. That recommendation discounts the many reasons why the technology has such a central position in contemporary life. Cell phones are primary means of communication and safety for many individuals. To ignore messages from the bully by turning off the phone means also missing messages from friends and loved ones that are important. Not checking e-mails or visiting one's usual websites has the same effect. Persons being victimized need to know how to block individual senders and how to report those who misuse websites; that way, the bully, not the victim, suffers the consequences of his or her behavior.

What is currently known about the consequences of being cyberbullied? Again, there hasn't been a sufficient amount of time to accumulate a strong body of empirical evidence on this question, but both anecdotally and rationally, one can make several assumptions. It is likely that the victim of cyberbullying will be distracted and have diminished attention and concentration at school or work. This consequence could be magnified by the intensity and frequency of the cyberbullying, so that if one fears future attacks, one is likely to be anxious and fearful. Until the attacker has been identified and stopped, the victim is likely to be in this hypervigilant state. There is also likely to be damage to the feeling of trust in others, particularly when the attacks are anonymous. Given that the offensive messages could be coming from any of one's classmates or coworkers, who among them can be trusted? The safest strategy would be to trust no one, making the school or workplace an unsafe and tense environment in which to function. Certainly some types of threatening cyberbullying can generate high levels of fear in the victim. And based on the examples given at the beginning of this book and others that have been covered in the news, it is apparent that depression and suicide are potential consequences for some individuals. Increased depression and suicidal ideation is associated with conventional victimization (Espelage & Swearer, 2003; van der Wal, de Wit, & Hirasing, 2003); hence, it is a logical extension to assume that these reactions to cybervictimization are also likely and should be monitored.

I believe that, depending on the type and intensity of the cybervictimization, some victims may develop symptoms of PTSD and/or depression and anxiety. If a client comes for counseling and mentions cybervictimization as an issue, screening for both PTSD and depression would certainly be in order. In some cases, a treatment plan that is based on protocols for PTSD would be the clinician's most appropriate response. Daniloff (2009) observed that many adults are too embarrassed to seek help for victimization; given the prevalence of this problem, it behooves the clinician to listen carefully for any hints that this has occurred.

Summary

- Estimates suggest that between 20% and 30% of students in U.S. schools are involved in school bullying in some way.
- The following types of bullying have been identified: physical, verbal, and relational. Another widely used classification is direct and indirect bullying. Relational or indirect bullying may be the most difficult for teachers to detect, but there is evidence that being victimized in that way has the most negative psychosocial outcomes.
- Bullying is no longer considered a dyadic encounter. Researchers have identified several bullying roles: the bully, the assistant, the reinforcer, the defender, the victim, and the outsider.
- Recently, interest has been focused on the role of bystanders and how they can intervene in bullying incidents.
- Victimization that begins in elementary school often continues through adolescence, which is also the case for bullying.
- Negative consequences are associated with involvement in bullying, including social, emotional, and behavioral problems. Depression has also been detected in victims and—along with anxiety and loneliness—may persist into adulthood. Poor academic performance and attendance problems have also been found among victims.
- Olweus proposed that victims may be either passive or provocative. There are also youths who are both bullies and victims, and they seem to have the most negative outcomes of all involved groups.
- When types of bullying are considered, boys tend to experience more physical bullying than girls. Relational victimization does not vary by gender at the middle school level.
- Although cyberbullying is similar to conventional bullying in that it describes intentional aggressive behavior designed to harm another repeatedly, it has unique characteristics that may increase the potential for harm.
- The perceived anonymity of electronic communication, in which people can hide behind screen names and aliases and can camouflage their identity in other ways, apparently creates a disinhibition effect, whereby the normal social controls on such behavior are diminished and people do or say things online they would not do or say in person.

- In conventional bullying, the power imbalance is a defining characteristic, but in the digital world, the attributes that elevate one to a position of power are altered. Conventional bullies are powerful because of their appearance or possession of other visible qualities; the cyberbully needs none of those accoutrements. The cyberbully needs to be knowledgeable about technology; the more knowledge, the more sophisticated the methods available to cyberbully others.
- In face-to-face interactions, the intent and nature of a message is conveyed not only in the words used but in gestures, facial expressions, and tone of voice. With the absence of these clues, some messages intended as jokes may be misinterpreted as aggressive and may provoke retaliatory responses. In addition, with cyberbullying, the bully is spared the chance to see the victim's reaction. In some cases, that reaction could be far more serious than the bully intended. Seeing the victim thus can promote empathy and reflection on the part of the conventional bully, but this is also absent in cyberbullying.
- The size of the audience for cyberbullying is immense. The victim's humiliation is visible to potentially millions of viewers, which contributes to the devastation.
- The absence of time and space restrictions on technological communication used in cyberbullying is an important difference from conventional bullying. The cyberbully can send the harmful messages at any time and from any place. Although some have suggested that a victim can stop the bullying by turning off such devices, that advice discounts the importance of technological communication in today's world.
- Even though empirical studies have not yet documented the consequences of cyberbullying, the many reports in the media are evidence that at least for some victims, the experience can be devastating. For most victims of cyberbullying, it is logical to assume that there will be diminished attention and concentration in school and in the workplace; decreased levels of trust for peers and colleagues because of the anonymous nature of many attacks; increased fear; and perhaps depression, anxiety, and other psychological disorders, including suicidal ideation of actions. When the cyberbully's tactics result in a large audience viewing the victim's humiliation, social isolation, elevated suspicion of others, and symptoms of PTSD may be consequences.

CHAPTER 3

Cyberenvironments

The bullying techniques described in the previous chapter can be used in a variety of environments. These techniques vary in ease of use, but one potential difference is the size of the audience. It is reasonable to assume that a derogatory e-mail received by an individual is less upsetting than a comparable message posted publicly on a website that can be seen by a potentially infinite audience.

Types of Cyberenvironments

IM

IM involves real-time communication in which messages are typed into a window and the participants respond back and forth. The images in Figures 1 and 2 show two different screens. The first one has numerous windows open, which means the viewer is engaged in several IM conversations at the same time (see Figure 1). The second one also shows several windows and includes a buddy list, which allows the user to quickly connect to those individuals if they are online (see Figure 2).

IM is a feature of many platforms and is available through some Internet service providers (ISPs; e.g., AOL, Comcast) and major web services (such as Yahoo and MSN). It is also a feature of social networking sites (described below). The next images show an IM on MySpace.com (see Figure 3) and on Facebook (see Figure 4).

Chat Rooms

Chat rooms can be seen as expanded IMs in the sense that the interaction occurs in real time. The difference is that the number of people is not re-

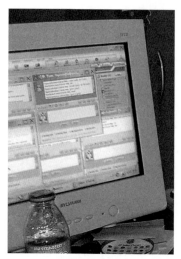

Figure 1
Simultaneous instant
messaging conversations.

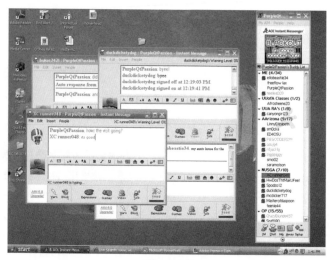

Figure 2
Multiple instant messaging screens open,
with buddy list.

Figure 3
MySpace chat.

Figure 4
Facebook chat.

stricted, and they may not know each other before convening in the chat room. Typically, the people who enter the room share some interest or theme or at least age group. Some chats are free, whereas others are part of a service that requires a subscription fee (e.g., MSN Chat) and has a large number of chats available. The view of the chat room varies by site, but most are easy to use, especially if one has used IM. Many chat rooms identify the user by a nickname that is selected by the user, but some allow the user to create an *avatar* (a graphic representation of the user, stylized and usually cartoon-like; R. O'Connell, 2001). The nickname can reveal as much or little about the participant as that participant is comfortable with. Some chats will not allow nicknames that are potentially offensive, but others take whatever the user chooses. When entering a chat room, one often sees a list of others present in the room. Some chats have moderators or hosts, who may be identified by a symbol near their name. Others are unmoderated, which means no one is monitoring the content. Sometimes people will be greeted when they enter a room, but in other rooms it is up to the user to say hello. One problem in chat rooms is that there can be private messages between participants, and some of those may be rude or offensive. Most chat rooms have the option to block or ignore a participant so that future messages from that particular person are not visible. Exclusion is also quite possible in chat rooms, where a user can be ignored by everyone in the room. An excellent overview of chatting is available at "Chat 101, the basics (and more) of chat . . ." (n.d.). There are several links from the home page that offer excellent advice and tips.

Trash Polling Sites

Perhaps the best known trash polling site is Juicycampus.com, launched in August 2007 and closed on February 5, 2009. The purpose of the site was to provide a space for users (by college or university) to post so-called juicy messages or comments anonymously and then to vote on the posting they considered the juiciest. Hostin (2008) reported on a college student who learned from a friend that she was the topic of posts on this site. She was described in rude and unflattering terms. She was so distressed when she saw these comments that she lost weight, could not sleep, became hypervigilant, and stated that her year at college (her freshman year) had been ruined. Many of the comments on this site were sexual in nature, to the point of commenting on specific body parts. The site was founded by an alumnus of Duke University who tried to conceal his identity. Hostin discovered that the Communications Decency Act (1996) protects website publishers from being liable for postings by a third party, even if those postings are libelous. The site portrayed itself as a place for anonymous commentary. So, if the student who was defamed on the site wanted to sue, she would have to identify the individuals who posted. The website owner is safe. However, if the student sued the anonymous poster(s), the website could be subpoenaed and required to provide its records, which might include the IP address of the computer from which the message was sent. Of course, that does not always identify the poster.

Although this site shut down, ostensibly for financial reasons, other sites have emerged, and it is impossible to say what the current version of Juicycampus is. It is also clear that the word gets around among college students very quickly, and it is likely that these sites will continue to promote mean-spirited and cruel attacks that are clearly an insidious form of cyberbullying. Discussion boards can also be used to publicly embarrass or derogate someone; chat rooms and even games can be venues for this behavior.

Another widely used site is Ratemyteachers.com; there is a comparable site for university professors at Ratemyprofessors.com. These are sites on which users can click on a numerical rating and also make comments. These are all available for anyone to view. I have not been rated on Ratemyprofessors.com (I'm not sure if that is good news or not), but I checked the ratings and comments for professors I know. Regardless of the ratings, I must say that the comments that I viewed all related to teaching and course characteristics; there were no personal attacks or defamatory comments, although some comments were rather extensive. That is not always the case. A teacher in Ireland checked his own ratings on Ratemyteachers.com and found two comments that were hurtful and personal (Coughlan, 2007). Web polls are easy (and often free) to create (e.g., www.micropoll.com) and can be placed on someone's website or social networking page. In addition, bullies can create their own websites and include defamatory content. In Pennsylvania there was a case in which a student created a website called "Teacher Sux" and posted insulting text about a particular teacher that disturbed the teacher to the extent that her functioning was impaired (Jonsson, 2008). The courts upheld the school district's decision to expel the student who created the site. They also awarded monetary damages to the teacher. This case was heard in court; interested readers may wish to view information about the case at *J. S. v. Bethlehem Area School District* (2000).

One final place that has been created primarily to allow malicious individuals to post anonymous comments on someone's wall in Facebook is an application created outside of Facebook called "Bathroom Wall." According to Perle (2009), this site is the most popular anonymous application, with over 150,000 active monthly users. What is interesting is that in order for a person to be able to use this application to post on your wall, the person must be someone in your "friends" list. I am very reluctant to use any of the applications associated with Facebook, but this one in particular seems insidious, and I am not interested in defaming my friends. Although the application could also be used to post praise and positive comments, it is clearly an avenue for devious intentions. Because the posts are anonymous, it is impossible to identify the friend in order to block or de-friend him or her.

Blogs

Blogs (or weblogs) are an individual person's thoughts (and photos and videos) that are available over the Internet. A blog can be a form of online diary, where one chronicles one's activities and musings, but many blogs are devoted to specific topics, such as new mothers, nutrition, travel, politics, and so forth. Sites such as Blogger.com or Blogspot.com provide the platform on which users, for no cost, create their personal blogs with a specific uniform resource locator (URL), or web address. There are professional bloggers who report news as it happens, and there are numerous individual blogs. One of the individual bloggers was George Sodini, who on August 5, 2009, entered a fitness club near Pittsburgh, PA, and killed three women. He also wounded

10 others and killed himself ("Police: Gym Shooter," 2009). Although the blog has been taken down from the Internet, one website claims to have the contents and has them available for viewing. The blog is a frightening window into Sodini's mental state and his plans to commit this horrible act ("PA Gym Killer George Sodini's Blog [Archived]," 2009). The contents are consistent with what the news reports say was found on the blog.

Most blogs have a mechanism by which readers can comment on the blog, and these comments are often as, or more, interesting than the blog. If anyone commented on Sodini's blog, those were not published. Although blogs can be informative and entertaining, both the blogs and comments can also be cruel and hurtful and can be appropriated as a vehicle for cyberbullying.

E-mail

E-mail allows people to send messages to others in electronic form. There are numerous advantages: It is free (no postage required), it is immediate (it arrives at the destination almost instantaneously), and messages can be saved for future reference. Most people believe that e-mail is confidential, but counselors and other professionals often include a disclaimer pointing out that in fact e-mail is NOT confidential and users should not put anything in an e-mail that should not be seen by anyone other than the recipient. E-mail can easily be used to cyberbully. I have repeatedly received nasty e-mails from individuals for a variety of reasons—many of these messages would probably qualify as cyberbullying. In one case, a student was not admitted to a graduate program and held me responsible. The student sent me numerous e-mails suggesting that the decision (which, in her view, was my decision) was unjust, that she was being unfairly treated, that I was biased against her, and so forth. There was also an incident in which I forwarded an e-mail (without permission) because it included what I knew to be untrue statements about another person's professional qualifications. The recipient of my forward meant to reply only to me (saying he was shocked), but he mistakenly clicked on *Reply All*, which meant the person who sent the e-mail to me also received the reply and thus knew I had forwarded it. That person was very angry and attempted to pursue the issue, saying I had violated confidentiality. We both learned that there is no confidentiality and that my action, although perhaps ill-advised, was not an offense of any kind. The e-mail policy at my university (and most other institutions, I suspect) states that the confidentiality of e-mail cannot be ensured. Counselors are particularly aware of this caveat and do not disclose any confidential information over the Internet. Clients who are receiving unsolicited and unwanted e-mail should, in addition to making sure their spam filters are up to date, block senders from whom they do not wish to receive messages. In Outlook 2007, I right-click on the e-mail message and see a drop-down menu that includes *junk e-mail*. By clicking on that, I see the option to *add sender to blocked senders list*, which means I will not get future messages from this e-mail address. Outlook 2010 (which runs on Windows XP, Vista, and

Windows 7, released in 2010) works similarly but has the junk e-mail drop-down displayed along the top of the page for easier access. In addition, in Outlook 2010 there is a feature that allows you to customize your site by using *Tools → Customize* on the *Commands* tab, choosing the *Action* category, highlighting *add sender to blocked senders list*, and then dragging that action to the toolbar where it is easy to reach. Then, to block a sender, simply select the message and click on the icon in your customized toolbar.

Texting

Text messaging—or texting or SMS (short message service)—is a feature that is increasingly common with cell phone users. In all age groups, the percentage of cell phone owners who use the texting feature increased from 2008 to 2009. For people in their 40s, 64% now report texting, as do 46% of those in their 50s (Vlingo, 2009). In addition to the increasing proportion of cell phone owners who text, the volume of texting has also increased, with those ages 13–19 averaging 500 text messages per month! One father discovered that his 13-year-old daughter had sent or received 14,528 texts in a single month (Hafner, 2009). Of all respondents to Vlingo's survey, 35% use their phones to text more often than they do to place voice calls. The appeal to cyberbullies of texting is the lack of time or location restrictions and the ability to avoid seeing the response of the victim when reading the message. Although text messages must show the caller's number, there are methods to circumvent this requirement that appeal to cyberbullies. For example, there are websites that allow one to send anonymous text messages (TxtEmNow.com), and there are services that allow the sender to alter the number that automatically appears to the number the caller selects.

In the two images that follow (both from my cell phone), you can see that the "real" message shows the number of the caller (see Figure 5), but the one I sent to myself from TxtEmNow.com lacks that information (see Figure 6). Websites such as the one I used enable a person to send a message anonymously and even offer applications that can disguise the voice in a voice call (a "spoof card" is available on TxtEmNow.com). So the de-

Figure 5
Cell phone screen with
typical text message.

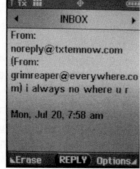

Figure 6
Cell phone screen
using proxy website.

termined cyberbully is not necessarily limited by the technological efforts to track one's identity.

In addition to sending cruel, obscene, threatening, or otherwise malicious texts, the caller can create groups in the phone's contact lists so that messages can be sent to several recipients at once. This feature is widely used to share photos and videos, and the bully of course is able to appropriate this feature to share supposedly confidential texts, photos, and videos with a wide audience with one call. This function is similar to creating address groups in e-mail and serves the same purpose. For example, when I sat on an organization's board and frequently sent messages to every person on it, it was efficient to create an e-mail group and type only one address to reach the entire board. Some people create groups on the phone to quickly notify members of a team or club that a meeting is cancelled. Again, the advantage of these features is clear, but the same mechanism allows a cyberbully to send a photo or rumor very quickly to a large number of recipients.

An important feature of texting that may stymie adults is that a unique shorthand or orthography has evolved to express information in the fewest characters possible. Adults may use LOL (laughing out loud) to show the recipient that the message was intended to be humorous or in a response to show they laughed at the original message. Other commonly used codes include BTW (by the way), IMHO (in my humble opinion), or BFN (bye for now). Young people have an enormous number of such acronyms and also have graphic codes to show emotions. Microsoft Word can create some of these common ones (e.g., ☺ ☹) using a combination of keys. Vigilant adults who insist the child use social networking sites only with direct adult oversight may still miss some of the exchanges. A widely used abbreviation is POS, which means "parent over shoulder," so the other party in the conversation knows that the writer is not able to communicate freely. There are other abbreviations with sexual content that a parent could easily miss. There are several websites that provide translations (e.g., www.techdictionary.com, www.netlingo.com). An excellent and very basic list of acronyms parents should know can be found at POS: Parents Over Shoulder (2009), and a short booklet for parents on texting (*Txt 2 Connect With Teens*) can be downloaded at docstoc.com (2009).

In addition to text messaging capabilities, most cell phones now have built-in cameras and can be used to send photos (pixts) and videos. Although this is delightful when one's puppy does something photogenic and the cell phone camera is easily used to take a shot to forward to the puppy's fans, it is a far different matter when the phone is used to surreptitiously photograph someone in an embarrassing state (e.g., in a locker room) and forward that to other viewers for the purpose of humiliating (cyberbullying) the subject of the photo.

Happy Slapping

The term *happy slapping* was coined in the United Kingdom to denote a practice of surprising a stranger by gently slapping his or her face while someone recorded the response on a cell phone. The original intent may have been similar to that of popular TV programs that engage unsuspecting persons in prank situations, which are filmed and aired. However, the practice has become more insidious: Fights are planned so that there is a person recording the incident, which is then placed on the Internet (on YouTube.com or on a social networking site). The victim is not only accosted and beaten, but his or her humiliation is made public via this practice. However, some victims have used the recording to their advantage in pressing charges. One youth was interviewed while in the hospital recovering from an assault that had been recorded and posted online and noted that she intended to use the recording as evidence in a legal case against the assailant ("Teen Beaten," 2008). In another case, when the video was sent to the victim, she posted it on YouTube.com and iReport (CNN.com user-generated content) to draw attention to the incident. She was contacted by a detective, who filed charges against the bully (Zdanowicz, 2009).

Social Networking

Social networking websites have become extremely popular and not only with youths. Social networking sites are platforms on the Internet that include a combination of the following features: (a) social interaction among two or more people; (b) the ability to create personal profiles with information they choose to display, including images; (c) methods to communicate with others within the site, such as IM and e-mail; and (d) search functions so the user can search for others with whom to communicate. More recently many social networking sites have applications (apps), which are programs developed by someone outside the site and made available on the site. These apps include games or quizzes that the user may use, and the user may agree to have the results displayed for others to see.

Most readers will be familiar with MySpace.com and Facebook.com, as these have the largest number of members, but there are numerous social networking sites, many of which appeal to a particular group. According to quantcast.com, as of May 31, 2009, MySpace.com had estimated monthly traffic of 63 million visitors from the United States and was the ninth most visited site on the Internet. The site attracts slightly more females, and 73% of visitors to the site are ages 12–24. Racial–ethnic minority groups visit the site at rates much higher than the Internet average. Facebook.com is ranked fifth in terms of visitors, with 95.5 million monthly U.S. visitors in September 2009 (Sydell, 2009), and about 500,000 new users worldwide are added every day (Parr, 2009). Data from quantcast.com show that the demographics of visitors to this site are almost identical to those of MySpace.com visitors. Teenagers who visit these sites are more likely to experience cyberbullying than their peers who do not visit such sites: 40% of social network users report being cyberbullied, compared with 22% of teens who use the Internet but not social networking sites (Lenhart, 2007).

The two sites have quite different styles. Figures 7 and 8 show the pages a non-member will see when first looking at those two sites. Note the emphasis on celebrities and music on MySpace.

Twitter.com

Twitter.com is a recent addition to the menu of social networking sites. On this site, users communicate with others using short (maximum 140 characters) messages known as *tweets*. Approximately 25 million tweets are posted every day (Cashmore, 2009). Users can "follow" other individuals and groups. The tweets from those persons are instantly available on one's Twitter home page (or cell phone—the site allows use by Internet-connected cell phones using the texting feature). Twitter users can contact specific individual users or, as is more common, post their tweets to all users. Privacy settings are available so that one can limit access to one's posts by protect-

Figure 7
MySpace home page.

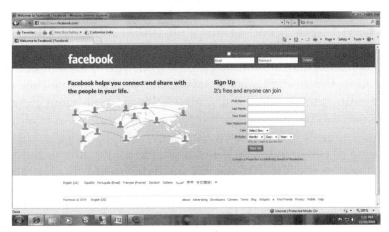

Figure 8
Facebook home page.

ing the profile so that one's approval of followers is required. The default setting is the public one, so users need to be careful to change this setting. In October 2009, Twitter added a feature called "lists" that allows users to follow everyone on the list by reaching the list instead of having to find each individual separately. The list can publicize its URL if it wants to be available for others to search.

Using Social Networking to Cyberbully

The potential for cyberbullying on these sites is great, as comments can be made about postings, photos, and videos on the site. An additional opportunity for cyberbullying is the creation of fake sites or accounts. Phony Twitter accounts can be set up; Twitter shows which accounts have been verified, but only those of persons most likely to be impersonated are checked. In a recent situation I was informed about, a student created a MySpace profile for a coach at the middle school. Because the coach is a public figure, the student was able to obtain an actual photograph for the profile and made a reasonable attempt at guessing the birth date and other details. The fake coach invited a number of students to be her "friends" on the site, which gave them the opportunity to comment, and so forth. Although there was nothing derogatory on the site, some of the attempts at humor could be construed as unflattering. For example, on the profile, *Coaching for Dummies* was listed under "Favorite Books." The student claimed she had created the site to entertain friends and was identified by a photo posted to the site. The principal at the school opted to have the student write about what she had done and the potential damage that could have been done to the coach, other students, and the school.

Other schools have been less tolerant of such behavior. Justin Layshock, a senior student in a high school in Pennsylvania, also set up a MySpace profile of the principal ("ACLU of Pennsylvania Urges Court," 2008). The profile proclaimed the principal smoked marijuana and kept a keg of beer in his office. When the student who created the site was identified, the school district suspended him and transferred him to an alternative program. He was also barred from attending his graduation ceremony. The American Civil Liberties Union (ACLU) sued the school district, the superintendent, the school principal, and the co-principal on the student's behalf. The court ruled in the student's favor, saying the profile was neither obscene nor threatening and invoked the student's First Amendment right to free speech. Since this decision was rendered in July 2007, an appeal has been heard, and the principal has sued the student (and several accomplices); the outcome of those actions was not available at the time of this writing.

Figure 9 shows my MySpace page. I show this to give readers an idea of how different MySpace is from Facebook (I include a sample Facebook page later). On MySpace, customizing layouts is important. The background graphics are called *skins*. Mine is a fairly basic layout—many are very elaborate—but readers can see the standard features of a profile here. The appearance and contents of the profile can be extensively customized.

Figure 9
MySpace profile of Dr. Bauman, including a poll feature listed
under "Interests" and a "Comments" section.

Music is a big part of MySpace, and my teenage friends have playlists on
their profiles to express themselves musically. It is common to have a song
play automatically when someone opens the profile (mine is a Paul Simon
tune). Note that I have also created a poll, shown under "Interests." It is
easy to see how such polls can be used to undermine a person's status. If
I were malicious, I would wait until I had accumulated many responses
and then show the results. The "Comments" feature is another place on
MySpace where someone could write derogatory things if cyberbullying
were an agenda.

Facebook profiles are much more uniform in appearance. If I put my own Facebook page here, my friends' posts and images would be visible, so I decided to show the profile page of a public figure, former president Bill Clinton (see Figure 10). The reader might want to visit the page and open the comments. They are very numerous and so are hidden (they open with just a click), but not all are favorable, to say the least. It would be interesting to see if any readers thought Mr. Clinton was being cyberbullied! In any case, you get a good idea of how different the Facebook platform is from MySpace.

Secretary of State Hillary Clinton's page is private, so I have to request that I be her friend (see Figure 11). The image shows how a Facebook friend

Figure 10
President Bill Clinton's Facebook wall.

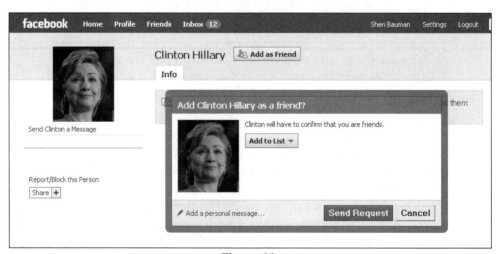

Figure 11
Requesting "friend" status from Hillary Clinton in Facebook.

request looks. Note that I can send Secretary Clinton a personal message (typically I will do so to greet a person I know but haven't seen recently and make the friend invitation less impersonal). Note also that there is a place to report this person, which I could do if she were cyberbullying me. You may be interested to know that Hillary did not confirm me as a friend, so I have been unable to see her private information!

There is so much to a social networking site that it is difficult to convey just the essentials so the reader can see both the positives and the potential for cyberbullying. Each of the websites has generated books, which are listed and described in Chapter 12.

Children's Websites

Websites that are created and designed for a youthful audience are described separately here because in many ways, they appear to be primarily a source of games and entertainment. Yet many of these sites have elements of social networking that present opportunities for cyberbullying.[1]

From their homes, schools, friends' homes, and the library, young children are flocking to websites that contain social networking features for entertainment and social purposes they've learned from family, friends, and peers. Data from 2007 showed that monthly visits to Club Penguin more than doubled to 4.7 million from the previous year (Buckleitner, 2008), with children spending an average of 54 minutes per visit; monthly traffic on Webkinz increased from 1 to 6 million in that same period (from April 2006 to January 2007), with the average visitor spending 2 hours and 8 minutes per visit (Hawn, 2007). Although the most famous and popular social networking websites are MySpace and Facebook, their membership is restricted to teenagers and adults, and so I will not focus on them in this section. However, I want to include the following comment by a youngster (with spelling as in the original), which illustrates that many younger children are eager to advance to these social networking services: "We should be aloud to use my space im only a little more than a year too young it's not fair at my age, we need to communicate! Everyone thinks life starts at 14, but it doesn't! it starts in middle school. Thanx a lot, tom!" (Tom is the owner of MySpace.com). This comment suggests that the commentator equates life with social networking sites.

More and more social networking sites are being offered to preteens (children of 12 years and younger), and such sites are continuously changing to generate features to improve their appeal and navigation on the sites. A recent listing of social networking websites that have no minimum age and are designed for young audiences listed 18 such sites ("February Roundup: Social Networking," 2008). Note that the information was cur-

---

[1]With permission of my coauthor and the American School Counselor Association, parts of this section were taken directly from a previously published article: Bauman & Tatum (2009).

rent at the time of this writing, but the interested reader is encouraged to regularly check the websites themselves or the resources listed in Chapter 12 for more information.

Club Penguin

Club Penguin, launched in 2005, has 2.8 million unique visitors per month as of January 2010 (www.quantcast.com).[2]

Although Club Penguin is primarily a game site, with a variety of children's games and activities and in which each player is a penguin (the penguin is an avatar), the site also includes IM and chats and allows users to accumulate clothing and furnishings for their igloos. The largest group of visitors is children ages 3–11 years old, with the next largest group ages 12–17.

Parental permission is required to play in Club Penguin. When a child opens an account, he or she must supply an e-mail address for a parent. The parent then receives an e-mail message with information about what the child can do on the site, along with disclosure of what information is collected and how it is protected. The parent must click on a link to allow the child to complete the registration for an account. The parent is also given the child's penguin name (similar to a login) and password. The parent has the ability to make changes to permissions on the child's account. These attempts to provide parental control are admirable, but savvy children can easily have the e-mail sent to their own (or a friend's) e-mail address and then approve the account. Users can chat with other penguins using prescripted content, or they can generate their own content with parental approval (which the parent decides when responding to the e-mail about the account). Although one can play on Club Penguin for free, a membership is available (monthly or annually) that gives access to many features unavailable to free users. Members with experience on the site can become so-called secret agents who patrol the site looking for bad behavior. Violators may be suspended from the site for days.

Figures 12–16 are screen shots that show what a new member sees when joining Club Penguin. Please note the many cautions that attempt to protect the user from abuse.

Once the child has an account, he or she can access the various options on the website. Two that I think are important to be aware of—because of the potential for cyberbullying—are the buddies feature and chats. Like other social networking sites, one has to request to be on someone's buddy list. In a brief experiment, my research assistant Tanisha Tatum and I opened free accounts in Club Penguin. I asked Tanisha to be my buddy and was happy when she agreed. For some children, not being accepted as a buddy is a passing disappointment; for others, it may be a terrible rejection. Some children see their buddy lists as validation of their social acceptance. If a child has one buddy request rejected, the child may be able

---

[2]Usage figures are updated daily. These figures were reported on quantcast.com on March 17, 2010.

Figure 12
Opening a free Club Penguin account.

Figure 13
Club Penguin rules.

Figure 14
Getting parental permission and password
to join Club Penguin.

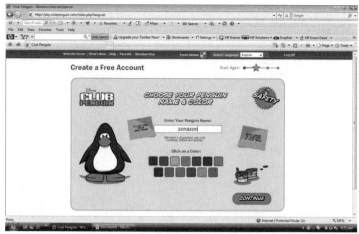

Figure 15
Creating a Club Penguin account.

Figure 16
Parents decide the chat mode available
to their child on Club Penguin.

to dismiss that. However, what if numerous requests are refused? Again, for vulnerable children, such experiences may be more emotionally significant than for others.

Next, Tanisha (Zonazoo) and I (Penguin94546165) entered a game. Within moments, we observed that someone had said something to hurt another's feelings ("That was not nice! Don't need to be that mean."). There's also an example of rejection when someone asks to join a party and is refused. We also observed such statements as "Ur weird" and "This place sux," suggesting that the filters still allow inappropriate statements to be posted (and posted by several penguins, or repeatedly), which can be hurtful to some children.

KidzWorld

KidzWorld has more features of a social networking site than Club Penguin, including message boards, chats, profiles, photos, and videos, and it reports more than 392,000 visitors per month, the majority of whom are under 18 years old. The home page of this site loads with video and music playing (see Figure 17). It is more like MySpace than the other children's websites

Figure 17
KidzWorld home page.

and has most of the features of the social networking sites, although it does
have some games, which makes it similar to more juvenile sites.

Webkinz

Webkinz are small plush toys that come with an attached secret code that
allows the owner to access the Webkinz World website. The secret code allows
the user to own a virtual version of the pet for virtual interaction. Webkinz
World began on April 28, 2005, and continues to grow on a daily basis; the
site is updated every 2 weeks (webkinz.com; see Figure 18). Webkinz currently has an estimated 3.6 million visitors per month (according to www.
quantcast.com). The largest group of visitors is children ages 3–11 years
old, with the next largest group ages 12–17. Webkinz World is an online
game area where users can play online games; shop for food, clothes, toys,
and furniture using KinzCash; and communicate with friends via the peer-

Figure 18
Webkinz home page.

to-peer network. Accumulating a large number of friends is important to many children, as can be seen in some children's comments listed below.

One teacher's response to a podcast about teaching kindergarten students how to be safe on the Internet is illuminating: "One of the kids had lost control of her Webkinz password for several months, and during that time someone (she never found out who) sold all her Webkinz furniture and did other things to mess up her account. The level of engagement of the students when we were discussing Webkinz was off the charts. Over 90% of the kids there in attendance (there were about 60) reported that they owned a Webkinz" ("Exploring Differences," 2008). The following are comments about Webkinz World found on www.topix.com, another source of child and adult reviews of websites.

- Webkinz rock except at 1:13 am a mesage comes up and does not let you log in!!!!!!! i mean COM ON give me a brake i always stay up late and play on Webkinz is all i want to do but i CAN'T!!!
- it is awesome! my username is jellita. please please please add me on your friendlist. bye.
- everyone stop talking sexual!!!!!!!!!!

Imbee

Imbee launched its social networking website in 2006 to offer a "safer" environment (as opposed to MySpace) for young children who wished to participate in social networking. Imbee most recently had approximately 8,000 visitors per month (according to www.quantcast.com), consisting of young children, parents, and teachers. Twenty-six percent of Imbee users ranged from ages 3–11 years, whereas 51% of users were ages 12–17. Adults compose the remainder of the membership. Billed as a safe social network for kids and lauded for its teacher features, it closed in May 2009. A primary reason for the closing of the site was the violation of privacy regulation in the Children's Online Privacy Protection Act (1998). The target audience for the site was the 8- to 14-year-old age group. When children registered for the site, they gave their full name, birth date, and e-mail address. After this information was provided, the parent received an e-mail invitation to activate the child's account (similar to Club Penguin). However, the information the child entered was retained by the site even if the parent never activated the account, which is a violation of the law. The site paid a $130,000 fine to resolve the problem. In addition, the site's founder was killed in a plane crash in 2008, which was a crucial blow to the site ("Imbee: First Safe Social Network," 2009).

Following are some comments about Imbee, obtained from mashable.com, a website with forums about social networking:

- yea i know it is much safer than myspace cause it is for kids like us
- you are doumb to have a my space
- N*** SHUT THE F*** UP [Words spelled out in the original post].

These comments illustrate how benign comments can easily escalate online. Note that the use of capitals is "netspeak" for shouting.

Kidswirl

A new entry into the websites for children is Kidswirl.com, a social networking site specifically for youths that was launched in March 2009. The home page proclaims that this is a "Kid Safe environment where kids can be kids!" All "bad language, inappropriate and suggestive phrases, and any other word usage that is requested by the parents and users" is blocked (Kidswirl, 2009). So far, it has a relatively small subscriber list (10,000 as of November 12, 2009). The appeal for parents is that the site is designed for children and youths: Member categories include age groups 2–12 and 13–18, Parent, Grandparent, Teacher, and Pastor. The site resembles the interface in Facebook and has many of the same features (marketed as convenience for parents, who can easily teach their kids how to use the site), but there are also links that are clearly appealing to children (e.g., "Pimp Your Profile"). Parental consent is required for children and teens, which is obtained via an e-mail entered by the user; parents also must approve any change, including adding friends. It remains to be seen whether children will find this site as appealing as parents will. Toward that end, on January 31, 2010, subscribers received an e-mail announcing that the site had been converted to a virtual economy, allowing users to accumulate Kidswirl Coins and to thus achieve status as the "richest" kid on the site. Despite the efforts to increase the appeal to young people, older children and teens may balk at the degree of control parents are given on this site. I encourage readers to visit www.kidswirl.com and to create an account in order to be able to explore the various features.

Aggression on Children's Websites

Greenfield (2004) expressed concern about aggression on some children's websites. Although many sites prohibit swear words or aggressive language, the quotations I have listed illustrate that despite the controls in place, children can make verbally aggressive comments on the site: "If I had to say, Club Penguin is mainly for pre-teens and teens (11 and up) because of the language. The moderators also don't work all the time, and swears do get through occasionally. Things also like, 'your a loser,' gets through very often" (Fiddle Didle, 2008). A mother who posed as a child and joined Club Penguin in order to evaluate the site reported being called a "weirdo" by other penguins and being excluded from a "party" that was for "members only" (Estroff, 2007). Although Club Penguin and some other sites have built-in mechanisms to monitor and control behavior, determined and tech-savvy children find ways around these restrictions. Estroff discovered that negative words are allowed if children describe themselves using those words (e.g., geek, nerd). Furthermore, penguins can tell others to "go away," display mean-faced emoticons, and throw snowballs at others. The fact that adults are not likely to witness these exchanges (and children are not likely to report them to parents for fear of the obvious solution: Stop going to the site) means that the cumulative impact of these events may be unnoticed by adults. The behavior exhibited on these sites might be called bullying if the same interactions occurred in real life. One concern about online bullying is that the anonymity afforded by these sites encourages some children to say or do things they would not do in a face-to-face situation.

Online Gaming

Online Gaming is not typically thought of in connection with cyberbullying. However, many of the games are interactive and people can be excluded or treated unkindly. These games often involve virtual worlds (described next) in which players have online roles. World of Warcraft (also known as WOW) and Runescape are examples of these interactive online gaming worlds. About 55% of U.S. teens have a portable gaming device through which they interact with others (Lenhart, 2009).

There are also several three-dimensional virtual worlds online; the best known site for adults is Second Life.com (see Figure 19). Other popular sites include IMVU.com and There.com. Monthly U.S. traffic on Second Life as of July 2, 2009, was 406,700 people, who viewed 17.2 million pages. This site also has a large international presence, with 1.2 million global visitors per month. Men (48%) and women (52%) are almost equally represented, with 30% of visitors in the 18- to 34-year-old age range and 23% in the 35- to 49-year-old range. Half of visitors reported no college education. On the site, so-called residents create avatars and are able to socialize, work, and date by voice and/or text chat. According to the frequently asked questions on the site, there are thousands of locations residents can visit by walking, flying, or teleporting to their chosen area. The site allows residents to own property, shop, build, play, start businesses, and perform other activities that mirror

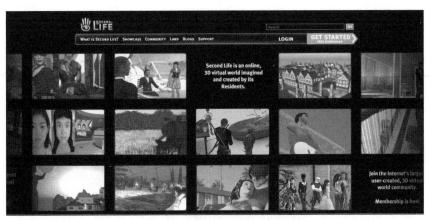

Figure 19
Second Life home page.

real life. A posting on Scientific Blogging.com reported on the findings of researchers at the University of Nottingham in the United Kingdom who conducted a cyberbased focus group of residents of Second Life. Residents reported such examples of bullying as being shot at, being hit, being harassed by noisy objects, having a house destroyed, and enduring swearing, with most of the bullying being directed at new residents (News Staff, 2007). Residents may not die or be killed, however. The site acknowledges that people can be harassed or bullied, but it allows users to mute offending persons. There is information available on further steps to take, including filing abuse reports (when terms of service or community standards have been violated), banning residents, or ejecting residents. Second Life requires residents to be at least 18 years old, but there is a teen version for those between the ages of 13 and 17. The site also is attempting to implement age verification features but acknowledges the difficulty of doing so.

Among the virtual worlds geared toward a younger audience, Whyville.com (see Figure 20) attracts about 3,000 visitors per month, 44% of whom are under the age of 18. The virtual world gaiaonline.com attracts 1.6 million U.S. visitors a month, 59% of whom are under the age of 18 (quantcast.com).

Video Sharing Sites

YouTube.com

YouTube.com merits specific attention because of its popularity (ranked as the fifth most popular site on the Internet in March 2010) and its potential for use in cyberbullying. Quantcast.com estimates that monthly U.S. traffic on YouTube is 104 million people! This figure is even more remarkable when one considers that the site was founded in 2005 and purchased by Google in 2006. Although the largest group of viewers is the 13- to 17-year-old age group, followed by the 18- to 34-year-old age group, the site attracts a considerable number of visitors in older groups as well. YouTube is a searchable site that contains viewer-posted videos (in addition to professionally recorded videos), which are rated and commented on by viewers.

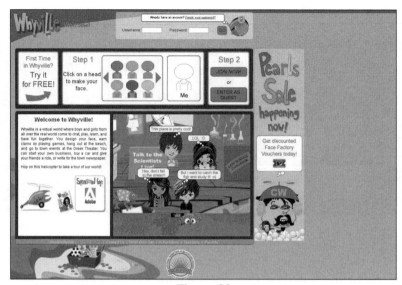

Figure 20
Whyville home page.

As a small experiment, I searched for "girl fights" on July 11, 2009, and got 164,000 hits. I also got some suggestions for search terms to get even more videos, for example, school fights and chick fights. The 2 minute and 4 second video that was first on the list had been posted 3 weeks earlier and had already had 101,376 views at that point. The fight was set to music and shown in four "rounds." More disturbing were the text comments about the video (there were 368 text comments and one video comment)—I was not willing to watch the video response.

YouTube, because it is populated by viewer material, also contains some wonderful clips that are edifying and entertaining. I was mesmerized recently by clips of a 6-year-old piano prodigy playing her own compositions (Emily Bear, if you are curious). I often use YouTube clips in my classes. YouTube was also instrumental in providing the world with images during the protests following the 2009 presidential election in Iran despite government efforts to censor news. Although there are numerous positive values for this site, the potential for cyberbullying is enormous. The video I watched was of a brutal, nasty fight. I don't know whether the girls did this for public viewing, but many such things are posted without the subjects' knowledge or consent. The comments can be as disturbing as the public viewing of one's humiliation. Some made rude comments about the pugilists' physiques; others judged who had "won," and so forth. I did not see a single comment (although I confess I did not read them all) suggesting this was not a good use of the site.

Summary

- A variety of cyberenvironments can be appropriated for malicious use. However, all cyberenvironments can provide positive experiences for users.

- IM allows for real-time conversation. It generally occurs online, although some phones and services have that capability. Some youths have multiple IMs at the same time; sensory overload can result in errors of judgment in the fast-paced conversation.
- Chat rooms are typically organized around a theme, and users select screen names for that environment. Some believe the anonymity leads to disinhibition, and individuals can be attacked verbally or rejected.
- Trash polling sites are designed to collect disparaging comments about an individual. Typically, the target is informed of the existence of the site after a sufficient number of comments have been collected so that the target finds a series of cruel remarks and comments.
- Blogs are similar to online diaries and express the writer's opinions. Many blogs are very informative, but some bloggers may take the opportunity to make comments about targeted individuals. In addition, viewers may comment on blog posts, which means there is yet another opportunity for cruelty.
- E-mail continues to be a popular method of communication, perhaps more so for adults. E-mails can be directly derogatory, but private e-mails can also be forwarded to an unintended audience, embarrassing or humiliating the original sender.
- Texting via cell phone has become increasingly popular. Although service providers do not allow users to hide their numbers, online services have been developed that enable people to send texts with their identities hidden. Anonymous texts can be very frightening when they include threats, direct or veiled.
- The practice of happy slapping, or filming incidents in which the target is beaten, is designed to humiliate the victim beyond the original incident by making the video available to a large audience. In some cases, those videos have led to the apprehension of the bully.
- Social networking sites provide many communication vehicles in one location. Many people enjoy using these sites to connect with friends and families and keep up with their lives. The sites can also be used for nefarious purposes in ways noted for other environments. Some websites designed for young children are primarily game sites, with communication options that allow children to be insulted or excluded. Adult sites have a minimum age for participation, but ages are not verifiable, so many youths participate.
- Virtual worlds are available for both young adults and children. These virtual worlds are fraught with all the hazards of real-world socializing, and bullying on such sites is not uncommon.
- Video sharing websites provide a wide variety of selections for viewers, including educational ones that can be used in classes. The sites also provide opportunities for people to post videos designed expressly to humiliate a target.

CHAPTER 4
Types of Cyberbullying

With the primary tools of the Internet and cell phones, there are a number of different ways in which cyberbullying is manifested. I describe them in this chapter, both to alert readers to the forms cyberbullying may take and also to begin to develop the vocabulary of technology.

Forms of Cyberbullying

Flaming

Flaming refers to hostile, angry, insulting interactions that frequently are hurtful personal attacks. Flaming can occur in a variety of environments, such as online forums and discussion boards, chat rooms, e-mail, and IM. The anger is often expressed by using capital letters, as in U R AN IDIOT AND I HATE U! Many flaming messages are vicious and cruel and tend to disregard fact or reason.

Harassment

Harassment on the Internet or by cell phone is the same as harassment using more conventional means. Harassment refers to hostile actions based on someone's gender, race, age, sexual orientation, and so forth and is against the law. Technology allows the perpetrator to perform these hostile actions more easily and persistently. The bully is not limited by time or space but is able to send repeated messages that threaten, upset, or defame the victim from any location and at any time. Although one can block e-mail and text messages when the sender is known, there are strategies the determined harasser can use to remain anonymous. For example, because cell phones do not allow someone to send a text message without showing the number of the sender, the malicious e-mailer may use websites set up just for this purpose. Those sites appear and disappear, but a Google search for "send anonymous text messages" will show a number of current sites. Many of the sites have an option for a person to block all messages that come from the site, but the individual would have to recognize that this is where the message originated. I provide more information about this topic later in the book.

Denigration

Denigration is the practice of demeaning or disrespecting another person using technology. This, like most variations on cyberbullying, can be accomplished in a variety of settings. In addition to involving rude or hurtful messages that are sent directly to the person, denigration is often done in a public setting by creating web pages specifically for the purpose of posting hurtful content and images about an individual. The most famous example of this form of cyberbullying is that of David Knight, a Canadian teenager. In 2005, a schoolmate of David's created a website called "Welcome to the page that makes fun of Dave Knight" (Leishman, 2005). The page was filled with hateful comments; some suggested David was a pedophile who used date rape drugs to ensnare young boys. David learned about the site when he received a message from a third party who suggested he visit the website. The page included a photo of David in addition to the offensive text. Nasty e-mails followed, with more invective. In an interview with Leishman, David's mother described his reaction to these events. He became extremely withdrawn and isolated. The police, contacted by David's parents, were unable to help. A discussion of the legal status of cyberbullying is given in Chapter 8, but suffice it to say that unless a direct, credible threat is made, the cyberbullying may not be against the law. In this case, the website was created on Yahoo, and the family attempted to get the company's cooperation in removing the site; however, the site was not removed right away. David was so distressed he left school and completed his last year at home. David's comment expressed what I suspect many victims feel: "Rather than just some people, say 30 in a cafeteria, hearing them all yell insults at you, it's up there for 6 billion people to see. Anyone with a computer can see it. And you can't get away from it when you come home from school. It made me feel even more trapped" (Leishman, 2005, para. 2). The offending site was eventually removed after the parents threatened legal action.

Masquerading

Masquerading is a technique that requires a bit of sophistication on the part of the perpetrator. It involves pretending to be another person and sending messages that appear to come from that person that cause harm to the person.

One way to do this is by somehow accessing (i.e., hacking into) an individual's e-mail account and sending the messages directly. This type of access is often accomplished by friends sharing passwords, but the sophisticated hacker may find other ways (e.g., systematically trying likely passwords). The useful website www.netsmartz.org has a section of real-life stories in brief video clips, and one of these, *Broken Friendship,* is an example of the harm inflicted on one young teen. It's well worth watching (and showing to teens). The victim shared her password with her best friend, who then gave it to other (popular) girls in an attempt to win their approval. These girls then sent provocative sexual images and messages to many boys from the victim's e-mail account. She was subjected to humiliating comments, and soon everyone knew of the shocking messages she had apparently sent. Her reputation was ruined, as was her original friendship.

Counselors can help clients (and communities) avoid this type of cyber-bullying by giving clear guidance regarding passwords. First, one should *never* share passwords with anyone, with the exception of children giving passwords to their parents or caregivers. Friendships change over time, and the best friend with someone's password may no longer value the friend-ship. Second, it is essential to create passwords that are not likely to be discovered by a determined hacker. For example, one's birth date, anniver-sary, children's names, house number, and so forth are common choices. Someone attempting to gain access to your account will try all the obvious choices—and it is imperative that those not work! Some sites requiring passwords now give a score for the difficulty of the password; choose one that is the most difficult to detect. Longer passwords with random digits or symbols are more likely to be safe. It is also important for the user to have a safe place, not on their computer, to store the passwords.

Counselors (and some clients) might benefit from having more than one e-mail account. One may be their business account for professional e-mails and personal correspondence. The other can be a so-called throw-away ac-count (Gmail, Yahoo) that is used for electronic mailing lists, online discus-sions, and so forth. If those accounts get unwanted or excessive numbers of messages, they can simply be closed down without interrupting essential e-mail. Counselors must decide whether and in what circumstances to give e-mail access to clients. This situation can present ethical dilemmas, which I discuss later in the book.

Outing and Trickery

Outing and trickery work in tandem. This method involves persuading an individual to provide confidential information or material—and then sharing it with others via e-mail, text message, or posting on a website. I have forwarded many e-mails without getting the consent of the sender, but in this cyberbullying tactic, it is done maliciously, and the information is actively sought with the intent of publicizing it. The cyberbully typically lies to the victim, swearing to keep the information confidential. One could consider the rash of sexting incidents as a variation on this theme. The bully persuades the victim to send a nude or very revealing photo via text, saying it is just for his or her personal use to admire. Then, or later when the relationship falters, the images are forwarded to many recipients, and the victim is humiliated and often subjected to nasty rumors. In an incident shared with me, this happened to a high school girl, who was charmed by her boyfriend into sending a nude photo. After they had a fight, the boyfriend sent the message to many students at their high school. It also happened that the girl was absent from school on the day he publicized the photo, and a rumor quickly circulated saying she was having an abortion. When she returned to school, she was subjected to verbal bullying (e.g., she was called "slut" and "baby-killer") and was so humiliated she wanted to drop out of school. This is not an isolated incident.

Social Exclusion

Social exclusion is a deliberate and pointed action to make it clear to individuals that they are not part of the group and that their presence is not wanted. On the Internet, this exclusion can happen in chat rooms quite easily. When using IM, a person can be removed from buddy lists and not included in discussions. On social networking sites, people can de-friend someone, which means their ability to view profiles, make comments, and so forth is no longer available. The message is clear: The victim is undesirable and an outsider.

Cyberstalking

Cyberstalking is the electronic version of stalking (repeatedly threatening or harassing someone). Because stalking is a crime, cyberstalking can often be actionable in the legal system. In most states, certain elements must be present in order to take legal action. Those elements include the presence of malice (the intention to terrorize and hurt the victim). The requirement that malice be present creates a problem for the victim when the cyberstalker is a possessive romantic partner who sends text messages many times per day. Premeditation is also necessary for legal action in many cases, and this is difficult to demonstrate unless the person sets up an elaborate system that can be shown to require planning. However, if the stalker is not a romantic partner and goes to great lengths to find identifying information about the victim in order to be more frightening—and perhaps to attempt in-person contact—premeditation is evident. The most salient feature of online stalking is the repetition. For actions to be cyberstalking, they must be repeated, typically many times. In some cases, former romantic partners become cyberstalkers, texting the individual every few minutes, leaving voicemails on the cell phone, making contact via social networking sites, and so forth. Cyberstalking also requires evidence that the victim is distressed and fearful. If a case is prosecuted, a counselor's testimony regarding the distress of the victim can provide this evidence. Sometimes cyberstalking actions are an immature person's idea of a prank, but the recipient has no way of knowing that. In one case, a student received numerous text messages over a weekend with messages such as, "You are going to die." The sender did not disguise his identity, and the police were contacted. The explanation given was that the sender (and a friend who was part of the scheme) thought it was a joke—a frequent response when cyberbullies are caught. The victim did not find any humor in the situation, nor did the police. Because of their age, the bullies were not prosecuted, but they received clear and stern warnings about the consequences of future behavior. Cyberstalking often includes these kinds of direct or implied cyberthreats, which are typically extremely upsetting to the victim. Some states require that there be "credible threats," which means the threat is one that the victim believes the stalker could carry out. In the case of the "You are going to die" messages to a vulnerable preadolescent, the stalker could argue that everyone dies, and there was no implied threat. Again, the victim interpreted the text to mean that the stalker intended to kill her. In some states, the victim would have to prove that the cyberstalker continued the behavior after being told it was unwanted. When the victim clearly sends a message saying "Do not contact me again," the stalker cannot argue that the contact was welcome.

Cyberstalking victims must learn how to identify, whenever possible, the perpetrator and how to reduce the harm. Counselors can provide information about the importance of blocking senders (this can be done in both e-mail and cell phones), saving evidence (such as e-mails with complete headers), taking appropriate actions (sending clear messages saying the contact is unwanted), contacting authorities when there are legal violations, and when necessary closing accounts and changing numbers and e-mail addresses. It is essential that counselors caution victims not to attempt to retaliate, as that is likely to accelerate the attacks and place the victim in legal jeopardy.

In Chapter 8, I review legislation on cyberbullying that helps the counselor recognize when bad behavior crosses the line into illegal behavior. In many cases, freedom of speech trumps victims' distress; counseling may be helpful when clients feel betrayed by the system. On the other hand, victims may not realize when they do have legal recourse, and counselors may be able to point that out.

Summary

- The types of cyberbullying are many, giving the cyberbully numerous tools to use. Sometimes these are used in combination, with additional effect. The primary tools are the Internet and the cellular phone.
- Flaming refers to sending angry (often with offensive language) messages technologically. Capital letters are used to show the equivalent of shouting.
- Harassment is the technological version of discrimination or hostile behavior toward someone based on his or her status (gender, race, religion, disability, sexual orientation, and so forth).

- Denigration is sending or posting defamatory information about someone.
- Masquerading is the tactic of using someone else's identity (e-mail, phone, and so forth) to send messages that are rude or inappropriate and making it appear that the message comes from someone else, so that person will be accused of perpetrating the behavior.
- Outing and trickery are ways of cajoling a person into revealing personal information, which is then publicized using electronic communication.
- Social exclusion is the practice of deliberately excluding someone from an electronic group, such as a buddy list, a chat room (by ignoring or blocking), a discussion board, or a game.
- Cyberstalking refers to repeatedly using electronic communication to annoy, harass, or threaten an individual.
- Cyberthreats are messages intended to convey that the recipient or the recipient's family is in imminent danger of harm.

CHAPTER 5
Theories of Aggressive Behavior

Because cyberbullying is a form of aggression, it is perhaps helpful to briefly review the major theories of aggressive behavior. Many volumes have been written on this topic, and a detailed explanation of each theory is beyond the scope of this book. The following is intended to give the reader a basic familiarity with the various theoretical positions.

Functions of Aggression

Aggression refers to behavior that is intended to cause harm to another. Most people tend to think of aggression as a negative behavior, but Swearer, Espelage, and Napolitano (2009) argued persuasively that developmental psychologists have not sufficiently addressed the fact that aggression serves a useful purpose for individuals and the social system. Bullying and aggression are used to establish dominance in peer groups, often bring increased popularity for aggressors, and frequently bring increased dating partners for middle school students. Smith (2007) looked to other species for the functions of aggression. He noted that aggression in primates and other mammals is often about competition for scarce resources. Establishing dominance hierarchies reduces the number and severity of conflicts, avoiding more serious injury or death. Challenges to dominance in these species often occur when a young animal is ready to assume a dominant position and does so by demonstrating his strength against an older adversary. Other challenges arise when new animals enter the group; their place in the hierarchy must be determined. Smith drew parallels to this behavior in humans and suggested that researchers must reconsider the view that aggression is always maladaptive. As Swearer et al. pointed out, neglecting to take into account the functions of aggression may doom prevention and intervention programs to failure.

Aggression can be classified according to the function of the behavior, and there are two types: instrumental aggression and reactive aggression. *Instrumental aggression* (sometimes called *proactive aggression*) refers to aggressive actions that are goal-directed and deliberate, such as assaulting a person in order to obtain the desired iPod or humiliating someone else in order to elevate one's social status in a group. With this type of aggression, the aggressor uses the behavior to obtain a goal and believes that aggression is an appropriate way of doing so. It is not a response to provocation. Small children can be observed pushing another child in order to obtain a particular toy, an example of instrumental aggression. *Reactive aggression* is an impulsive, often emotional and uncontrolled, response to a perceived attack. A person who strikes out after being hit by another is engaging in reactive aggression. Cyberbullying likely involves both types of aggression. The calculating bully who seeks to win approval from others by attacking a teacher online, for example, is engaging in instrumental aggression. The victim who sends an angry, expletive-ridden message in response to a hurtful e-mail is reactively aggressive. This distinction is helpful for counselors in devising appropriate interventions for cyberbullies. For example, cyberbullies who are proactively aggressive in order to gain social status or approval from peers can be taught new skills to accomplish those goals. The reactively aggressive cyberbully–victim will benefit from developing a repertoire of ways to respond when bullied, other than retaliation.

Forms of Aggression

Aggression can also be categorized by the form of the behavior. *Overt aggression* is direct and readily observed: hitting, pushing, name-calling. *Covert aggression* (also called *relational aggression* or *social aggression*) is directed toward harming the target's friendships, social relationships, or social status. Excluding someone from an activity is one such behavior. Some have suggested that cyberbullying is related to covert or relational aggression because of its anonymity and the absence of physical contact. On the other hand, some cyberbullying is quite direct and involves name-calling and deliberate humiliation of the target. Cyberbullying is therefore likely to encompass both forms and both types of aggression.

Theories of Aggression

Why are people aggressive? One theory proposes that humans have an innate, biologically based aggressive instinct. This perspective has origins in Freudian psychology and finds support in the early emergence of aggressive behavior in children. Others note that aggression is common in other animals as well, citing evidence from the field of animal ethology. Drive theory has also been proposed as an explanation of aggression. This theory proposes that when frustration builds, aggression occurs. The frustration occurs when attempts to satisfy basic needs (food, water, sleep, sex, love, recognition) are impeded by an outside force. If the frustration is accompanied by anger, aggression is likely.

Bandura (1973) found both instinct and drive theories lacking. He explained aggression in his broader theory of social learning. He believes that aggression is a learned behavior. The developing child learns about aggression by observing it in others (adults, peers, media) and noting whether it works (the aggressor gets his or her goal) or leads to negative consequences (the aggressor is punished). As children use aggression themselves, the learning is reinforced (or not). This theory has been the basis of considerable research on the influence media violence has on children's behavior, suggesting that observational or vicarious learning is quite effective. For counselors working with cyberbullies and victims, understanding how and where these behaviors have been learned and reinforced may lead to strategies to replace these behaviors by learning and reinforcing more prosocial ones.

Most current views of aggression incorporate aspects of all three major theories (Baron & Richardson, 2004; Huesmann, Guerra, Miller, & Zelli, 1992). Researchers know that some children may inherit aggressive predispositions and that their interactions and observations of the social environment are powerful influences on their behavior. These theories need to be considered when working with all aspects of cyberbullying, but perhaps it is most important when working with the cyberbullies who are engaging in aggressive behavior.

Social–Ecological Theory

The social–ecological perspective of bullying (Swearer & Espelage, 2004), based on Bronfenbrenner's (1979) ecological model, is very applicable to cyberbullying. This theory situates bullying within contextual layers: The center of the model is the individual, but bullying occurs within the social context of peer networks, classrooms, schools, communities, and so forth, sometimes depicted as a series of concentric circles. The importance of this framework is that it reminds us counselors that we cannot view this problem with too narrow a lens. That is, if we focus only on the individuals (the cyberbullies and cybervictims), we are ignoring the influence of family, school, peers, community, culture, and so forth. Bronfenbrenner described several systems that interact and affect an individual: the microsystem, with whom an individual has direct contact (family, peers, and school); the mesosystem, which encompasses the interactions between elements of the microsystem (if a family uses harsh discipline and is critical of a young person, that young person might turn to peers for affection and approval); the exosystem, which involves the relationships between other systems (the family's response when called to a school conference); and the macrosystem, the largest system that includes culture and society.

Swearer and Doll (2001) described the social ecology of bullying. Applying this approach to cyberbullying, one sees that the individual is the center of the model, and individual characteristics are relevant. However, research in cyberbullying has not identified the characteristics that may predispose someone to cyberbully or to be cybervictimized. Conventional bullies tend to be aggressive and impulsive and to view aggression as a useful strategy to get one's needs met. Victims may be shy and depressed and have a tendency to internalize problems. Whether these characteristics also apply to cyberbullies and cybervictims has not yet been empirically established. In their early study of cyberbullying, Ybarra and Mitchell (2004) found that those who were both aggressors and targets reported the most difficulties, including problem behaviors, drinking, smoking, and overall poor psychosocial functioning. Aggressors were more likely to be high school age than middle school age (the opposite is the case for conventional bullying). They were also likely to rate themselves as expert or nearly expert at Internet skills and to use the Internet 3 hours per day or more. The only characteristic of targets who were not also aggressors was intense daily usage of the Internet. Note that cell phone use was not part of this study. Given the differences between conventional and cyber forms of bullying and victimization, it may be that a different individual profile emerges. In any case, the individual's decision to engage in these behaviors is influenced by individual traits and characteristics.

Families contribute to the dynamics of cyberbullying in the way they model interactions with technology. Do parents talk about negative online interactions and discuss aggressive responses? Do they talk with children about the safe and appropriate use of technology? This modeling also applies to workplace cyberbullying. What do other adults in the family model in terms of how to respond to aggressive technological communication in the workplace? How is aggression expressed in the family? Is it ignored, encouraged?

Because a good deal of cyberbullying involves peers from school, the behavior of peers and teachers is also part of the equation. For example, if a cyberbully brags to friends (or shows friends electronically) about an action that embarrasses a classmate, do the friends respond with approval, or do they discourage the behavior? Do friendship groups engage in cyberbullying? How do teachers respond when cyberbullying is detected or reported? Do they intervene or ignore the situation? The workplace contains similar dynamics, with colleagues in the position of friends and supervisors in the role played by teachers with adolescents.

The next level involves school (or workplace) policies regarding cyberbullying and how consistently those are enforced. Are the policies clear and well-publicized? Are students or employees asked to sign a copy of the policies to indicate they understand them? Is aggression of any kind tolerated in the school or organization? Do leaders model bullying or cyberbullying?

Not only is our society infused with technology (note the advent of Twitter, which had 1.4 million monthly visits in January 2009 and almost 27 million people visits in June 2009, according to quantcast.com), it seems as though interpersonal communication via technology has become the norm. Although cyberbullying is not condoned at the societal level, both the fascination with and the rapid adoption of new ways to communicate are strongly embraced. Thus, as concerned counselors consider how to reduce cyberbullying, the solutions must address the multiple interrelated systems that are involved in contributing to that behavior. Furthermore, the enormous complexity apparent when one takes a social–ecological perspective suggests that eliminating cyberbullying is not likely to happen in the short term; harm reduction strategies and strategies for responding when cyberbullying occurs are necessary components of a solution.

Social Information Processing Theory

The social information processing theory provides insight into how children process social information. The model has undergone several revisions since it was first proposed by Dodge (1986); the primary source of the following description is Crick and Dodge (1994). The steps to be described are predicated on the assumption that children bring biologically defined capacities along with memories of past experiences (the individual database) to a social situation. Those memories are integrated with others so that there are more general cognitive structures, called *schemata* or *scripts* that can be used to guide the process in subsequent situations. Such cognitive structures improve the efficiency of the process but may also result in errors.

When a social situation is encountered, children process the social information in a series of discrete steps that occur at the unconscious level and are often automatic. Although this automaticity allows for more rapid social information processing, it also means that the neural pathways in which these responses are encoded become strengthened, making it more difficult to access novel responses.

1. In the first step, the cues (sensory input) are encoded. This process involves attending to salient details in the social situation, and this step can be influenced by emotional arousal, which provides internal clues.
2. Next, those cues are interpreted, and a mental representation of the interpretation is created. The interpretation is made with the undergirding of the database information (memories of past events) that the child has stored.
    a. The interpretation is based on the selective attention that occurred in Step 1. That is, it is based on the elements of the scene that the child noticed.
    b. The interpretation may be influenced by the emotional response to the situation. A child who is feeling fearful is likely to interpret a situation differently than if that child were feeling calm.
    c. The interpretation may include a determination of the cause of the situation.
    d. The interpretation includes conclusions about the intent of others in the situation (these are known as *attributions*, which are discussed in more detail below).

    e. The interpretation may consider whether the goal in prior social exchanges had been achieved.

    f. The interpretation may include an evaluation of outcome expectations and self-efficacy predictions in previous social exchanges with this peer.

    g. The interpretation includes an assessment of the meaning of this social exchange for the child (self-evaluation) and the peer (other-evaluation).

3. Based on that representation, a goal is selected.

    a. The goal is a particular outcome the child wants to achieve in this situation (e.g., gaining status, getting even, making a friend, and so forth).

    b. Children bring tendencies toward certain types of goals to a situation (e.g., staying out of trouble) but may construct a new goal in a new situation.

4. A menu of possible responses is accessed or created.

    a. The child retrieves from memory a repertoire of possible responses or creates new responses.

    b. The ability to access a sufficient number of options can be influenced by the child's emotional state.

5. A decision is made regarding the best response, given the goal and predicted emotional reactions of self and others.

    a. When evaluating responses, children consider their expectation for the outcome of each possible response (outcome expectation).

    b. They also consider whether they have the skills or abilities necessary to enact a particular response (self-efficacy).

    c. They also consider their beliefs regarding how appropriate a given response seems to be (response evaluation).

6. The chosen behavior is enacted.

    a. Based on the processing that has occurred, children select a behavior.

    b. Children are likely to check the reactions they receive from enacting a particular behavior, and that information is stored for retrieval in a future similar situation.

Although the description of the process appears linear and singular (i.e., one situation at a time), in reality the process is cyclical, and there may be several social information processing steps occurring simultaneously. Crick and Dodge (1994) pointed out that these processes also occur on a neural level, but the connection between the two is difficult to determine.

In terms of development, as children grow older they have a larger set of experiences in social situations and thus have larger repertoires of possible responses. They also acquire more adaptive skills as they grow, such as negotiating with a peer rather than using physical aggression. The increased experience makes each step of social information processing more efficient and, generally, more appropriate. Children also continue to receive messages and modeling from adults about how to manage social situations.

Attribution Theory

In developing their model of the social information processing theory, Crick and Dodge (1994) drew on attribution theory. Attribution theory (e.g., developed by Heider [1958], extended by Kelley [1967], applied to education by Weiner [1986, 1992]) proposes that human beings tend to want to explain events in their lives—positive or negative—based on several types of beliefs (attributions) about the cause of those events. The locus of the cause can be perceived to be either (a) internal, or dispositional (i.e., something within the self); or (b) external, or situational (i.e., something in the environment or in someone else). For example, when victimized by cyberbullying, the victim might believe this happened because he or she is flawed in some way or less worthy of respect than others (internal) or that this happened because the bully is callous, cowardly, and pathetic (external). The victim also has underlying beliefs about whether the cause is something that is stable (i.e., enduring, such as a physical trait or disability) or unstable (i.e., a behavior one has chosen, such as not wearing trendy clothing). Causes are also controllable or uncontrollable. If one is targeted because of severe acne or a large nose, those traits are not easily changed (uncontrollable), whereas if one has been targeted because of a behavior (being unfriendly or rude), the cause is controllable.

This theory has been widely applied to academic motivation, and a basic principle is that individuals will interpret events in order to maintain their self-esteem. The classic example is test performance. Weiner maintains that when students do well, they are likely to attribute their success to internal ("I'm intelligent"), stable ("I'm diligent"), and controllable ("I studied hard") variables, whereas when they do poorly, they are likely to perceive the cause to be external ("The test was unfair"), unstable ("I was having a bad day"), and uncontrollable ("The subject is boring").

Attributions have been studied in relation to bullying because there is evidence that people tend to develop attribution biases that affect their behavior (Graham & Juvonen, 2001). It is reasonable to assume that this same process will apply to cyberbullying. The theory proposes that one develops a tendency to consistently evaluate all similar events with the same attributions of causality rather than examining each event separately. Developmentally, as children acquire social understanding and skills, they develop mental templates for solving social problems (Epps & Kendall, 1995). The child may develop a general belief that the world is hostile (known as *hostile attribution bias*; Crick & Dodge, 1994; Nasby, Hayden, & DePaulo, 1980) and, when presented with a new situation, will focus on those elements in the situation that confirm the bias and will act in accordance with that bias. This hostile attribution bias is particularly problematic when the event is ambiguous: When there is insufficient evidence to determine whether another's actions were intentionally hostile, the person with a hostile attribution bias will tend to evaluate the event as if it were definitely hostile. This pattern tends to be self-reinforcing, so that without intervention, the hostile attribution bias tends to become quite ingrained and may persist into adulthood. An interesting study by MacBrayer, Milich, and Hundley (2003) observed hostile attribution biases in mothers of aggressive children, suggesting that this pattern might be learned by observation.

When victims perceive the cause of victimization to be internal (i.e., within the self as opposed to within the bully), they may have what is known as a *self-blaming attribution.* Two variations of this bias have been described: *Behavioral self-blame* fixes the blame on something one has done in the situation ("I gave my password to a friend"), which is then controllable and unstable, whereas *characterological self-blame* attributes the cause of victimization to some "permanent" quality of the self ("I am so stupid"; Graham & Juvonen, 2001). It is obvious that behavioral self-blame can lead to behavioral changes to avoid a repetition of the event ("I'll change my password and not give it to anyone this time"), whereas the characterological self-blame leads to a sense of helplessness and hopelessness ("I can't help it if I wasn't born with much in the brains department"). Empirical studies have revealed that victims of bullying and harassment tend to report more characterological self-blaming attributions than their nonvictimized peers (e.g., see Graham, Bellmore, & Mize, 2006; Kingsbury & Espelage, 2008), and characterological self-blame is associated with greater maladjustment in response to hypothetical bullying scenarios (Graham et al., 2006) and cyberbullying scenarios (Bauman, 2009).

What is important is that attributional biases affect not only behavior but also psychological reactions. The hostile attributions made by bullies lead to their aggressive behavior; the self-blaming attributions of victims lead to psychological distress. This finding has important implications for interventions, which are discussed later in the book.

Moral Disengagement

Bandura (1999, 2001, 2002) and his colleagues (Bandura, Barbaranelli, Caprara, & Pastorelli, 1996) proposed a theory of moral disengagement consistent with his broader social cognitive theory that provides a way of understanding aspects of bullying. From this perspective, people behave in ways that are satisfying and validate their self-worth. Hence, once people have developed moral standards, or beliefs about what is right and wrong, they do not behave in ways that are contrary to those standards because that would result in negative self-evaluation. However, those negative self-judgments can be avoided by a process Bandura called *moral disengagement.* This process involves the following cognitive mechanisms by which the individual disengages those moral standards: cognitive restructuring, minimizing one's role, disregarding the harmful effects, and blaming the victim. Bandura (2002) observed that this process is incremental, whereby a person gradually uses more of these mechanisms or uses them more frequently over time, each time slightly reducing the self-censure that would cause the person to stop the behavior.

Each of these categories of cognitive mechanisms includes several different but related tactics. Cognitive restructuring includes the practice of moral justification, that is, explaining the behavior by higher principles, such as honor or loyalty. Using this strategy, the bully tells himself that he attacked the victim because the victim had defamed a friend, so that loyalty to a friend justifies the aggression. Euphemistic language, or describing a morally unacceptable behavior in terms that mask its nature, might be used by a bully who describes aggression as "fooling around." The third mechanism of cognitive restructuring involves advantageous comparison: The bully diminishes the harmfulness of the action by comparing it to something more serious. The bully might think, "Teasing isn't anything like beating someone up."

The next group of mechanisms that involves minimizing one's role is about denying self-responsibility: "It's the teacher's job to keep us in line" or "Everyone was telling me to do it" or "Everyone was teasing her, not just me." In general, people feel less responsible for something when they are part of a group than when they act as an individual. The mechanism of disregarding harmful effects includes cognitive strategies minimizing the negative consequences of one's actions and focusing on positive ones. For example, the bully might believe, "I'm just toughening him up so he can protect himself from real bullies." Note that to use this mechanism, the bully must avoid focusing attention on the harm that's been done (such as the victim's tears, the black eye, and so forth).

The final set of strategies involves mentally transforming the actions so they are the fault of the victim. One may dehumanize the victim, a favorite of racist aggressors, so that the victim is perceived to lack human traits. Another approach is to attribute blame to the victim, by saying for example, "If she had not given me her password, this wouldn't have happened" or "If he hadn't insulted my sister, I wouldn't have had to beat him up."

Bandura et al. (1996) tested the model and a questionnaire designed to measure moral disengagement on elementary, middle, and high school students. They found that for all groups, the higher the ratings (self, peer, or teacher) for peer aggression, the higher the score on moral disengagement and, conversely, the lower the ratings for prosocial behavior.

Other research has had similar outcomes. Researchers in three different European cities used peer nomination to classify 179 children as bullies, victims, or outsiders (Menesini et al., 2003). The students were interviewed using cartoons to illustrate bullying situations and were asked about their emotions if they were the bully in the scenario. The emotions of guilt or shame were considered to reflect moral responsibility, whereas indifference or pride was coded for moral disengagement. The researchers then asked the children about the reasons they would feel the emotions they described. Responses reflecting moral responsibility were classified into three categories: (a) Egocentric responsibility was coded when the reason given showed the child was trying to avoid negative consequences, (b) conventional rules was used when the response showed the child was focused on the rules of normative behavior, and (c) empathy was coded when the child's response showed concern for others. Responses reflecting moral disengagement motives were also classified into three categories: (a) Egocentric disengagement was coded when the response focused on the positive consequences for the bully or reflected disregard of the negative consequences to the victim, (b) deviant rules was coded when the response evidenced diffusion of responsibility or avoidance of personal responsibility, and (c) absence of empathy was coded when the response showed a lack of interest in others. The results showed that bullies identified moral disengagement emotions significantly more than victims or outsiders. In addition, the researchers found that egocentric disengagement was the most common type of moral disengagement used by bullies. Other than for conventional rules (which younger children reported more often than older children), age differences were not detected. Despite some differences between cities, the authors noted that the profiles of bullies with respect to the two major variables (moral disengagement and egocentrism) did not reveal any cultural differences.

Hymel, Rocke-Henderson, and Bonanno (2005) studied 494 Canadian students in Grades 8 and 10 using a self-report survey. They found that 38% of variance in self-reported bullying behavior was explained by the moral disengagement score. Additional analyses by bullying and victimization frequency revealed that students who reported most frequent bullying had the highest mean scores on the moral disengagement measure. Another interesting result was that among those who engaged in limited or infrequent bullying, levels of moral disengagement dropped when their personal victimization increased. The researchers speculated that it is more difficult to use moral disengagement when one has experienced first-hand the harmful effects of bullying. The reader should keep in mind that the students in the study were predominantly White and from middle- to upper-class families; future research will have to inform us of results with a more diverse sample.

Gini (2006) examined social cognition and moral cognition in bullying in a sample of 581 children ages 8 to 11 years in an Italian elementary school. Students were mostly (96%) White. In order to balance participant role groups by gender and number, Gini randomly selected 204 students to compose six groups of 34 children, with an equal number of boys and girls in each group. The finding was that all the aggressive roles (bullies, reinforcers of the bully, and assistants of the bully) had significantly higher moral disengagement scores than did defenders. Bullies also had significantly higher scores than outsiders and victims.

The response, or lack thereof, of witnesses or bystanders when bullying occurs is related to this discussion, but it has not been studied as closely, and not at all with respect to cyberbullying. Salmivalli (1999) identified participant roles: assistants to the bully, who join in; reinforcers of the bully, who encourage the behavior; outsiders, who do nothing but are seen to give passive approval by their inaction; and defenders, who actively take steps to stop the behavior. Menesini et al. (2003) found that bystanders tend to display indifferent attitudes when observing bullying, and they tend to remove themselves from the situation without taking steps to intervene in any way.

Previous research showed that about 85% of playground bullying episodes were observed by peers (Craig & Pepler, 1997; P. O'Connell et al., 1999), and about 25% of the time peers intervened on the victim's behalf. Those interventions stopped the bullying in 75% of cases. In the United Kingdom, researchers found that 66% of 2,308 students (ages 10–14) acknowledged having observed bullying at school: Of those, 47% tried not to be involved, 34% told bullies to stop, and 18% asked an adult to intervene (Smith & Shu, 2000). Craig and Pepler's work illuminated the reasons children as bystanders are reluctant to intervene: When other children are also present as bystanders, there is a tendency to avoid individual responsibility; they fear retaliation from the bully; they lack necessary skills; and they fear that intervening may make the situation worse. These processes are very likely involved in cyberbullying as well and, in fact, may be magnified in cyberbullying, given the large audience. For example, if many people see the offending website, it may be easy for each viewer (bystander) to justify inaction by believing someone else will take care of it. If the cyberbullying act is egregious, the bystander might imagine what the bully would do if an intervener caused trouble. Given that many people lack knowledge and skills for what to do when the offense is technological, ignorance may be another way to justify inaction. The good news is that knowledge and skills can be learned, and counselors can be instrumental in imparting them.

Along with attribution theory, the moral disengagement component of social cognitive theory is relevant to understanding the behavior of those involved in cyberbullying and also suggests treatment approaches for counselors.

Summary

- Aggression can be either (a) instrumental, or proactive (deliberate, designed to achieve a goal); or (b) reactive (impulsive aggressive response to a real or perceived attack).
- Aggression can be either overt (direct physical or verbal) or covert (indirect, designed to damage relationships or social status).
- There are three major views of aggression: It is an instinct that is inborn, it is a response to accumulated frustration of drive satisfaction, and it is learned via modeling and observation and is reinforced (social learning).
- Social information processing theory proposes a six-step process by which children and youths cognitively process social cues: (a) encoding, (b) interpreting, (c) clarifying goals, (d) generating response options, (e) deciding on an option, and (f) enacting the chosen behavior.
- Attribution errors have been detected in those involved in conventional bullying and may be relevant in cyberbullying as well. Perpetrators may have hostile attribution biases—a tendency to interpret neutral or ambiguous situations as aggressive—which then leads them to respond aggressively. Considering the reduced visual cues in much of technological communication, this tendency could play an important role in

cyberbullying. Victims may have self-blaming attributions, assuming that they have unalterable, permanent characteristics that cause the bullying.

- Moral disengagement has been associated with bullying behavior. A component of Bandura's social cognitive theory, moral disengagement describes a series of cognitive justifications that allow people to act in ways they believe are wrong. Those justifications include thinking the behavior serves a higher purpose (such as loyalty to friends), labeling an action euphemistically ("It was only a joke"), making advantageous comparisons ("It's not as bad as beating someone up"), distorting the consequences ("He didn't even mind"), dehumanizing the victim ("She's just a slut"), or blaming the victim ("It's his fault for acting so smart").

- Bystanders who observe bullying or cyberbullying also use cognitive mechanisms for not intervening or seeking help. They may tell themselves, "It's not my problem" or "I could be next" or "I'm not able to stop this anyway."

CHAPTER 6

Developmental Factors in Cyberbullying

The popular media has conveyed the impression that cyberbullying is a phenomenon that is the province of teens. Many of the highly publicized incidents involve teenage victims. Although there are certainly reasons why this age group may be more highly involved than others, there is no age group that is immune from the problem of cyberbullying. In the following sections, I describe the unique characteristics of each developmental stage and relate those characteristics to that age group's experiences with cyberbullying.

Young Children (Ages 2–9 Years)

One might presume that young children are safe from cyberbullying, that it is not until later that one needs to be concerned.[1] Obviously, in order to be involved in bullying via technology, one must use that technology and be engaged in bullying behaviors. Unfortunately, both the behavior and the technology are widely used by young children. Although assessing bullying and victimization in preschool and kindergarten is challenging methodologically, there are studies that have demonstrated that this behavior is already present by that time (Perren & Alsaker, 2006). Two hundred kindergarten children from the Midwestern United States were participants in a longitudinal study that included victimization by peers in kindergarten. Data were collected in interviews with the children in spring and fall. In fall, 21% of participants met criteria for being victims (being victimized more often

---

[1] With permission of my coauthor and the publisher, parts of this section were taken directly from an article: Bauman & Tatum (2009).

than sometimes). The same percentage was found in the spring assessment, but there were only 9% of children who were classified as victims at both time points. An interesting dissertation examined victimization by bullying in a K–5 school, with participation of 465 students from all grades (Fuller, 2006). The researcher collected data four times during the school year. Because the study was testing the effectiveness of a curriculum, there were two groups, each of which received the curriculum at different points in the year. Descriptive data were reported by group and testing time. Table 1 shows the percentage of kindergarten students who reported in individually administered surveys that they were victimized in each way.

Fuller (2006) observed that older children in Grades 1 through 5 reported more victimization than did the kindergarten students. Note that response options at the older grades included "1 or 2 times per week," "1 or 2 times per day," and "many times per day." At all grade levels, there were more students who reported being victimized than who acknowledged perpetrating the behaviors.

In their study of 344 Swiss kindergarten students (ages 5 years to 7 years, 11 months), Perren and Alsaker (2006) conducted interviews—including peer nomination with photographs—with the children and also administered teacher questionnaires. The children were in two classes: a younger class (first year of kindergarten) and an older class (second year). Of the 257 children who could be categorized on the basis of available data, approximately 15% were classified as bullies, 8% as victims, 14% as bully–victims, and 64% as uninvolved. Girls were more frequently uninvolved, and boys were more frequently found in the bully–victim group. The older children were overrepresented in the bully group.

In addition to this evidence that very young children are exposed to bullying, there is also evidence that they are having experiences that introduce them to technology. In a study of 1,065 parents of children from 6 months to 6 years old, parent reports indicated that 21% of children ages 2 years and younger had used a computer; of that group, 14% said the child used it every day (Calvert, Rideout, Woolard, Barr, & Strouse, 2005). On average, children began to use the computer at age 2.7 years and did so on a parent's lap. Independent use began at 3.7 years of age,

Table 1

Percentage of Kindergarten Students Who Reported Being Victimized From a Little to a Lot Over Four Time Points During the Year, by Group

Behavior	Time 1		Time 2		Time 3		Time 4	
	Group 1	Group 2	Group 1	Group 2	Group 1	Group 2	Group 1	Group 2
Been hit, kicked, pushed	37	30	46	37	36	31	14	44
Excluded from play	46	26	50	50	28	32	42	33
Teased by others	29	35	27	32	21	19	28	44
Called mean names	38	35	38	23	35	12	21	33
Laughed at	15	35	25	27	14	6	14	33

and the use of a computer mouse for pointing and clicking began at age 3.5 years. Forty-two percent of young children who used computers had looked at websites for young children, and 60% had asked to go to a particular site. The older the children were, the more likely they were to have asked about specific websites.

By about age 2, children begin to think about the world and to use symbols (including words), major advances in cognitive development (Broderick & Blewitt, 2006). Research on brain development indicates that in children ages 2 to 5 years, sensory processing abilities are similar to those of adults, but young children lack the ability to analyze complex visual data (Thomas & Johnson, 2008). The ability to predict the goals and intentions of others also has not fully developed. Impulse and emotional control are quite poor in children at this stage of development. In 5- to 7-year-olds, even though the cortical structures needed for basic functions of the sensory areas of the brain are fully developed, and language and memory systems are continuing to develop, impulse and emotional control are still incomplete. Although the areas of the cerebral cortex that respond to visual stimuli are similar to those of adults by ages 8 to 10 years, the ability to discern faces is not as selective as it becomes by ages 12 to 14 years. These characteristics are important to keep in mind when considering the young ages at which children are interacting with complex visual images and other people on Internet sites.

In the few studies on cyberbullying that have included young children, there is evidence that it is a problem in elementary school. A study conducted in primary and secondary schools in the Netherlands found that the rates of cyberbullying and victimization were higher for the primary school sample than for the secondary school group (Dehue, Bolman, & Völlink, 2008). The percentage of the 1,211 students in the study who were cyberbullies was higher for boys than girls, but girls were more often victimized. In this sample, most of the cyberbullying behaviors took place at home rather than at school, and the most popular environment in which this occurred was IM. Almost 40% of victims did not know the identity of their cyberbullies. Similar to my own findings described in Chapter 1, very few bullies or victims told teachers or parents about their cyberexperiences. They responded most often to cyberbullying by either pretending to ignore the situation, actually ignoring it, or bullying back. An interesting aspect of this study was that parents were also surveyed, and this survey revealed that the majority of parents set rules about Internet use; however, the parents greatly underestimated their children's experiences with cyberbullying. There was no information about whether children followed the rules set by parents or circumvented them.

When are children introduced to technology? In the crib, it seems, in some cases. Several parents acknowledged that they used their cell phone features to soothe their distressed children (Associated Press, 2009). A rattle application available for some phones couples graphics and chimes with the traditional rattle sounds. Parents also give cell phones to children to play with and find they are intrigued by the interesting buttons and sounds and flashing screens. Other preschool children will view photos or play games on their parents' smart phones (phones that have additional features, such as Internet connectivity, cameras, and other applications). Some parents report that even preschool children are very quick to figure out how to work the phones. In addition to real cell phones, toy phones appeal to children with the sounds and graphics and the resemblance to adult devices.

Although few U.S. children younger than 12 years of age currently have their own cell phones, that number is increasing. According to one 2008 report, experts estimate that 54% of 8- to 12-year-olds will have cell phones within 3 years (Wilson, 2008). Another report put the percentage of 8-year-olds with a cell phone in 2008 at 8%, with more than 50% of 12-year-olds having cell phones. The report also noted that many of these youngsters do not have (or want) cell phones designed for children (with numerous parental controls) and that they respond to aggressive marketing campaigns targeting young children (Media General News Service, 2008). Technology and parenting blogs abound with debates about the age at which children should get their first cell phone, with frequent mentions of safety (the child can be located easily in an emergency or can call for help) and health concerns (health concerns about effects of radiation associated with using the phones). It is clear that although safety may be the parental motive (worries about finding a lost child, a child feeling ill, and so forth), many children avail themselves of all the features, including texting.

If we Americans can learn from other countries, the United Kingdom and Australia have reported increasing use of cell phones with young children. In the United Kingdom, more than 50% of children ages 5 to 9 years have their own cell phones (Naish, 2009), and in Australia, 40% of children ages 4 through 7 years have mobile phones ("Child Mobile Phone Use," 2009). A major network is expanding its product line to include phones designed for use by children as young as 4 years of age (Naish, 2009). Even more alarming, an Australian survey found that 25% of elementary-aged school children were allowed to have their mobile phones in their rooms at night. A noted Australian psychologist found that to be extremely troubling, saying that these children stay up and text friends and thus are chronically sleep deprived, with all the attendant mental and physical health consequences. One parent interviewed by Naish was the divorced father of a 7-year-old, with whom he stays in touch using the cell phone. This father wants the child to be able to reach him at any time but insists the child does not use the phone to communicate with friends.

The Firefly Mobile, designed for young children, is making inroads in the European market, and other phones are available in the United States, such as Cingular Firefly (along with others, such as the Verizon Migo and Tictalk by Enforma). France, on the other hand, has introduced laws to stop sales of mobile phones to children younger than 6 and to ban advertising such phones to children younger than 12 (Naish, 2009). It remains to be seen how this trend will unfold in the United States, but given the appetite for technology here, it seems only a matter of time before we see widespread use of cell phones by the younger set. Keep in mind that young children are not immune to peer pressure; it is not difficult to imagine preschoolers and kindergarteners saying they "need" cell phones to be like their peers in the same way they already recognize certain types and brands of trendy clothing. Fortunately, most children in preschool and of early elementary age do not have the literacy skills to use the phone for cruel texting, but if their phones (and parents) allow them to communicate with other children, the potential for bullying exists.

Many children are now introduced to computers at a young age and use them for both entertainment and educational purposes (Mazzarella, 2005). One survey found that 18% of children under age 7 years go online (Rideout & Hamel, 2006). Children ages 2 to 6 years are able to manipulate the mouse, and on the older end of the range, they can type short words or phrases. However, the use of currency systems to acquire things on many of the children's game sites is beyond most of their cognitive abilities at this age (Buckleitner, 2008). Critics have argued that early access to computers threatens to replace the normal social interactions essential to social development and to promote inappropriate patterns of thinking and relating (Attewell, Suazo-Garcia, & Battle, 2003). Very young children have little understanding of computer problems and may become very frustrated if their play is interrupted (Buckleitner, 2008). This early involvement with computers worried Professor Susan Greenfield (Derbyshire, 2009), who observed that children's websites engage children's brains in the same manner by which the sites engage the external world—using sounds and lights to capture the children's attention, which encourages short attention spans and immediate gratification. Developmentally, young children must first learn to assimilate detail and context in an image in order to understand meaning. Greenfield commented that she fears that the brain itself may develop differently in children who spend a great deal of time on these activities. Her fear is supported by studies using recent advances in brain neurobiology. Davidson (2007) demonstrated that the brain changes (in both structure and function) in response to experience, a feature known as *plasticity*. Another expert observed that although technology and computers have positive contributions, children should have ample experience with in-person relationships before they start using social networking sites (Derbyshire, 2009). Face-to-face interactions are the "most emotionally maturing experiences" (Cordes & Miller, 2000). Referring to the work of Turkle (1995), the National Science Board (1998) observed, "Computing and cyberspace may blur children's ability to separate the living from the inanimate, contribute to escapism and emotional detachment, stunt the development of a sense of personal security, and create a hyper-fluid sense of identity" (pp. 8–24).

Children who are between the ages of 6 and 8 years have more advanced skills. They understand that an avatar represents a person that they can compete with or befriend. They pay attention to rules and may be distressed when rules are broken. Their tolerance for frustration has increased some-what. They are also now more skilled at computer use in general and may use bookmarks, right mouse-clicks, and passwords proficiently (Buckleitner, 2008), making navigation of the sites easier and more efficient.

Addie Schwartz, an executive with a company geared toward preteen girls, observed that preadolescents (ages 8 to 12) are very interested in MySpace and Facebook, although those sites are designed for, and technically limited to, adolescents and adults. She described this age group as follows: "Born with a mouse in her hand, today's tween is more comfortable online than ever before. Some kids learn to use the Internet before they can read" (quoted in "Too Old for Webkinz," 2008, para. 7, p. 6). Schwartz continued, "Sites like Club Penguin and Webkinz are giving children a taste of social networking, whetting their appetite for the more sophisticated fare" ("Too Old for Webkinz," para. 8).

Livingstone (2008) described a developmental trajectory for use of technology. Early childhood (up to about 8 years old) is a time of high physical activity and low media use, with media use at home increasing beginning at ages 9 through 11. However, Shellenbarger (2006) observed that social networking sites compete for subscribers as young as 8 years of age. A video guide to Webkinz for parents (commonsensemedia.org) recommends that 8 years old is the minimum age at which children should use the site, but usage data from quantcast.com suggest that not all parents follow that recommendation.

As with adults, face-to-face communication among children involves many clues to the speaker's intent that enable a listener to interpret the content. Nonverbal gestures and facial expressions convey a considerable amount of information during usual communication; in fact, even in audio-only situations (such as when using the telephone), variations in tone, emphasis, and so forth augment the semantic content. Because young children have less experience with social communication than adults, these young children might have more difficulty interpreting messages that lack these additional clues. A child may mistake a joke for an insult, for example, and respond in kind, escalating a benign interaction to a hostile exchange (Dwyer, 2007).

New Zealand has a wonderful resource for safe computing for children that includes animated videos that would be useful for parents and teachers to watch with children, especially younger children. *Hector's World*, which the site states targets 2- to 9-year-olds (with the focus on 5- to 8-year-olds), includes educational animated videos, lesson plans, and other resources, but one worth considering as a download is the Hector's World safety button—a program to be installed on any computer. After the program is installed, a cartoon character appears on a corner of the screen; then, if children see something upsetting, they can click on the image and the screen content is replaced by an underwater scene along with a written affirmation for clicking and encouragement to get an adult. Children can use this feature any time they are upset by an interaction in a game or if they accidentally view something inappropriate. The deluxe safety button is available in many languages.

Parents often ask counselors for advice and may consult with them on the pros and cons of the technology in which their children are interested. Counselors will be more helpful if they are well informed and can be specific when making recommendations. Parents may need support for establishing rules and boundaries despite the pleas of children. With both young children and adolescents, counselors should work with parents to help them build solid relationships with their children so that their children will come to them when something happens online and will listen when parents teach them safe practices. Parents may also need support for taking active measures, such as close monitoring of computer and cell phone use, even when the child objects. Authoritative parenting, with high control and high warmth, will help children feel secure and facilitate compliance with parental rules.

Tweens and Early Adolescents (10–13 Years)

One variable that is important in understanding the attraction to cyberbullying that 10- to 13-year-olds (and teenagers) have is the incomplete development of their prefrontal cortex (Walsh, 2004; Weinberger, Elvevåg, & Giedd, 2005). This part of the brain, which is the locus for decision making, planning, predicting consequences, and controlling impulses, does not develop fully until early adulthood (mid-20s). Recent research has shown that youths process emotional information differently than adults, so that they tend to have a more impulsive response rather than a thoughtful response (Weinberger et al., 2005; Yurgelun-Todd, 2002). This impulsiveness means youths may not think through a message carefully before sending it or passing it along. They may not think about potential consequences; although they send something expecting it to be private, they may not consider the possibility that they have lost control of the material once it enters cyberspace. I asked a group of high school students whether they had anything on their MySpace or Facebook pages that they would not want their mothers to see, and they all immediately said, "Yes." I told them I had heard that college admissions officers and employers often search these sites for potential students or employees and that some have lost opportunities because of inappropriate content. They said they were aware of that, but they knew it would not happen to them. I said, "Isn't that what girls say about getting pregnant when they have sex without protection?" and they all laughed and said, "Exactly!" So, at some level, they understood the absence of logic in their thinking, but their adolescent sense of invincibility apparently prevailed.

In addition to the incomplete development of the prefrontal cortex, youths at this time in their lives tend to experience (although probably not recognize) sensory overload. In the photos displayed previously in Figures 1 and 2, which show the multiple IM conversations on the computer, it would not be a surprise if the teen was also sending text messages, listening to music, and watching TV. The multiple sensory inputs call for very rapid responses and quick attention shifting, which may cause impulsive responses to an ambiguous e-mail, for example. Youths are constantly hooked up to technology—their phones (many with Internet access), music, and so forth are part of their lives. Nevertheless, it is questionable whether the brain can effectively process so much sensory input at once.

Youths also desire to be current and fit in with their peers. A recent Harris Interactive survey found that after clothing, the cell phone a teen carries is most important in determining his or her social status (Campbell, 2005). Teens use cell phones for texting as much as talking and say that if they did not have texting, their social lives would end or at least deteriorate; 57% believe their cell phone has improved their life (Harris Interactive, 2008). In addition to the need to be part of the youth culture, teens use cell phones (texting) as the key to their social world. Social networking sites also allow teens to be aware of the social activities and moment-to-moment unfolding of friends' activities, thoughts, and interests. It is astonishing to note the number of "friends" that many teens have on their social networking sites. Numbers into the hundreds are not unusual. This number, too, is a marker of one's social status. It is also apparent that one cannot know that many people very well, and so with each friend added, one is giving information to that person (and often all their friends as well) that can be used for cyberbullying purposes.

During this developmental stage, peer relationships assume great importance. As youths become teens, they begin to individuate and create identities outside the family. A part of that identity development process involves social comparison, determining where one ranks in the social milieu. For example, "I am smarter than Susie but not as smart as Joe" or "I will never be as good as Chris in basketball." In addition, adolescent behavior is sensitive to social norms, which means adolescents make choices about their own behavior based on what they believe is normal for their peers. The concept of social norms has become a popular strategy for campaigns attempting to reduce risky behaviors like smoking (Eisenberg & Forster, 2003) and college student alcohol consumption (Wechsler et al., 2003) and to increase condom use by adolescents (DiClemente, 1991); it has also been examined in relation to conventional bullying (Björkqvist, Ekman, & Lagerspetz, 2008) and rumor spreading (J. E. Cross & Peisner, 2009).

Technology is instrumental for young people for maintaining friendships. In fact, online and offline worlds are no longer separate spheres, and technological communication appears to promote more intimate self-disclosure among friends (Valkenburg & Peter, 2007). Because of the widespread use of these devices, youths often communicate with friends using IM, text, chat, or social networking sites. Valkenburg and Peter studied the impact of technology (IM) and chat on friendships of preadolescents and adolescents with 794 Dutch students ages 10–16 years. The authors described many similarities between Dutch and U.S. students' access to and use of technology, so although the research was conducted elsewhere, the findings may have implications for U.S. trends and preteens. Data were collected in

2004; the focus was on IM and chat, which were the most common methods of technological communication among youths at that time. The researchers found that 88% of youths who used these technologies communicated with real-life friends rather than with strangers. For those participants who communicated primarily with their offline friends, online communication was positively related to the closeness of those friendships. This relationship held for preadolescents, early adolescents, and middle adolescents in the study. In addition, those participants identified as socially anxious were less likely to use online communication, but that group was more likely to believe that online communication is helpful for increasing the breadth and depth of communication. Those socially anxious adolescents who endorsed this belief were more likely to use online communication and report closeness with friends. The researchers speculated that socially anxious adolescents may find that the absence of visual and auditory clues to how they look or sound during interactions reduces their anxiety in interpersonal communication. McKay and her colleagues said that these technologies are "not replacing, but enhancing social interaction" (McKay, Thurlow, & Zimmerman, 2005, p. 191).

Given the importance of such communication to preteens and teens, it is clear that there are many ways in which these tools can be appropriated by the cyberbully. The vulnerability of some young people to being mocked, embarrassed, or insulted in these ways is apparent in the outcomes of the cases described at the beginning of this book. Although there are adults who have suffered extreme humiliation in these ways (e.g., teachers taking early retirement in response to cyberbullying [Coughlan, 2007]), adults are usually better able than children to evaluate a variety of solutions to a problem and have more experience with problem solving in general. Preteens and teens who are attacked by cyberbullies may resort to extreme measures, and counselors must be attuned to the possibility that symptoms of depression and other psychological symptoms may be related to technological experiences.

Adolescents (13–18 Years)

A recent study painted a picture of the ways in which adolescents (ages 13–18 years) are using social networking (Common Sense Media, 2009). The study was conducted in May and June of 2009 with a nationally representative sample of 1,013 students in Grades 7–12 and 1,002 parents of students in those grades; it was conducted by an independent research firm. The results are so illuminating that I include many of them here. The following findings are quoted from the report:

- 51% of teens check social networking sites more than once a day.
- 22% check social networking sites more than 10 times a day.
- 54% use the sites to complain about or make fun of their teachers, and 37% make fun of other students.

- 28% have shared personal information they would not usually share in public.
- 25% have created a fake profile.
- 24% have hacked into someone else's account.
- 16% have posted false information or lies about others.
- 13% have posted naked or semi-naked images or videos of themselves or someone else online.
- 18% have been humiliated online; of those, 23% retaliated by doing something similar to the offender.
- 19% say they have been harassed or cyberbullied online, and 38% know someone who has been cyberbullied.
- 12% of teens who have Facebook or MySpace accounts say their parents are unaware of the account.
- Given these data, it is interesting that 4% of parents report their teen checks social networking sites more than 10 times a day, and 23% say their child checks more than once per day.
- 16% of parents think their teen has shared more personal information online than they would usually share publicly, and 2% say their child has posted naked or partially naked images of themselves online. Compare these to the student figures above.
- 14% of teens say their parents know their passwords for social networking sites, but 51% of parents say they know them.
- 37% of teens say they have been surfing the web without parental supervision since age 10, whereas only 11% of parents think their child started at that age. Forty-nine percent of parents think their children were 13 or older before they began surfing without supervision, but only 14% of teens say they waited until age 13.
- 28% of teens who have accounts on social networking sites say their parents check their profiles at least occasionally; 82% of parents check regularly.
- The following percentages show the types of sites visited more than once per day by teens: social networking sites (51%), sites with streaming video or TV (33%), online gaming sites (30%), sites that host chat rooms for teens (14%), sites for homework help (7%), and sports sites (7%).

These data point out the importance of online interactions for teens and the discrepancy between their reports and those of their parents. Consider that this study did not examine cell phone use, and it becomes very clear that teens' lives are technologically immersed. Adults—parents and counselors—are rarely as consumed by their technological lives. This difference contributes to the feeling by those victimized in cyberspace that they are not able to communicate with adults about problems they experience in their technological world.

Older Adolescents and Young Adults (18–25 Years)

This age group considers technology essential, rather than optional. They have grown up with much of the technology and have difficulty imagining life before computers and cell phones. To them, such life seems prehistoric! Because this technology has been part of their lives since childhood, it is also an integral part of their social lives.

The essential task of adolescence (and young adulthood) is developing a stable identity. In that process, many young people experiment with different versions of themselves, adopting different styles of clothing and appearance, listening to different musical genres, and socializing with different cliques. Because the Internet in particular allows one to socialize without having to be visible to one's social group (as in a chat room), many youths find the Internet a relatively safe place to explore various identities. In a chat room, a male can assume a female persona, an overweight youth can describe him- or herself as an athlete, a young person in a wheelchair does not have to mention that, and so on. One's acne or skin color are not known, so one is less likely to be self-conscious about real or perceived physical barriers to social acceptance. A shy and socially anxious adolescent can "practice" socializing in this setting, acquiring skills and learning about the communication styles of peers. The downside is that the opportunity to explore one's identity is coupled with the opportunity to be victimized. Although one's physical appearance may not be an issue, one's comments (or lack thereof) can be cause for ridicule or ostracism. Again, depending on one's overall well-being, some will dismiss those events as learning opportunities or use the information to select another chat room where members are move civil, but others may feel personally devalued and may invoke self-blaming attributions that then result in depressed mood and, over time, decreased self-esteem.

At this stage in life, romantic relationships are part of the quest for intimacy, and many marriages are begun at this point. How can cyberbullying emerge in romantic relationships? One can say cruel and hurtful things in an argument that occurs over technology just as one can in person. A difference is that the remark can be preserved and revisited, which often happens. For some, the re-reading of the painful comment is a futile effort to find something (positive) that was missed at first read. What often happens instead is that the person experiences the same emotional response (shock, hurt, betrayal) each time the message is read, magnifying the harm.

In addition, the technology allows a jealous or insecure partner to maintain contact at all times, even when that contact is not welcome. Partners may call or text incessantly, demanding to know where the partner is, what he or she is doing, whether there are eligible singles around, and so forth. Aside from the intrusion, such behavior smacks of stalking and can interrupt one's work. As with other problems, one can turn off the phone, but that means one will not be able to receive other calls. The solution is to block the sender and tell the sender that you will do so in order to function in daily life without being harassed. In these situations, victims may be afraid of the partner's anger if the calls are blocked or other measures taken. The counselor will recognize the signs of an unhealthy relationship with the potential for abuse (verbal or physical), if it has not happened already. The counselor can help the client to see the danger signals such behavior entails and, it is hoped, to make changes in or leave the relationship.

Ending a relationship is often difficult and awkward, and unfortunately, such actions are now sometimes done technologically. It is not unheard of, particularly among teens, for break-up messages to be transmitted electronically. The sender is protected from witnessing the reaction of the one who is being dumped, but the person getting the message is likely to feel doubly wounded. Not only is the relationship being terminated, but the courtesy of a face-to-face announcement has been discounted. For most, the loss of a romantic relationship is an emotional blow; whether that blow is more painful when delivered electronically is unknown.

The final concern regarding technology and romantic relationships is the possibility of aggressive reactions using technology if a relationship sours. A former partner may disclose intimate secrets, post private information, send out provocative photos to a wide audience, post insults on social networking sites, and so forth. This means that the pain of a lost relationship may be both extended in time and exacerbated in degree by using technology to perpetrate hostile behavior against the former partner. Counselors must be prepared to consider how technology may be involved in a relationship, both during the relationship and after it is over.

Risk taking in adolescence is normative; the degree and types of risk taken distinguish normative from dangerous behavior. Adolescents (including college students) may post photos on their social networking site profiles that appeal to their peers but that present them in a less than optimal guise. It is quite common to see photos of parties that show consumption of alcohol (sometimes to excess and sometimes including underage imbibers). In addition, photos that would be seen as sexually provocative by most adults are commonplace. A 2008 survey of 31,000 employers undertaken by CareerBuilder.com (Havenstein, 2008) found that more than 20% of employers screen potential hires by searching the Internet, particularly social networking sites. These employers also reported that in one third of the searches, information was located that caused the candidate to be excluded from further consideration for the position. The types of information that were cause for not considering the candidate included alcohol or drug use (41%), inappropriate photos (20%), disparaging comments about former employers on their sites (28%), unprofessional screen names (22%), and several others. Most adolescents and college students—who will soon be in the job market—do not believe their sites will be scrutinized for this purpose, despite warnings from adults and in the media. Counselors can present these data to young people in an effort to help them avoid long-term negative consequences from their participation in online sites.

Summary

- Young children have been found to engage in conventional bullying and may develop attitudes and behaviors that predispose them to cyberbullying. Young children are very familiar with computer technology and may even have their own cell phones, arguably for safety purposes. Some games for young children have components that allow them to bully others, and adults are often unaware of this potential. Young children often imitate behaviors of older children, and the omnipresence of technology is likely to pique their interest in technological communication.

- Early adolescents, sometimes referred to as tweens, do not have the cortical development to always make good decisions or to anticipate consequences. They also frequently have multiple forms of technology in use at any one moment, and sensory overload may interfere with decision making that occurs very rapidly in technological situations. At this stage of development, young people are eager to fit in and be current, which now means they believe they need the latest technology. They also want to be part of the social networks that are now maintained by technology. Peer relationships are very important, and socializing online allows tweens to experiment with identity where their physical characteristics do not define them.

- Late teens and young adults live technological lives and are rarely out of reach of electronic communication. Identity development is the main task of adolescence, and technology can provide tools to help that process (social networks, virtual worlds, blogs, and so forth). Romantic relationships are often enhanced by technology (loving texts at random times) but also can be vulnerable to cyberbullying if the partner is jealous or if the relationship sours.

CHAPTER 7

Strategies to Prevent and Reduce Cyberbullying

Although I have mentioned some options to respond to cyberbullying, I now turn to several general strategies to prevent or reduce cyberbullying in schools and workplaces: acceptable use policies (AUPs), technological strategies, anonymous reporting systems, and counseling services in schools.

AUPs

Policies that clearly enumerate a school's or employer's policies regarding the use of technology must be developed, and all stakeholders must be made aware of those policies. In her book *Cyberbullying and Cyberthreats* (2007b), Nancy Willard, who is an educator and a lawyer, included a sample school district Internet use policy and a sample student Internet use policy and agreement. These samples are useful models for educational institutions seeking a template for their own AUP. A useful guide for employers can be found at the Electronic Frontiers Australia (2000) website. Some states (e.g., the Virginia Department of Education, n.d.) also provide guidelines for these documents. Although such guidelines are very useful, it is important to make the document relevant to the specific organization and to consider it as a guide for employees or students, rather than a list of prohibitions and penalties. It is also important to include representatives from all stakeholders when crafting the document. This inclusion will increase stakeholders' investment in promoting the document and will ensure that the needs or circumstances of a particular group are not overlooked. Both management and end-users (e.g., students) need to be involved in the AUP development process if it is to be a document all will respect and follow.

Rather than making broad statements about what is acceptable, an effective AUP lists specific activities or uses that are violations of the policy, and it does so in clear language that the lay user, to whom the policy applies, can understand it. Hence, all terms that may be unclear should be defined. It is also important to make the document flexible, because technology is evolving at a very rapid rate and an AUP may need to be revised to address new issues. Thus, it is a good practice to have the committee that is charged with developing the document also conduct an annual review to check that the document is still current.

There is a risk that many people will tend to ignore lengthy, presumably in-comprehensible documents, much as they ignore the terms of service agreements on many Internet sites. It is up to the employer or school to devise strategies to attenuate this risk and to make employees or students aware of the importance of carefully examining the AUP's contents. Although institutions or employers will have to develop their own programs for ensuring compliance, there are several practices that might be considered. Reminders at appropriate meetings may be helpful. Schools or employers can (and many do) require that anyone who will use their computers or other communication technology sign a statement indicating they have read the policies, understand them, and agree to abide by them. The statement can add that violations of the policy will be referred to the appropriate authority (internal or external if a law has been broken). At the very least, such a short statement, with the full title of the AUP, is written evidence of the user's intention to comply. It is essential that the school or employer *not* issue an account to anyone without that person having this signed document, which signals just how much importance the employer or school places on this policy. An excellent model for such a form for schools is available at the U.S. Department of Justice's (n.d.) website.

If organizations place a priority on preventing cyberbullying, they may want to require that employees demonstrate some kind of understanding of the organization's AUP. For example, one cannot obtain a driver's license without passing a written test of understanding of the rules of the road. If one is a university researcher, most universities require that some kind of assessment or test of the rules regarding research with human subjects be passed before undertaking any research. If it is truly important to protect employees from cyberbullying, a similar procedure could be used.

In schools and workplaces, the existence of the policy must be prominently displayed. Reminders can be included in newsletters, on bulletin boards, in handbooks, and so forth. It is also possible to have a reminder message—or an additional confirmation of intent to abide by the policy—appear on the login page for computers and a link on employee sections of a website to the AUP. For schools, students and employees both need to have links to the policy prominently displayed.

Technological Strategies

As concerns about misuse of technology emerged, efforts to find technological solutions followed close behind. The easiest technological strategy may be installing filter software. These programs allow the computer owner (or parent) to control the type of content that is displayed, to block certain sites, and to require passwords for use. Some of the software will allow chat room monitoring. Microsoft Windows has a family safety component available for free download to Windows users that has most of these features. There are websites, such as "Top Ten Reviews" (n.d.), that review such software so that novices—or parents wanting to keep current—can determine which program best meets their specific needs. The reader should also realize that some such features are available from some ISPs (e.g., MSN, AOL, Earthlink) at no charge. Internet Explorer has built-in controls for content. To access those, click on *Tools* and then select *Internet Options* from the drop-down list. Select the *Content* tab and click on *Enable*. There is a list of categories, and the user can click on any of those categories and adjust the slider to set the restrictions, from *none* to *limited* to *unrestricted*. In this way, control over content can be exerted without the use of any additional software.

A national telephone survey of U.S. households in which a person age 10–17 years who used the Internet on a regular basis resided found that 33% of the parents interviewed used filtering software (Mitchell, Finkelhor, & Wolak, 2005). They were more likely to use this technology if the children were younger than 15 and if they were especially concerned about potential exposure to sexual content online. In addition, parents who were more aware of the child's online activities or had concerns about the child's ability to be responsible online were also more likely to install filters. An interesting finding was that if the child used the Internet for school assignments, parents were less likely to have filters.

There are also usage control options for cell phones. For example, with my service I can limit the total time available for voice calls and the number of texts, restrict the time of day or night when calls can be made, and install both blocked and trusted numbers; in addition, for phones with Internet access, content filters are available. The basic parental control package for my service costs about $5 per phone. With these features, youths can have a phone that looks grown-up (most chafe at the idea of kiddie-phones, even kiddies!), but parents can oversee how the tool is used. There are also so-called chaperone features that allow a parent to determine the physical location of the phone (and presumably the child). Youths and especially teens will probably be less than enthusiastic about any parental control, but parents will have to determine what is in the best interest of their children. An acquaintance of mine told me her teenage son was incensed when she insisted that his cell phone be in her possession after 9:00 p.m. She said that he could choose not to have a phone, but if he did have it, that was the rule. The teen chose to keep the phone and turn it in at night. The parental control, by the way, could restrict the times calls were allowed.

Most schools have installed extensive filtering software, and some schools block specific sites (high on the list are YouTube, MySpace, and Facebook). I caution schools and parents against complacency. Although these filters and blocks definitely reduce access to inappropriate sites or those that might be particularly useful for cyberbullying, they are not foolproof. In fact, students seem to delight in finding ways around those blocks and filters.

Anonymous proxy websites allow the user to go to that site and then connect to any URL the user types in. It someone checks the history of the site, the proxy site's URL will show, not the URL of the site ultimately visited. These sites change frequently (as they are discovered and blocked, they are shut down, and new ones appear), but of course there are sites that provide lists of currently active anonymous proxy websites. So, students do this to visit prohibited sites while at school, and workers do the same while at work. Figure 21 shows one I tested (it worked).

Another strategy—explained to me by a teen—to access blocked websites is to use the existing browser (for which the blocks and filters are installed) to download another browser. For example, if the computer has Explorer as the browser, going to the Mozilla.com website to download Firefox (another browser) is an easy step. Then the new browser (without blocks installed) can be used to go to whatever sites are blocked on Explorer, and when the person leaves the computer, he or she will put Firefox in the trash bin and empty it. This strategy could be detected, but one has to be suspicious or extremely vigilant to check every visitor to every computer. I will discuss this situation in more detail in the next chapter.

A tip I discovered online (Arrowsmith, 2008) may be useful if someone attempts to remove offensive material in order to avoid consequences and the victim needs evidence of the offensive posting. Search engines like Google take digital snapshots of every web page they visit. When you see the results of your search, the main link is at the top of the listing. At the end of the listing is a link to *Cached* (next to *Similar*; see Figure 22). If the cyberbully has posted something (a comment, photo, and so forth) and then later removed it, you may be able to locate the previous versions in the cache.

Some strategies parents can use to find out if their teen or tween is on a social networking site (and to monitor their behavior) if the teen refuses to tell them (or uses an alias) are described in a brief video clip at Common Sense Media (search for "Facebook for Parents"). Another tactic used by a parent I know is to request "friend" status with his child's friends. If only

Figure 21
Shadowsurf.com is one of several anonymous proxy websites that one can use to avoid detection of the websites one has visited.

Figure 22
Locating removed text from cached information.

one accepts, the parent can link to his own child's website by clicking on wall posts or other communications from the child. This is the sort of tactic that adolescents will resent, but parents who have reasons to be concerned about their child's activities online may find themselves resorting to such methods. Parents should not be complacent if their child friends them, however. It is possible to adjust one's privacy settings to exclude certain individuals from access to specific information. So, your child might friend you but ensure that you don't see photos or videos, for example, that you would find objectionable—or cause for disciplinary action!

A final technological method to prevent cyberbullying is the use of PSAs. Several of the anticyberbullying websites have these 30-second attention-grabbing videos available at no cost. These videos can be set to come up randomly on computers in a school or company as reminders of the importance of not using technology to hurt others. In Australia, the antibullying website bullyingnoway.com/au posts anti-cyberbullying mobile movies (PSA-type) on their website for everyone to see and use.

Anonymous Reporting Systems

Victims often do not report incidents of cyberbullying because they fear retaliation and worry that they will be ostracized if it is known that they reported. In fact, these fears are not unfounded. Bullies and cyberbullies often make it clear to their targets that if they tell anyone about what has occurred, they can expect further, more damaging incidents. Our culture has many derogatory terms for "tattling," "narcing," or reporting misbehavior, to such an extent that the reporter can be scorned more than the offender.

Various types of anonymous reporting systems have been set up in schools and workplaces and may include a telephone number where messages can be left (or text messages sent) or a website where reports can be left without identifying the source. Some schools and workplaces have set up such programs, but I could find no data reporting the effectiveness of such options.

I recently learned of an integrated system for schools that includes anonymous reporting: www.schooltiponline.com. This service provides Internet and telephone reporting with so-called managed anonymity. That is, there are controls in the system to prevent false reporting and to allow follow-up in an emergency (students login with an id number that could identify the student if, for example, the report contained suicidal or homicidal statements). When the program is first implemented, the students receive training that includes information about the degree of anonymity they can expect. The service immediately refers reports to administrators or counselors, who can use the system to interact with the reporter without knowing his or her identity. At some point, the counselor could invite the reporter to discuss the matter in person, but the reporter makes the choice. The system also includes an emergency notification system (put in place by many colleges and universities after the shootings at Virginia Tech), a survey on school climate that provides baseline and ongoing data, and the capacity to create other surveys. The system provides data collection so the school can have and use data on the number of contacts, role of the contact (parent, teacher, student), and so forth. Schools pay an annual fee for the program, depending on enrollment.

School Counseling Services

I will say more about how counselors can help prevent and reduce cyberbullying in Chapter 9, but I want to note here that students, employees, and citizens may not know where or from whom they can seek assistance with cyberbullying. Just as many counselors use posters or symbols to convey their acceptance of diverse clients, I believe counselors in all settings need to make their willingness to work with cyberbullying very clear. That may include using a poster of some kind, a statement in one's professional disclosure statements that clients get, or announcements in a newsletter and other forms of public information about services. When someone is victimized and struggling with the emotional reactions, the feeling of helplessness that arises from not knowing where to turn can compound the negative feelings.

Certainly in schools, most of which have a school counselor (or several, in the case of high schools), students may not consider that the counselor is knowledgeable and may fear that disclosure would result in some kind of disciplinary referral. Students also fear that confidentiality may not apply to this kind of situation, and so they choose not to seek help. If counselors are proactive in publicizing that they are prepared to help with cyberbullying, students are more likely to come to them for help. In addition, as part of informed consent, school counselors should advise students of any limits to confidentiality that might apply to this situation so the student can decide how much to disclose. Workers (especially digital immigrants) may be completely unmoored by serious incidents. Counselors should do all that is possible to make it known that they can help.

Summary

- Schools and organizations should have well-crafted AUPs that are constructed by various stakeholders (students, teachers, parents, administrators, community members, supervisors, managers, employees from different levels or divisions), and counselors can take the leadership role in initiating this process. Policies need to be officially adopted and publicized and should be reviewed at regular intervals. It is prudent to have all who are affected by the policy sign a copy of the document to acknowledge having read and understood it. Several sources (including Willard, 2007b) have model policies that can be used as guidelines.

- Blocks and filters for the Internet are helpful but not foolproof, and schools or organizations should not be complacent if they have software installed. Reminders of the AUP can be posted on the organization's or school's computers, and the AUP should be prominently covered in school or employee handbooks.
- PSAs can keep attention on the AUP and can be helpful to remind users of the dangers of cyberbullying. In schools, students can produce their own PSAs, which can then be shown on school computers. Some websites have contests for the best PSA produced by students, which is potential outlet for student productions.

CHAPTER 8

Responding to Cyberbullying

In the previous chapter, I described some general remedies that are useful in combating cyberbullying. In this chapter, I provide more specific information to use when an issue arises.

Browser Histories

First, I suggest a strategy for schools, employers, and parents to use that is somewhat controversial because it smacks of overcontrol. I argue that when school computers or computers that are the property of a business are used, the individual user should consider that the owner of the computers has an obligation to make sure they are used responsibly. Company or school practices used to ensure responsible computer use are policies that should be made clear in the AUP, discussed in the previous chapter, so that the practice is transparent and does not appear to be clandestine. An Internet browser keeps an account of websites that have been visited by that browser.

- In Mozilla Firefox, there is a drop-down menu along the top of the screen that includes *History*. When that menu is opened, a list of recently visited sites appears.
- At the top, there is also a place to click on *Show All History*.
- To change the time period for which history is retained, click on *Tools* → *Privacy*. Note that the first item on that screen allows the user to set the time period.
- In Internet Explorer, there is a star on the bar above the current page. Clicking on that star brings up three tabs, one of which is *History* (see Figure 23).

Figure 23
Viewing browser history in Internet
Explorer.

- There are choices regarding the time frame for the history.
- It's also quite easy to delete the history by clicking on *Tools* and then on *Delete browsing history.*
- The user can set how long items are kept in the history by going to *Tools → General.* On that page, there is a section for browsing history.
- Clicking on *Settings* brings up a new screen, at the bottom of which is the setting for how many days to keep pages in history.

So, the school or employer or parent can view the history for a given period and set the time period for the specific situation. For example, in a school computer lab, students can be required to print the browser history when they sign off from a machine (or on a random basis, to save paper). If the history is missing, that is a signal that the student has removed it, probably to conceal a site that could bring closer scrutiny. Even if this browser history check is done only occasionally (think about the most effective reinforcement schedules), the practice may alert students that staff are both savvy and vigilant. The same is true in a workplace.

E-mail Headers

Headers are records of the route taken by an e-mail message, which typically passes through a number of servers on the way to its destination—the recipient's inbox. It is easy to falsify or obscure the identity of the sender as shown in the "from" line of the message. However, it is also easy to determine the identity (or IP address) of the actual sender by viewing the complete header. I will provide instructions for both tasks.

When one sets up an Outlook 2007 account, required information is entered, including how you want your name to appear in messages. The entered information is saved, and the user can return to edit that information at any time. The name that appears in the "from" line on an e-mail can be changed by clicking on *Tools* along the top of the page and selecting *Account Settings* from the drop-down list. Your e-mail account is listed, and by highlighting and double-clicking on the listing, a dialog screen opens called *Change E-mail Account.* In the *Your Name* field, you can type whatever name you want to appear in the *From* field of your e-mail. You can also create a fake e-mail address, which is what the recipient will see in the message. In Outlook 2010, *Mail Account Settings* is accessed from the Office logo in the upper left corner, from which you can get to *Section Information* and navigate to the account settings.

To access the complete header showing the source of an e-mail message, do the following: In Outlook 2007, right-click on the message listed in the inbox and then click on *Message Options* in the drop-down menu to see the *Internet headers* showing the path taken by the message. This information includes the IP address of the computer from which the message was sent. In Outlook 2007, one can also access that dialog from the opened message using the small arrow in the lower right-hand corner of the *Options* section of the menu bar. In Outlook 2010, one must open the e-mail message, go to *View*, and then click on *Options* to see the information. To learn how to view the header in other programs, go the University of Delaware Police (n.d.) website.

When you receive unwanted, harassing, or offensive e-mails, cell phones calls, or text messages, the first step is generally to make a very clear statement to the sender that you do not want to receive any further communications from him or her. Then, after saving the evidence in case the situation continues, the best strategy is to block the sender. Each e-mail service has its own mechanism to block e-mails from a particular sender. My university e-mail account includes a *Block Sender* tab at the top of every message, so if I open a message that offends me and I do not wish to receive any further e-mail from the sender, I click that tab.

In Outlook 2007, I right-click on the message, choose *Junk E-mail* from the drop-down list, and then select *Add Sender to Blocked Senders List.* For cell phones (both calls and text messages), each provider has its own way to block calls. For my provider, I do this online. In this way, it is possible to block not only incoming messages, but also outgoing messages. This feature may be something parents want to investigate.

Every communication system is different, but all have ways to control the content you receive. For example, if I received a text message from an "anonymous" sender, and I did not want to continue to receive messages sent from the website, I could go to my online account with my cell phone service provider and block Internet domains or e-mail addresses. I could also block messages from a cell phone number by entering it in the appropriate place. Blocking is a feature of every communication device, and if the user is unsure how to enable it, a Google search or a search of the provider's website usually provides the answer.

Reporting Problematic Content on Social Networking Sites

All social networking sites have mechanisms for reporting offensive content. It can be frustrating to access that information, though, because it is not always prominently displayed. On Facebook, for example, one must scroll down to the very bottom of the page and click on the small word *Help* on the extreme right side of the page. Once at the Help Center, the easiest way to access information is to search for *report abuse* to read the answers to questions about reporting.

Although the information found there is useful and explains what the reporter needs to do, it is not easy to access that information. This lack of reporting ease is even more frustrating when one realizes that Facebook, MySpace, and other major social networking sites in Europe have abided voluntarily by the "Safer Social Networking Principles for the EU" (2009), which were signed on February 10, 2009, and includes the section listed as 3e in the list below. The purpose of this agreement is to protect children by reducing risk from four sources: illegal content, age-inappropriate content, inappropriate contact, and conduct, which is relevant here. The principles define *conduct* to include bullying or victimization by others as well as behaviors of children that put them at risk (disclosing personal details, posting images that portray themselves inappropriately, lying about one's age to gain access to sites that are prohibited, and meeting online contacts in person). I think the principles are a model and one that counselors should advocate for in the United States, so a summary of each follows:

1. Raise awareness of safety practices and AUPs among users, parents, and teachers in a *prominent* [emphasis added] manner.
2. Take steps to ensure that sites and services are suitable for the intended audience, including efforts to verify ages and prevent rejected users from re-registering by changing age.
3. Provide users with ways to take charge of what they see on the sites. Prominent among these actions are the following:
   a. Work to make sure private profiles of underage users (minors) can not be searched;
   b. Set default profiles to private for underage users (or all users);
   c. Include controls so that users can block someone from accessing their profiles, and allow users to "reject" individual friend requests;
   d. Allow users the option to preview comments before they are public;
   e. Provide easy-to-use tools to report infractions; and
   f. Educate parents about filtering and other types of controls.
4. Provide easy-to-use methods to report inappropriate content, conduct, or violations of the AUP. Reports should be acted on promptly, and the reporter should receive acknowledgment of the receipt of the report.
5. Respond promptly to reports of offending material by taking action, including removing content and reporting illegal behavior as needed.
6. Provide a range of privacy settings with sufficient information about each so that users can make informed decisions for their own material. [Please note that in December 2009, Facebook took steps to implement this recommendation: Users were advised several times to check their privacy settings and were given instructions for doing so, and privacy choices were expanded.]
7. Conduct periodic assessments of the effectives of their practices for protecting children and have a system in place to make changes or additions as needed.

As is quite obvious, I would be delighted if such an agreement could be established in the United States, but the main point here is that when an individual is cyberbullied via a social networking site, that person should be assisted to access the internal reporting mechanisms within the site itself.

Additional reporting should be made to the ISP, who also may be able to assist its customers. Most have some filtering software of their own, but individual sites can sometimes slip through. The next (or concurrent) level of reporting is the school or organization. Reporting would ideally be facilitated by an anonymous method, so that the victim does not have to fear retribution. All stakeholders should know how to report and what the procedure will be for handling reports—and how false reporting will be handled as well.

If one is victimized on a website, one strategy worth attempting is to use the website www.whois.com, which can help identify the owner of the offending site. This tool is particularly effective when dealing with a website that was designed by savvy individuals for the purpose of defaming others, or even a single person (e.g., the person mentioned in Chapter 1 whose face had been superimposed on the hippo's body), while remaining anonymous. In such cases, the identity of the responsible party can be determined, and the victim can then decide whether to report the offense to the police (if the offense was illegal) or to others, such as the parents if the case involved a student.

Legislation

Counselors are not lawyers and should not be expected to know all the technicalities of legislation that might apply to their clients. On the other hand, they should have enough working knowledge of the legal system that they know when it might be useful for a client to consult a lawyer or even to call the police. Many clients are unaware of the options for redress for cyberbullying, and the sense that they have no recourse may exacerbate any existing distress or diagnoses.

In response to concerns about cyberbullying, particularly the high-profile tragedies reported at the beginning of the book, legislators have made attempts to provide legal protection for victims. In this section, I review the existing and proposed legislation specific to cyberbullying and note what types of laws can be applied to cyberbullying even if cyberbullying is not specifically mentioned in the statute. Although there are numerous laws on the books regarding cyberbullying, taken as a whole, "current remedies are either inefficient or non-existent" (Cheney, 2009, p. 5). Currently, there are federal laws against stalking and harassment that theoretically could be used to prosecute some cases of cyberbullying, and there are state statutes that vary widely and that apply to bullying, cyberbullying, or both.

In response to the Megan Meier incident, Representative Linda Sanchez of California, along with 17 cosponsors, introduced the Megan Meier Cyberbullying Prevention Act (H.R. 1966, 2009) to the U.S. House of Representatives on April 2, 2009. If passed, this bill will amend the federal criminal code "to impose criminal penalties [fine or imprisonment for up to two years or both] on anyone who transmits in interstate or foreign commerce a communication intended to coerce, intimidate, harass, or cause substantial emotional distress to another person, using electronic means to support severe, repeated, and hostile behavior" (H.R. 1966, 2009). At the time of this writing, the bill was still in committee and had not yet come to the floor for a vote. A previous version of that bill (H.B. 1628) was introduced in 2008 and did not come to a vote, but Representative Sanchez said in a radio interview on April 5, 2009, that she is confident that the bill will come to a vote in the current session of the legislature. Predictably, the bill has both supporters and detractors, and the ultimate outcome of the legislation is uncertain. Opponents criticize the language of the bill as too vague, noting that "substantial emotional distress" and "severe" are open to interpretation. They also suggest that there could be a deluge of cases that could overwhelm courts and worry that bloggers whose columns might offend someone could be sued under this law.

The Children's Internet Protection Act (2003) applies to schools and libraries that receive funding from the federal E-Rate program for Internet access or connections. That program reduces costs for communications technology for participating schools and libraries. Those schools and libraries are required to certify that they have an Internet safety policy including blocks and filters to block pornographic sites, obscene images, or material that is harmful to minors. They are also required to have and enforce a policy that monitors online activities of minors and prohibits the unauthorized disclosure of personal information about minors. The law does not apply if the organization receives E-Rate funding only for telephone service. It allows authorized persons to disable the blocks or filters to allow adults to conduct lawful activities online, and it does not require tracking of Internet use. Although this legislation was ostensibly designed to protect minors, critics argue that the broad category of material that must be blocked has the effect of blocking much material that is protected by the First Amendment. Although this act has been upheld by the U.S. Supreme Court, researchers Jaeger, Bertot, and McClure (2004) emphasized that the nature of this ruling does not prevent future legal challenges to this law.

On October 10, 2008, President Bush signed the Broadband Data Improvement Act (2008), which is designed to increase the availability of high-speed Internet access to all geographic areas of the country, particularly those that do not currently have high-speed connectivity, by collecting current data on availability and providing funds for groups that will increase Internet access (Bosworth, 2008). Data collection is emphasized in the bill, which includes a requirement that the 2010 Census questionnaires include questions about Internet access. This bill should increase access to high-speed Internet, which means that individuals in areas of the country who have been neglected to date will gain the opportunities—and hazards—of readily available activities on the Internet.

Harassment

Harassment is one offense that might apply to cyberbullies; the legal definition refers to hostile conduct (physical or verbal) toward another person because of that person's status or membership in a protected group and that serves no legitimate purpose and causes substantial emotional distress. Categories to which harassment applies are age, sex, race, ethnicity, religion, national origin, and disability. Shariff and Gouin (2006) claimed that gender and sexual harassment were found to be the most common bases for cyberbullying among both adolescents and adults. State and federal laws will typically provide more specifics about the type of actions that constitute harassment (and whether specific groups, such as gays and lesbians, are protected) and the penalties for offenders found guilty of such actions. The federal legislation was amended in 2006 by adding "any interactive computer service" to the text (Cheney, 2009). Cheney also observed that federal laws apply only when the attacker and victim are in different states. Recall that in the Megan Meier case, the suit was filed in California, where MySpace offices are located. They could not apply federal antiharassment laws because the cyberbully (Lori Drew) and victim (Megan) lived in the same state.

Counselors should be familiar with the laws in their states that might be the basis of legal action against a cyberbully. I live in New Mexico, where there are separate statutes for harassment and stalking (and harassment is also listed as a form of stalking); harassment is a misdemeanor, but stalking can be either a misdemeanor or a felony depending on whether the defendant has a prior conviction for stalking. In addition to other penalties, the court is required to order counseling for the victim at the defendant's expense if the defendant is convicted. I am concerned that in most states, the victims are not encouraged to seek counseling. I hope that victims will do so of their own accord, but the legal system does not address this need. When electronic communications are specified as a means of harassment (or stalking) in the law, it may be somewhat easier to prosecute, but the law may still apply to harassment by technology when it is not specifically stated.

Most states have laws against harassment and stalking. Those laws can be applied to cases of Internet or cell phone harassment as well as other forms of message delivery. The National Conference of State Legislatures (NCSL; 2009) provides a list of state electronic harassment or cyberstalking laws, with links to the statutes. Alabama, Arizona, Connecticut, Hawaii, Illinois, New Hampshire, and New York have added electronic communications to existing harassment laws; Alaska, Florida, Oklahoma, and California have added it to stalking laws.

An example of prosecution for using electronic devices to harass or stalk is the case of James Murphy of South Carolina, who received a sentence of 5 years probation, 500 hours of community service, and $12,000 in restitution for his conviction on two counts of using a telecommunications device with intent to annoy, abuse, threaten, or harass Joelle Ligon. Years after the end of a romantic relationship, Murphy sent numerous harassing e-mails and faxes to Ms. Ligon and her coworkers. The e-mails included both threats and false information about Ms. Ligon. Eventually, Murphy masqueraded as Ms. Ligon and sent pornographic e-mails to her coworkers that appeared to come from her. Ms. Ligon was able to identify Murphy as the sender, and she obtained a court order forbidding contact from him. He violated that order by sending her an e-mail denying he was the one harassing her. Restitution was paid to Ms. Ligon's employer for hours of work time spent by workers dealing with the harassment.

Stalking refers to conduct that puts the victim in fear for his or her safety or the safety of a household member. According to federal law, "the term 'stalking' means engaging in a course of conduct directed at a specific person that would cause a reasonable person to—'(A) fear for his or her safety or the safety of others;' or '(B) suffer substantial emotional distress'" (Violence Against Women and Department of Justice Reauthorization Act, 2006, para. 24 (Definitions), § 4002). This act made online harassment and cyberstalking criminal offenses under particular circumstances. The law specifically prohibits using a telephone or telecommunications device "without disclosing [one's] identity and with intent to annoy, abuse, threaten, or harass any person at the called number or who receives the communication" (§ 223[a][1][c]). This law attempts to address the harassers who use the perceived anonymity of the Internet to conduct their malicious behavior.

Cyberstalking

Cyberstalking is involved in 20%–40% of all stalking cases, according to the NCSL (2009). The definition varies somewhat by source, but in general it refers to using electronic communication to stalk someone. Stalking is generally defined as repeated harassing or threatening behavior. In some states, the law states that the offender must have made a "credible" threat of violence against the victim or the victim's family. In others, an implied threat is sufficient. There is also evidence that suggests that most stalkers are men and most victims are women, but the reverse definitely occurs ("Cyberstalking," n.d.). It may be that because cyberstalkers do not have to be in the physical presence of their victims, there is less resistance to engaging in stalking behavior. The technology also can make the stalking more ominous. For example, cyberstalkers can use software to send threatening or harassing e-mails at prescribed intervals.

There are already laws that allow victims to sue for actions that involve the "intentional infliction of emotional distress" (Auerbach, 2008–2009, p. 1669), which may be the best avenue for victims to pursue. There are four conditions that must be demonstrated for such a case to prevail: The defendant must have known or should have known that the actions would cause serious emotional distress, the actions must be outside the norm of acceptable behavior to the degree that it would be "considered intolerable in a civilized community" (Auerbach, 2008–2009, p. 1669), the offender's actions must be the direct cause of the emotional distress, and finally the emotional distress must be serious enough that no one should be expected to endure it. Although this is a high bar for many incidents, there are certainly some that would qualify. Counselors could even be called on to testify on the final requirement. If a client receives services from a counselor because of the severe emotional distress he or she experienced as a direct result of cyberbullying, the counselor may want to recommend that the client seek legal counsel. If a lawyer took such a case, it is likely that the counselor would be asked to testify.

The good news is that law enforcement personnel are becoming much more aware of the severity of this type of harassment and stalking and are much better equipped to respond now than just a few years ago. Several large cities have specialized units to work on such cases, and many other agencies have technology specialists who can assist even when specialized units do not exist.

In the educational arena, cyberbullying has been added to the existing antibullying legislation in many states. Table 2 summarizes the key points. Notice that in some states, jurisdiction is restricted to incidents that occur on school property or at school-sponsored activities, whereas other states may take disciplinary action when the events cause substantial disruption of school functions. I found only one state law that made mention of the victim's needs.

In some places where there are no applicable state laws dealing with cyberbullying, school districts have nevertheless taken measures to address the issue. For example, Bullitt County, Kentucky, experienced several incidents of online threats that created significant disruption in the school ("Students to Be Punished," 2007). In January 2007, several hundred students left the school after threats were posted on MySpace. In April 2007, two high school students threatened a middle school student; one posted a photo of himself holding a gun on MySpace. The students were arrested. And in the previous year, a student had committed suicide after repeated MySpace threats. In August 2007, the school board passed a policy stating that students could be suspended or expelled (in addition to being subjected to any criminal charges) for messages posted on MySpace. This policy came to the attention of the ACLU because of concerns regarding the First Amendment rights of students. That organization promised to closely monitor the situation.

According to Auerbach (2008–2009), "Neither federal nor state law provides sweeping redress for individuals suffering from Internet-based harassment" (p. 1645). The biggest challenge for schools attempting to intervene in cyberbullying cases is ensuring First Amendment rights. There are three rulings by the U.S. Supreme Court that have bearing on this issue. The earliest was *Tinker v. Des Moines School District* in 1969 (cited in Auerbach, 2008–2009; Beckstrom, 2008; and Willard, 2007a). During the Vietnam War, some students chose to wear armbands showing opposition to the war during school hours despite a policy created by the school district saying that students who wore such armbands would be asked to remove them, and if they refused they would be suspended. The policy was enforced on several students. The ruling in this case established that there are restrictions on the First Amendment (guaranteeing freedom of speech) in the school setting. The ruling allows schools to restrict free speech when it creates a substantial disruption to school function or if it "invades the rights of oth-

Table 2

Existing State Legislation on Cyberbullying

State	Main Provision	Year	Comments
AK	Added cyberbullying to existing legislation requiring school districts to have harassment prevention policies.	2007	School districts also directed to include statement in policy that covers off-campus electronic acts that cause "substantial disruption" of the educational environment.
CA	Includes bullying by electronic act in the definition of bullying.	2008	Students who cyberbully may be suspended or expelled.
DE	Schools must create a bullying prevention policy that includes a bullying prevention program and a system for reporting incidents to the state Department of Education.	2007	Electronic communication is included in the definition of bullying. Off-campus bullying is actionable if there is a "sufficient school nexus."
FL	Bullying or harassment (including via technology) of students and employees is prohibited. Schools must have procedures in place in order to receive Safe School funds.	2008	BullyPolice.org rates this law as the best in the country. The state department must provide a model policy; minimum requirements are specified in the legislation. Policies must include a procedure to refer bullies and victims for counseling and a procedure for reporting to victim's parents on how victim is being protected. Reporters are immune from liability.
ID	Schools can suspend students who disrupt school by bullying, including bullying by technological methods.	2006	This is an amendment to a previous law, adding the suspension provision. A student who bullies or conspires to commit bullying "may be guilty of an infraction."
IA	School must adopt antiharassment and antibullying policies. Bullying definition includes electronic means. The law prohibits bullying on school property, at school functions, or at school-sponsored activities, regardless of location.	2007	This is an amendment to previous law, adding technological means. Components of the policy are specified in the law. Districts must collect data on incidents. Reporters are granted immunity.
KS	Added cyberbullying in July to antibullying law passed in January.	2008	School districts must adopt a policy that prohibits all forms of bullying on school property or when using school property. The districts also must implement a plan that includes training for students and staff.
MD	Revised statute includes "an intentional electronic communication" as an example of cyberbullying.	2008	Specifies offenses occur on school property, at a school activity, or on the school bus. Incidents must be reported using a form created by the state department. State board must develop model policy by end of March 2009. School employees are granted immunity from civil liability.
MN	School districts are required to develop written bullying policies, including cyberbullying.	2007	The law does not have any other provisions.

(Continued)

Table 2

Existing State Legislation on Cyberbullying *(Continued)*

State	Main Provision	Year	Comments
MO	Modifies existing law regarding stalking and harassment to include electronic means. School boards are required to have a written policy. Employees are required to report any bullying of which they have "firsthand knowledge." Policy must state consequences of bullying. Policy will include training for employees in the policy requirements.	2008	Electronic harassment is now a crime.
NE	Districts must adopt a policy by July 1, 2009, regarding bullying prevention and education. Definition of bullying includes "electronic abuse."	2008	Law applies to school property, school-sponsored events or activities, and designated school bus stops. It does not apply to off-campus cyberbullying.
NJ	The law requires districts to amend existing policies to include cyberbullying. The policy applies to behaviors on school property, school functions, or school buses.	2007	After passage of this statute, the state department of education developed guidelines that allow districts to discipline cyberbullies when off-campus cyberbullying "substantially interferes" with the functioning of the school.
NC	Electronic communication included in definition of bullying. Restricts bullying to actions on school property, at school functions, or on a school bus. All school districts must adopt a policy prohibiting bullying and harassment by December 31, 2009. The law specifies required components of the policy, including a provision for "consequences and appropriate remedial action" for the bully.	2009	Definition includes actions that "the victim subjectively views . . . as bullying . . . and [in which] the conduct is objectively severe or pervasive enough that a reasonable person would agree that it is bullying." Victim is not prohibited from seeking civil or criminal "redress."
OK	Updates an earlier bill. Includes electronic communication in the definition of bullying and requires districts to investigate complaints of bullying.	2008	The law also permits school boards to recommend mental health services.
OR	Adds cyberbullying to existing laws on bullying. Districts must adopt a policy prohibiting cyberbullying.	2007	No guidelines for components of the policy are provided in the legislation. The law states that an emergency exists, and the act was necessary to protect public safety.
PA	Definition of bullying includes cyberbullying, which is prohibited in school settings (on school property, including in school vehicles, and at school activities).	2008	
RI	Definition of bullying in school discipline codes expanded to include electronic communication.	2008	

(Continued)

Table 2

Existing State Legislation on Cyberbullying *(Continued)*

State	Main Provision	Year	Comments
SC	School district required to adopt policies prohibiting bullying, harassment, and intimidation. Electronic communication is included in definition.	2006	Components of the policy are specified by the law. The policy must include consequences and "remedial action" for someone found to have falsely accused someone else. The state board of education must develop model policies and teacher preparation program standards. Districts are encouraged to develop bullying prevention programs.
WA	By August 1, 2008, districts were required to amend existing policies to include electronic communications. The policies were required to include a statement that materials are available to educate parents and students about cyberbullying.	2007	If a district has an acceptable use policy, it must include statements that bullying, harassment, or intimidation online are prohibited.
WI	The act added a section on "unlawful use of computerized communication systems" to an existing law. This statute itemizes offenses using computerized communication systems and makes them a Class B misdemeanor. Prohibited are actions intended to "frighten, intimidate, threaten, abuse, or harass" another person using computerized communication systems. Included in the prohibited actions are messages that use "lewd or profane language, or suggests any lewd or lascivious act" or attempt to conceal the identity of the sender. It also prohibits allowing or directing another person to send such a message.	1996	This law is not specific to schools, so is applicable to a broader range of settings. The classification of offenses as Class B misdemeanor may not be serious enough.

Note. Laws go into effect after some specified period of time after they are passed by the legislature and signed by the governor. Information in this table came from National Conference of State Legislatures (2009), "State Action on Cyberbullying" (2008), Beckstrom (2008), and Auerbach (2008–2009). When possible, the statutes were read to verify information.

ers" (Beckstrom, 2008, p. 297). The Court ruled against the district in this case, saying the armbands did not rise to that standard.

The next important ruling was in the 1986 case of *Bethel School District No. 403 v. Fraser* (cited in Auerbach, 2008–2009; and Beckstrom, 2008). In this case, the student gave a speech at a voluntary assembly that contained inappropriate graphic sexual language. He was warned by teachers that giving the speech would have serious consequences and was disciplined for this behavior. In this case, the ruling was quite different. The Court decided that the rights of students in a school setting are not the same as those of adults in other contexts, and that schools could decide that certain offensive language would be prohibited. So in this case, the Court ruled in favor of the school district.

The most recent case, *Hazelwood School District v. Kuhlmeier* (cited in Auerbach, 2008–2009; and Beckstrom, 2008), was filed by students who worked on the school newspaper. The students claimed that their First Amendment rights were violated when the school's administrators deleted articles that their advisor thought were inappropriate. The school newspaper was considered by the Court to be a "non-public forum" because it was part of the school curriculum and paid for by the school district. The ruling in 2007 by the U.S. Supreme Court again favored the school district. So, in two of the three cases, the schools were allowed to restrict student speech, although the *Tinker* case provided standards by which some speech could be evaluated. The fact that the rulings have not been entirely consistent makes it difficult to predict how attempts to deal with cyberbullying will be treated by the courts.

No cases dealing specifically with cyberbullying have yet reached the Supreme Court, but in one case, *J.S. ex rel. H.S. v. Bethlehem Area School District* (cited in Auerbach 2008–2009; Beckstrom, 2008), the lower court ruled that the discipline administered to a student who created a website on his home computer that posted derogatory and offensive comments and images about a teacher and the school principal was not a violation of the student's rights. The teacher in this case was sufficiently distressed that she did not return to school for the remainder of the year. The school district first suspended and then moved to expel the student, and the parents sued the district on the basis of a violation of the student's First Amendment right to freedom of speech. An important thing to note is that the court ruled there was a "nexus" between the website and the school such that the offense could be considered "on campus," and, using the *Tinker* standards, ruled that the website caused a substantial disruption; hence, the court ruled against the student. Similarly, in the *Layshock v. Hermitage School District* case discussed earlier, the court again found that a "substantial disruption" was created by the website, and thus the school's disciplinary actions did not violate his right to freedom of speech.

These cases provide little comfort for school districts that are concerned that if they intervene in cases of cyberbullying they will have no legal standing. Many if not most incidents that happen will not "substantially disrupt" school operations (although some students may be upset), and thus school actions when the incidents originate off campus may not be supported. Recently, a U.S. District judge in Los Angeles ruled against a school that had suspended an eighth-grade student for posting a YouTube video in which a group of girls insulted another student and called her derogatory names (Kim, 2009). The student who had been the target of the video complained to her school counselor, feeling humiliated because the video had been seen by many students who were alerted technologically about it. The counselor brought the situation to the attention of the school's administrators, who suspended the girl who posted the video. The girl who had been suspended sued, saying her First Amendment rights had been violated. The judge agreed and commented, "The court cannot uphold school discipline of student speech simply because young persons are unpredictable or immature, or because, in general, teenagers are emotionally fragile and may often fight over hurtful comments" (Kim, 2009, para. 6).

There have been several rulings (e.g., *Coy v. Board of Education, Killion v. Franklin Regional School District*) in which students disciplined for creating websites that made rude or offensive comments were found to have had their rights to freedom of speech violated (Beckstrom, 2008). One other case is relevant to how schools might respond to incidents of cyberbullying without violating students' rights. In *Watts v. United States* (as cited in Beckstrom, 2008), the U.S. Supreme Court ruled that a "true threat" is not protected by the First Amendment, and that the location from which a true threat is made is not relevant. Whether communication qualifies as a "true threat" is determined by whether the person receiving it could reasonably conclude that the message really presented a real threat. Or, as another court determined, the standard to be applied can be whether a reasonable person would believe that the recipient would interpret the message as a serious intent to harm (Beckstrom, 2008). Thus, although there is not absolute agreement, it is apparent that with the exception of several cases to which the *Tinker* standards apply, or when a realistic threat has been made, schools will need to be cautious about taking disciplinary measures when cyberbullying occurs. School counselors may be the best people to work with both offenders and victims in these cases. In the following chapter, I discuss some methods that may be useful in these cases and for which school counselors are uniquely qualified.

Lawsuits

Another legal strategy for dealing with cyberbullying involves the victim suing the service provider. However, the Communications Decency Act of 1996 essentially protects service providers from liability. The law says that "primary publishers," the authors of the content, are liable, but distributors and "conduits" (ISPs) are not liable. The law was intended to protect ISPs because legislators wanted to maintain the Internet as a place for honest exchanges of opinion while ensuring that First Amendment rights were protected online. A small window of liability applies if it can be proven that the distributor had knowledge of the defamatory statements. This is one reason that notifying an ISP of offending material is important.

A major difficulty with legislation is that it takes time for a problem that can be addressed by legislation to be recognized, legislators informed, legislation crafted, voted on, and so forth. For example, someone created an anonymous blog on www.blogger.com called "Skanks in NYC," on which photos of a well-known model were posted with derogatory captions (Tan-neeru, 2009). The model sued Google (owner of blogger.com) to learn the identity of the blogger. The Supreme Court ruled that Google had to reveal the name, and it did so. Several lawsuits have been filed but had not been decided at the time of this writing. A clothing designer who provided clothes to Courtney Love is suing her because Love made derogatory and defamatory (according to the suit) comments about the designer on Twit-ter.com. In a similar case, a woman made a comment about her former landlord on Twitter.com and is being sued for $50,000 in alleged damages by the owner of the apartment (Tanneeru, 2009).

Stacy Snyder was completing her student teaching, the last step in obtaining a degree in education, in 2006. Millersville University, where she was a student, decided not to award her a degree, and Ms. Synder sued. In her complaint, she alleged that the reason the university withheld the degree was because of a photo on her MySpace page in which she was wearing a pirate's hat and drinking from a cup. The caption on the photo was "Drunken Pirate." The court decided in favor of the university, which provided other reasons for denying the degree (Tanneeru, 2009). Regardless of the outcome, this incident highlights how material posted online can be viewed and used by others.

Another case that had not been decided at the time of this writing is intriguing because a high school is being sued for punishing students for suggestive photos on their MySpace pages that were taken and posted during their summer vacation ("School Sued," 2009). The ACLU filed the suit against Churubusco High School in Indianapolis, Indiana, because the girls were initially banned from all extra-curricular activities for the year and were required to apologize to the coaches' board and to obtain counseling because of suggestive photos posted on their MySpace pages—photos that the girls said were a joke. Although the punishment was modified (to being banned from 25% of fall activities) after the apology was tendered and the counseling completed, the suit was filed. The photos were taken on a summer outing and posted on their pages with privacy settings set so that only "friends" could view the images. It is not known how the photos reached the principal (a good reminder to everyone that there are *no* guarantees of privacy on the Internet), although it is likely that a "friend" copied it and sent it. The principal claims he was implementing the athletic code that permits the principal to ban students from activities if their behavior in or out of school "creates a disruptive influence on the discipline, good order, moral or educational environment at Churubusco High School" ("School Sued," 2009, para. 7).

Adults in the workplace should be aware that organization e-mail accounts can be inspected by the employer if their employees have been informed that this could happen (Shariff, 2005). Employees who use their company computer to cyberbully another cannot claim any rights to privacy in that situation.

Summary

- Computers keep track of websites visited, and the history function of the browser can be used to monitor the user's online behavior.
- E-mails can appear to come from one sender but actually originate elsewhere; viewing the full header allows the user to identify the actual source. This header can be evidence of cyberbullying.
- Senders of unwanted or bullying messages can be blocked both online and on cell phones. This blocking is a way to limit cyberbullying without depriving the victim of other electronic interaction.
- Cyberbullies should be reported. Schools and agencies may have systems for doing this reporting, but websites and ISPs should also be contacted, as they can remove offensive content and bar offenders from certain sites or access.
- Several states have amended existing antibullying legislation to include cyberbullying. However, some laws restrict school jurisdiction only to actions using school equipment or on school grounds. Other states allow schools to take action when the cyberbullying seriously disrupts school functioning.
- Several cyberbullying cases have been heard in court. The issue is often whether First Amendment rights apply. In a school setting, there are limits on freedom of speech.
- A federal law to prohibit cyberbullying has been proposed by Rep. Linda Sanchez of California, but the bill has not moved out of committee. Critics say the law, if passed as proposed, could censor bloggers and others who express unpopular opinions.
- Legal scholars suggest that current laws may apply to cyberbullying (typically antiharassment or antistalking laws or laws dealing with the intentional infliction of emotional distress).

CHAPTER 9

Counseling Strategies to Combat Cyberbullying

I have reviewed the laws that may provide recourse to victims of cyberbullying. It is clear that although extreme actions may be prosecuted, "lesser" incidents will need other remedies. In this chapter, I review some nonpunitive strategies that may be helpful. I begin with a discussion of punishment and discuss why it may not be the most effective way to deal with cyberbullying incidents, especially those that are less severe. I then describe the most widely used nonpunitive approaches in school and workplace settings. Many of these strategies are most effectively implemented by counselors, whose training provides the skills in communication and consultation that are the basis of these approaches. Finally, I include some suggestions for working with parents.

Punishment

When punishment (or sanctions or consequences) is imposed on an offender, there are potential outcomes that are not what the punisher intended. First, punishment teaches the offender what *not* to do, not how to behave appropriately. And, it may be that what he or she learns not to do is to get caught. That is, the offender may associate the punishment with getting caught and become more clandestine and devious in his or her future behavior. Punishment is likely to result in temporary cessation of the behavior, but it is unlikely to result in lasting change. Cyberbullies may become more careful about how they hide their identity and may increase the threats to others who might report them. They may also change strategies.

When the cyberbully is punished, he or she may blame the victim or the person who reported the behavior. The cyberbully may even blame the person who imposes the punishment. If this is the case, the likely outcome is anger, resentment, and retaliation—the cyberbully wants to get even with those who cause him or her unpleasantness. For the victim, this may mean increased (although less observable) torment; for bystanders, threats may be made; and for teachers or managers, other disruptive behaviors may be the bully's way to retaliate. In any case, these were not the desired outcomes when punishments were imposed.

In addition, when punishment is administered aggressively, the child may reason that it is appropriate to behave aggressively only when the target is smaller and/or weaker than oneself. If a child becomes very upset at a punishment, that child may become so emotionally aroused that the reason for the punishment is forgotten, so the intended lesson about appropriate behavior is completely missed (Baron & Richardson, 2004).

These comments may imply that punishment never works, and that is not true. However, there are many considerations that affect the way punishment influences behavior. First, the punishment has to be greater than the reward in order to be effective. Whatever gratification cyberbullies obtain from their actions may be greater than the consequences (e.g., temporary loss of access to technology). It is also a well-known principle of behaviorism that the closer in time the punishment is to the offense, the more likely it will be to have an effect. Often, given the procedures in place in many schools and workplaces, the punishment does not follow closely enough on the offense, and the impact of the punishment is diluted. This delay is also often present in the legal system. Many cases take years before they are finally settled. The impact of punishment also depends to some extent on the importance of the person administering the punishment. A person who is highly valued may only have to look disappointed to have an effect on one's behavior, whereas a person one does not respect might impose severe penalties with the only effect being a reinforcement of one's belief that the person is unjust or cruel. Given the hostile attribution biases of many cyberbullies, this latter outcome is quite likely.

What alternatives are there to punishment? I will describe several non-punitive counseling-based strategies, beginning with those that are suitable for the school setting. There are several aspects of nonpunitive approaches that enhance their value. First, they are primarily interpersonal approaches. That is, rather than isolating the cyberbully, these approaches promote cooperative and collaborative behavior. It has been well-established that cyberbullying is usually more than a dyadic encounter. There are often bystanders and others who are aware of the activity, and in these nonpunitive methods, the larger group is involved in generating solutions. This process promotes a wider investment in developing a positive climate, and it helps all parties develop both skills and moral standards. Second, most of these strategies capitalize on the therapeutic variables (Yalom, 1995) that are present in groups. These variables include the following:

- Altruism—the satisfaction that comes from being helpful to others
- Cohesiveness—the positive feeling of belonging to a group

- Instillation of hope—the sense that problems can be solved, that things can get better
- Universality—the sense that one is not alone (both cyberbullies and cybervictims learn that others have similar needs and feelings)
- Identification— similar to modeling, learning from positive role models
- Guidance—receiving suggestions from peers about possible solutions
- Interpersonal learning—discovering how one's behaviors are perceived by others

Third, these strategies are generally strengths-based. They identify and expand on positive characteristics rather than focusing on the problematic behaviors. Thus, cyberbullies are helped to use their assets to overcome negative behaviors, which is consistent with the current focus in the field on wellness and positive psychology. Rather than being punished, cyberbullies receive positive reinforcement (praise, satisfaction) for behaving in more socially appropriate ways.

Philosophically, these strategies are based on the belief that the most effective strategies not only stop the bullying but also have long-term effects so that all parties involved learn different ways to deal with each other. The strategies must work quickly and be easily mastered by staff. They must be understood by parents, students, and other employees. Because many people may at first be wary of an approach that doesn't punish the cyberbully (in the usual sense), you, the counselor, may have to convince them of the value of nonpunitive strategies. I suggest emphasizing that the goal is to stop the cyberbullying and to create long-term positive change in the school or organization. As that is everyone's goal, the message is clear. If punishment does not have the desired effect, are not other approaches worthy of consideration? Punishment has been well-tested in most schools, and yet bullying problems have rarely been much reduced.

Typically, before punishment can be applied, there must be an investigation with clear evidence produced. In schools and workplaces, this process takes a great deal of time, and often the circumstances cannot be completely clarified. Some of the legislation discussed in the previous chapter requires that no action be taken against a bully until proof of the offending action has been obtained. In reality, this requirement is not likely to be met all the time. The requirement also places school personnel and workplace managers and human resources personnel in the position of investigators, which is neither their role nor their training. I propose that when a case of cyberbullying is not legally actionable, has not caused a serious disruption of school or workplace functioning, but nevertheless has caused distress for the victim, nonpunitive methods should be considered. I hope the reader will be open-minded and reflect on how some of the nonpunitive counseling-based strategies could provide a more helpful process for all concerned.

I have not included peer mediation as one of these suggested strategies. The primary reason is that peer mediation is based on presumed equality of the parties in the conflict. By definition, bullying means there is an imbalance of power between the bully and the victim, placing the victim at a disadvantage (at best) and replicating the power dynamics of the bullying (at worst). In many schools, peer mediation is conducted by students (peers) who have been trained in a specific protocol for conducting the meetings. Although not having school authority figures present reinforces the notion of mediation, student mediators may not be able to recognize when an agreement is insincere. Adult mediators may not recognize such insincerity either. Details of a bullying that was covered by the media (Zdanowicz, 2009) indicated that the school resource officer (a police officer stationed at the school) and principal conducted a peer mediation session with two girls and believed the situation had been resolved. The next day the bully attacked the victim.

Brief Solution-Focused Individual Counseling

Brief solution-focused counseling (BSFC) for individuals is most appropriate for responding to incidents of low-level severity. This counseling approach will be familiar to many readers; the basic premises are to focus on exceptions to the problem (times when the problem does not exist), build on client strengths, and envision life without the problem. As applied to bullying or cyberbullying, the assumption is that the cyberbully or victim has been referred to the counselor as a first step in resolving the issue. The problem is framed as being in trouble at school (for the bully) or being unhappy at school (for the victim). This framing removes the need for clients to be defensive or to justify their behavior. Young and Holdorf (2003) reported excellent results using this approach with students in schools, both bullies and victims. Of 134 referrals received for bullying in 2000–2001, individual BSFC was used with 118 referrals (66 boys, 52 girls; 26 elementary age, and 92 secondary students). Twenty-six students had only one session, which is consistent with the BSFC approach. Of the 92 students who had more than one individual session, 92% reached a point at which support was no longer needed. Using the students' own scaling, 8% stayed at the same level on scaling, made insufficient progress from their own point of view, or discontinued the sessions. The average number of sessions until a successful termination was met was 2.8. Young and Holdorf indicated that re-referral for bullying was "very low" (p. 278).

Briefly, the steps of the process are as follows:

1. Establish rapport with nonproblem talk.
2. Use scaling (1–10) to rate the severity of the situation from the client perspective.
   a. The rating is generally not 1, so the counselor inquires how the client has been able to reach whatever level is reported (e.g., "How do you manage to be a "4" when all this is going on?").
   b. This strategy identifies strengths and areas of current success.
   c. The client is asked what the rating *will* be in a week. (This wording is very purposeful. The *presuppositional* language conveys the message that the client *will* be better.)

3. The client is asked to provide detailed descriptions of times when the problem is *not* present. (Typically, the client reports he or she is doing something other than bullying, such as playing a game, having lunch, and so forth.)

4. Use the so-called miracle question, a basic tool of BSFC. The client is asked to assume the counselor performs a miracle while the client is asleep, and the problem has disappeared. The client is asked how he or she will know it is gone, who else will notice, what is different about him or her, and so forth. This process helps clients see how the positive changes will affect their lives and relationships with others.

5. Compliment the client on what he or she has done well.

6. If necessary, offer tentative suggestions (with client permission), but these should come from what the client has already said that can be applied to improving the situation. "I have an idea of something that might help. Would you be interested in hearing about it?"

7. Arrange to review progress at an agreed-upon time (usually a week). The client is instructed to pay close attention to successes to report to the counselor at that time. Again, this encourages clients to focus on the times, even brief moments, when they are managing the problem well.

8. Some practitioners of BSFC like to end sessions with a written note that includes a positive affirmation of what the client has already accomplished and expresses confidence that change will occur.

Counselors who work with adults may already be quite familiar with this counseling approach. With incidents of low-level severity, the intervention may not only resolve the current problem but also equip the client with strategies that can be used for similar situations in the future. It is essential that the problem be framed in a way that avoids defensiveness on the client's part. "Being in trouble" or "being unhappy" is much more palatable that "being a bully" or "being bullied."

Although there is some research evidence for the effectiveness of BSFC in the school setting, additional controlled studies are needed. Single-case designs have been recommended and used to evaluate this approach (Franklin, Biever, Moore, Clemons, & Scamardo, 2001). Franklin and her colleagues used this approach with fifth- and sixth-grade children who had learning disabilities and were having behavior problems in school. Seven children received between 5 and 10 sessions of BSFC, with each session lasting 30 to 45 minutes. Teacher consultations occurred for approximately 10–120 minutes per week. Three solution-focused methods were included in each session: the use of the miracle question, scaling, and compliments. All sessions were videotaped to ensure adherence to the treatment plan. To be included in the study, at least half of baseline scores on the Conners Teacher Rating Scale had to be above the level considered clinically significant ($T > 69$). The research design was AB case study, replicated in the seven children. In AB case study research, observations of the child are made during a baseline period (no intervention) and during the treatment phase. The data from the two observation periods are compared. Of the seven cases, five showed definite positive behavior changes at the end of the intervention, and the changes were maintained at follow-up 1 month after treatment. The researchers concluded that the results add weight to findings of previous studies demonstrating positive behavior changes using BSFC with children in the school setting.

Support Groups

A number of experts have promoted support groups for dealing with conventional bullying incidents in schools; there are some variations in the method that will be apparent below. Although these approaches were developed for and have been used with conventional bullying, there is no reason that they would not work as well with cyberbullying. In fact, because the cyberbully may be more difficult to identify than a conventional bully, this method could prove even more beneficial.

Evelyn Field's Approach

Evelyn Field, an Australian psychologist and expert on bullying in both schools and the workplace, has devised several support group programs in which victims are not only supported but also taught skills to combat bullying. Her books also give guidelines to parents for helping their children when they are victimized (e.g., Field, 2007). She shared six "secrets" for blocking bullying that apply to cyberbullying as well:

1. Regulate feelings (respond assertively vs. passively or aggressively).
2. Understand your role (why you are bullied).
3. Build self-esteem.
4. Become a confident communicator.
5. Create a personal "power pack" (e.g., retorts to use with the bully).
6. Develop a support network.

These skills are effectively taught in a group, where there is also an opportunity to practice and get feedback from others. In addition, the group is a step toward building a support network. Many of the exercises in *Bully Blocking* (Field, 2007), written with child victims in mind, can be readily adapted for use with adults.

Robinson and Maines's Approach

Robinson and Maines (2008) have proposed a model that uses a skilled facilitator, most often a school counselor. The current version of their approach has evolved over time, refined by the experiences of the authors and other professionals using the system who provide them with feedback. The approach was initially called the *no-blame approach*, but that term was misunderstood and politically unpopular, so they now refer to their approach simply as the *support group method.* An evaluation of the approach used in the United Kingdom reported that 45 of 47 interventions in secondary schools were successful, and 7 of 7 interventions in elementary schools were also deemed successful (Smith & Sharp, 1994).

The process involves a series of steps to be implemented:

Step 1: Meet with the target. Cyberbullying may come to the attention of the counselor through either self-report or reports from friends, parents, teachers, and so forth. The target (victim) is invited to meet with the counselor. There are specific goals for this initial meeting:

- One goal is for the counselor to understand how the bullying has hurt the victim and how the victim has been feeling.
- The counselor then explains the support group method and gets the victim's permission to proceed. For people who have been victimized, it is essential that they not be placed in a position in which they again feel powerless, so gaining their consent is essential to reinforce that they have control at this point.
- If the student agrees to proceed, the counselor gathers the names of those involved, including the cyberbully (if known), others who knew about the cyberbullying, and also friends and allies or potential allies of the victim who would be helpful in the process. If the victim says, "I have no friends," the counselor asks for the names of people he or she would like to have as friends.
- In this step, the counselor is careful to confirm with the victim what information can be shared with the group, protecting the victim's right to privacy. The victim is invited (encouraged) to compose or draw something that portrays his or her distress at what has happened. Poetry is often suggested. The victim will not be included in the group meetings until the end of the process, so the artistic creation is used to convey the harm the victim experienced. The victim is also invited to see the counselor at any point during the process.

Step 2: The counselor brings together the people identified in the previous step for an initial meeting. It is important that there be a good balance between those involved in the incident and those who support the victim and can model positive responses. The atmosphere should be friendly and welcoming, and all students should be thanked for coming.

Step 3: The counselor tells the group about his or her concern for the victim (e.g., "I'm worried about Suzie; she's been having a hard time lately"). The purpose of the meeting is explained as helping the counselor with this concern. At this point, the artistic creation can be used to enhance the counselor's story of why the counselor is so concerned. It is important that details of bullying incidents are not disclosed and that no blame is affixed. The session is not an investigative one, so it's essential that the counselor not focus on the specifics of the incident—the counselor doesn't want to give the impression that he or she is seeking information or trying to identify the bully. The counselor may say, for example, "Suzie has been receiving very upsetting text messages. She drew this picture of how she is feeling."

Step 4: The counselor explains that no one is in trouble. The counselor wants to help Suzie feel happier in school but believes that additional help is needed and that those present can be helpful.

Step 5: The counselor asks the group members for their ideas to help Suzie. This step is treated as a brainstorming activity, with no judgments of the suggestions. The counselor tries to elicit a suggestion from each person. Sometimes, when a student cannot think of an idea, others can be invited to help. The result is often that the student is enlisted to help with someone else's plan, for example, "I'm going to sit with her at lunch. You could sit with us too."

Step 6: The counselor thanks all the members and expresses confidence that the situation with Suzie will improve. No promises or contracts are elicited, but the counselor does say he or she will check back with the group members in a week and get their assessment of progress.

Step 7: At individual follow-up meetings with each participant (including the victim), the counselor asks how the ideas are working. If necessary, more meetings can be scheduled.

Sue Young's Approach

Young (1998) provided a rationale for her support group approach based on findings from social psychology and group psychology. She observed that individuals are more likely to help or intervene when the following conditions are present: they have been asked to help and agree to do so, the need for action is very clear to them, they have been given responsibility and know that their individual action is helpful, they have witnessed harm, they have had their empathy elicited, they expect feedback on the results of their efforts, they have a specific task, and they feel guilty (p. 38). The group component amplifies these effects because of the following: Each individual has had validation for his or her suggestions from the group or leader; others will be likely to follow after even a single member of the group takes a helpful step; each individual's commitment to help has been made to the group, so he or she is less likely to be anonymous; members increase their own self-esteem by being part of a successful group; group norms develop that disapprove of unhelpful actions; group cohesiveness promotes mutually helpful behavior; the public nature of the commitment to help promotes cooperation; and members are less likely to leave the group when the group has expectations of a positive outcome.

Young's (2002) support group approach is similar to Robinson and Maines's (2008) but has several important differences. I admit to a personal preference for this version, which applies solution-focused principles to the advantages of peer support. In this variation on the support group theme, the first step is similar to that of Robinson and Maines's approach, with the exception that no artistic representation of the emotional pain is requested. The target is asked to identify the bullies and others involved and also to identify either friends or peers he or she would like to have as friends. The student's permission to proceed, once the plan is explained, is also obtained, but consistent with Young's solution-focused perspective, the counselor first expresses confidence that the situation will improve and then asks the target to pay close attention to anything that is better between now and next time they meet (usually a week interval is used).

When the meeting is convened with the group identified by the student, the counselor first assures them that no one is in trouble. They are advised that the counselor has asked them to meet because she needs help with a situation, and they have been invited because she is confident in their ability to help. Regarding the target's situation, the group is told only that the target is unhappy at school, and any comments about what is happening are deflected. The next step is the one that Young (2002) has added and that I believe is very critical to the success of the approach. The counselor elicits empathy from the members of the group by asking if any of them have ever been unhappy at school. As they share their personal examples, the counselor focuses on how the student felt at the time and may say, "I wonder if that is how John is feeling now."

Then the counselor asks for suggestions from the group. The counselor can lead into this phase by noting that the students, unlike the counselor, see John all the time, so they are in the best position to think of how to help him be happier at school. The counselor should write down the suggestions to demonstrate that they are being taken seriously and should reinforce them ("That seems like a good way to help"). Again, members are not asked to make a commitment but are told the counselor is confident they will be able to make a difference with the victim. The counselor mentions that he or she will check back in about a week to see how things are going. The group members are thanked for their willingness to help, and the meeting is adjourned.

In a short period, a day or two, the counselor meets again with the victim and asks *what* (not *if*) he or she has noticed that is better than the last time they talked. A second follow-up meeting is recommended so that the progress can be checked once more.

A meeting is also held again with the support group, and the members are asked whether they think the victim appears to be happier in school. If individuals mention what they are doing, they should be complimented. They are asked whether they would like to continue "helping" for another week, and another review is scheduled. Young (2002) indicated that two reviews are usually all that are needed, but the counselor should make an informed decision about how long the process should be maintained.

The value of this approach is that without a mention or investigation of the cyberbullying incident, the cyberbully and others who may have supported or encouraged the cyberbully's actions are now engaged in helping the victim be happier at school. The suggestions are likely to include such ideas as "I won't send him any text messages, even as a joke." Thus, the bully receives support and encouragement for behaving nonaggressively toward the victim, and the victim gains a social support network.

Young (1998) evaluated this approach as applied specifically to bullying. She reported that of 51 primary-school cases handled using this method, 100% were successful, with 80% having immediate success—no problems reported once the support group was established. Another 14% were successful after three to five weekly meetings, with the bullying either stopping completely or the victim no longer feeling the need for support. More limited success was reported in 6% of cases—there was definite improvement, although the victim still reported incidents of concern. In those few cases, the support group continued until the situation stabilized at a "tolerable" (Young, 1998, p. 36) level, but the victim was referred again later for situations involving different bullies. Four cases from secondary schools were reported, two of which had immediate success and two of which were incomplete because students did not continue in the same school.

Method of Shared Concern

A related, but again slightly different, strategy is called the *method of shared concern*. This method was originally devised by Pikas (1989, 2002) but has been modified slightly and widely promoted by Ken Rigby (2005) in Australia. An evaluation study was conducted in Scotland after Pikas provided training to 14 professionals there (Duncan, 1996). Practitioners indicated in surveys that they had used the method 38 times since the training with students ranging in age from 7 to 16 years. Practitioners reported that the method was either very successful or successful in 34 of the 38 cases, with the remaining four reporting no change in the situation. Experts have stated that this method has had an "impressive success rate in Australia, England, Spain, and Finland" and in the United States (Jarvis, 2007, slide 8; Morrison, Blood, & Thorsborne, 2006).

This method differs from the others described so far in several ways. First, the method assumes that the bullying is a group activity, even if one member of the group is the instigator and primary bully. Second, in this method, talking with the victim before meeting with any of the bullies is *not* part of the process. In fact, it is recommended that the counselor learn about the situation by other methods—observation, reports, and so forth. The idea is to avoid any kind of contact with the victim that might suggest to others that the victim has informed "authorities." This point may be more important with older students, for whom this intervention is most appropriate.

Once the counselor has sufficient information to proceed, each of the cyberbullies is interviewed individually. The purpose of these individual meetings is to begin to individuate members of the bullying group. The bully (or associate) is informed that the counselor is concerned about the victim and has heard from others that the victim is not doing well at the moment. The counselor waits for some type of acknowledgement of that statement, even a nonverbal nod. Then the counselor inquires what the student knows about the situation, which is likely to result in a general "kids are picking on him/her, posting mean things on MySpace" response (at best). At this point, the counselor asks what might be done to make things better. Any positive suggestions are commended. This process continues with the individual bullies until all have been seen individually, at which time the counselor meets with the target (victim). In this meeting, the counselor hears about how things are going at school and, it is hoped, hears about the situation from the victim's perspective. Using basic counseling skills and expressing concern and support, the counselor also attempts to discover if there is anything the victim is doing to provoke the actions. This step is quite controversial—some argue that this can be seen as blaming the victim. Rigby believes that often the victim *has* done something, however minor or unintentional, and that acknowledging that can move the process forward. The counselor meets individually again with each of the bullies to assess progress in making things better for the victim. The next step is a meeting of the "bully" group, at which the bullies are commended for any progress that has been made. At this point, a meeting *may* be scheduled including the victim, but only if the counselor believes it would be productive. Sometimes these meetings end with written agreements.

It is clear that all of these approaches are time consuming, which is often an argument against using them. I invite counselors to think about the time that can be spent investigating allegations of bullying or cyberbullying in order to justify a punitive action. In such cases, the time invested may not lead to a resolution and may result in recriminations and even more secretive or anonymous attacks on the victim.

Restorative Justice and Restorative Practice

The final method I propose, restorative justice, is usually more formal and might be reserved for the most serious cases that are just below the level that would involve the legal system. This method should not be confused with peer mediation, which is not recommended for use with bullying situations. In peer mediation, the two parties (bully and victim) meet with a trained mediator (often a student or coworker) to resolve a conflict. Because of the power imbalance, most bullying experts believe that the mediation puts the victim at a disadvantage at best, and it may create another victimization experience at worst. Restorative justice differs in several ways, including the presence of supporters of both parties and the goal: to restore relationships and give the bully an opportunity to make amends. These elements are not present in peer mediation. In addition, restorative justice conveners (facilitators) are highly trained and are not peers of the parties involved.

Restorative justice approaches are often contrasted with the retributive justice thinking that is more widely applied—the focus being on punishment of the offender. The restorative justice method originated within the criminal justice system as an alternative to criminal prosecution. It is widely used in Australia, New Zealand, and Canada, with excellent results. In one evaluation of community conferencing in schools, 89 conferences were conducted in response to serious incidents, such as assault, serious victimization, property damage, and theft (Cameron & Thorsborne, 1999). A review concluded that participants were highly satisfied with the method and that there were high rates of compliance to the agreement on the part of offenders, who had a low rate of re-offending. In addition, offenders felt more accepted and cared about, and victims felt safer than they did prior to the conference. All school administrators and most parents also had positive evaluations of the process.

The theoretical basis of this approach is that the harm that has been done is to relationships, and the goal of the intervention is to restore those relationships. The relationship is not just between the bully and victim but with the entire school or local community and all those affected. For example, in a school situation, parents and even siblings of the victim may be present and talk about how they have been affected (worried, afraid, angry). The aspect of this approach that I find is missing from all the other approaches, including punishment, is that of making amends. Even if one is jailed, the offender rarely has to directly repair the harm done to the victim (of any crime). Sometimes there are victims' compensation funds that can provide some monetary relief to the victim, but the offender's role in that process is distant from the victim (he or she is required to contribute money to the fund). This approach can be used not only in schools but in organizations and communities as well, and it treats all involved with dignity and respect.

Morrison (2007) emphasized what seems to make the restorative justice approach so powerful. In a restorative justice conference, the offender has an opportunity to gain insight about the effects on others, including the victim. It also provides a learning opportunity for the offender, who can take responsibility for the consequences of his or her actions and work to change behavior in the future. In this approach, victims, who often are neglected in other approaches, have the opportunity to express their thoughts and feelings and to be heard. Unlike in peer mediation, which is generally discouraged because of the power differential between bully and victim, in restorative justice there are supporters present and the parents of both parties if the parties are juveniles. There is also the opportunity for the families and representatives of the larger community to be involved in the process, which works toward restoring the damaged relationships. The participants at the conference can become supporters of both the offender and victim going forward. The opportunity to restore the relationships involves making it right, or making amends, in a manner that is acceptable to the victim. This step is, to me, the most likely to ensure success and the one not considered in most other approaches. Barton (n.d.) considers one of the beneficial aspects of the approach to be the reversal of moral disengagement, discussed earlier. It seems to me that the cyberbullying actions (forwarding material that is embarrassing, creating defamatory websites, harassing a classmate or colleague via text message) are very suitable for this approach.

What follows is a very basic overview of this approach. Many counselors and others who use it get extensive training to be sure it is implemented faithfully. I think being trained is ideal, but I also believe that the basic structure of this approach can be adapted and used by counselors because of their unique professional training. The formal process is very precisely structured. The steps I describe below are detailed in Barton (2003), but I strongly recommend that a school or organization send the counselor in charge of the process for training sessions, which are held frequently around the country. If attending a training session is not possible, watching the available videos and reading the manuals that include step-by-step instructions are necessary to be fully prepared.

Step 1: The first step in this approach is preconference preparations. That includes the logistics of finding a convenient time and suitable location and the important task of inviting participants. Given the goals of this process, it is essential that no one feel coerced to attend. However, if people are unfamiliar with the process, they may need clear and specific information about the purpose and process of the meeting. Making sure that there is strong support for both victim and cyberbully will ensure that there is not a power imbalance that destabilizes the meeting. The location should be neutral so that all parties feel safe. The meeting protocol uses a circular seating arrangement, so finding a room that allows for this is necessary. If restorative justice were adopted as standard practice within a school or organization, it would be helpful to dedicate a room for this purpose so that it is not necessary to spend time seeking a location for each meeting. Meetings may be lengthy, so having water and perhaps a snack shows attention to participants' needs. The seating arrangement is very purposeful (with victims and their supporters to one side of the facilitator, bully and supporters on the other side, and other involved persons further from the facilitator), so the counselor should make some kind of labels for the table or chairs indicating where each person should sit when entering the room.

The counselor (or *convener*, in restorative practice language) needs to have all papers ready, including the script, the blank plan, and so forth. There are several books that provide templates for these documents; the school or organization can select the ones that are most applicable to its needs. When this preparatory stage has been done carefully, the next step—the conference proper—is more likely to be successful.

Step 2: Holding the conference itself is the next step. The facilitator's job is to create an environment in which open and respectful discussion will lead to an outcome that is genuinely accepted by all parties. There are three phases to this step: exploration, transition, and agreement (Barton, 2003).

In the exploration phase, the offender speaks first and describes (with the facilitator's prompting) the events leading to the conference, with attention to the explanation for the behavior. The following script comes from T. O'Connell, Wachtel, and Wachtel (1999). The questions for offenders are as follows: What happened? What were you thinking about at the time? What have you thought about since the incident? Who do you think has been affected by your actions? How have they been affected? Next, the victim and the victim supporters respond. For the victim, the questions are as follows: What was your reaction at the time of the incident? How do you feel about what happened? What has been the hardest thing for you? How did your family and friends react when they heard about the incident? There are similar questions for supporters.

In the transition phase, the offender is asked whether there is anything he or she wants to say at this time. To prompt an agreement, the victim is asked what he or she would like from the conference. The offender is given an opportunity to respond, and supporters' thoughts are also solicited. This process continues until there seems to be an agreement.

In the agreement phase, the facilitator checks with all participants to be sure the agreement accurately reflects what has been decided before preparing a written agreement. All participants are invited to make comments, and all are thanked for their work. Typically, some refreshments are available while the facilitator prepares the written agreement, which is signed by the parties present.

Step 3: Step 3 is follow-up. The facilitator conducts follow-up interviews with victims to check on their status following the conference and to provide information about any further services that might be needed. It is important to check on ongoing support systems the victim has in place.

The United Nations has several publications about restorative justice that are available at no cost. These sources are listed in Chapter 12. I created Table 3 as a guideline for which type of intervention might be best suited to an individual case of bullying; although it was created for use in conven-

Table 3

Selecting an Intervention for Cyberbullying

Incident Severity	Method	Group Sessions	Participant Criteria	Outcome
Very high	Sanctions	None	Offense is legally actionable	Police are contacted
Moderate to high	Restorative justice	Multiple	Harm to target is severe, parents need to be involved	Amends are made, relationships are restored, bullying stops
Moderate	Method of shared concern	Multiple	Target's functioning is affected in multiple areas (attendance, school engagement, and so forth)	Bullying stops and does not re-occur
Low	Support group	Multiple	Target shows distress, feels isolated	Bullying behavior stops. Social support for target increases, self-esteem of supporters increases
Low	Individual brief solution-focused counseling	None	Target shows little distress	Bullying behavior ceases. Self-efficacy of target increases

tional bullying, the model is, I believe, very appropriate for most instances of cyberbullying. Note that although there are reports from Australia, the United Kingdom, and Canada of success using nonpunitive methods, there are as yet no rigorous scientific studies comparing these methods with more traditional methods in U.S. school settings. A case study examining the efficacy of restorative justice practices at West Philadelphia High School (Mirsky, 2009) reported that serious disciplinary incidents declined 52%, as did rates of suspensions and expulsions. In addition, the school reported a more positive overall climate. The school implemented classroom circles, a less formal approach to conferencing, to ameliorate problems before they escalated. The website (Mirsky, 2009) has a short video about the changes the school has observed.

Not all situations merit the full restorative community conference. In less serious incidents, a counselor can conduct a small group conference—parents do not participate but are informed of the process. Classroom conferences can also be used when the cyberbullying incident has disrupted learning in the classroom. They are likely to be most effective when a counselor assists or supports the teacher, who may not be familiar with the process (Armstrong & Thorsborne, 2006).

Working With Parents

Research conducted in Australia to evaluate the effectiveness of antibullying programs found that parent involvement was a key ingredient (D. Cross, Hall, Hamilton, Pintabona, & Erceg, 2004). Parents of bullies and victims (and cyberbullies and cybervictims) may be distressed and upset when learning of incidents involving their child, so sensitive responses are essential to ensure that a positive relationship with parents is built and sustained. Field and Carroll (2006) offered suggestions to counselors working with parents, and the following section is based primarily on their recommendations.

Counselors need to understand that the parents of victims may be quite emotional when learning of their child's mistreatment. Counselors need to understand their feelings and ensure that parents' concerns are heard and taken seriously. When the parents are very angry, it is often because they believe that the school (often school administration) has not protected their child and then did not treat the parents respectfully. Their anger may lead them to (a) encourage their child to retaliate, (b) take retaliatory steps themselves, (c) withdraw the child from the school, or (d) threaten lawsuits. Examples of all of those behaviors have been given earlier in the book. It is therefore particularly important that counselors work with angry parents, validating their experience, expressing empathy, and most clearly expressing concern for the child and a willingness to address the problem. In some cases, the parents may not have complete information, and they need reassurance that the matter will not be ignored or their concerns trivialized. With this type of parent, it is essential that the counselor maintain frequent contact with the parents to keep them informed of steps the school is taking to resolve the situation.

Some parents, often victims themselves, may not respond to the child's situation because they feel powerless. Counselors should communicate to these parents that by not taking action or being involved, they are modeling powerlessness to their child. It is important that counselors convey their optimism that a solution will be found to stop the cyberbullying and that the parents' support is important.

Some parents are adamant about wanting to know the cyberbully has been punished. If the counselor or the school is using nonpunitive strategies, this may present an obstacle. It may be helpful to tell these parents that you know how much they care for their child and how much they want the cyberbullying to stop. If you explain the negative aspects of punishment, discussed early in this chapter (such as concerns about retaliation and ostracism by other students), and also explain the rationale behind using the nonpunitive methods, many parents will reconsider.

Parents of some victims of conventional bullying, particularly boys, have been found to be overprotective. Although family therapy may be useful, it is beyond the scope of school counselors to provide that. However, parenting workshops are often offered by school counselors, who can teach and promote parenting practices that are more likely to foster resilient children.

School personnel may find that parents of cyber- (and conventional) bullies may be aggressive themselves. In approaching such parents, it is essential to note that the child is a valued member of the school community whose current behavior in this situation is not acceptable. Some parents will deny their child would ever be involved in such behavior. Again, remind the parents that you are concerned about the behavior, but you know the child has many good qualities. You also want to be alert for signs that the parent intends to punish the child severely at home. Instead, tell the parents that you believe you can help the bully learn more appropriate ways to communicate and that you will inform them so that they can collaborate with the school. This reassures them that the situation will be handled and, it is hoped, decreases their interest in handling it punitively or aggressively at home.

Other parents of bullies may truly be ignorant of what their child is doing with technology, particularly if the child has not been a conventional bully. In such cases, the new behavior may be a complete surprise to the parents. As noted many times in this book, youths are much more sophisticated about technology than their parents and may be able to carry out many incidents of cyberbullying without their parents' knowledge. These parents need to be informed about the problem and need to understand the negative outcomes that could ensue if the behavior doesn't stop.

Field and Carroll (2006) highlighted general principles for working with parents in bullying situations: Communicate with parents regularly about the situation; provide information to parents about bullying and cyberbullying (e.g., handouts, pamphlets); offer workshops or information about workshops on parenting; have books and other parenting materials available for parents to use, including those on teaching children assertiveness, conflict resolution, and anger management; provide training to teachers and other school personnel on how to communicate effectively with angry or frightened parents; and provide information about resources, including counseling and therapy, available in the community.

I hope this chapter has provided counselors with new approaches that can be applied to cyberbullying situations. Several of these approaches (individual BSFC and restorative justice practices) can be used with adults as well.

Summary

- In addition to punishing cyberbullies, there are other methods for handling cyberbullying that may avoid some of the unintended consequences of punishment (retaliation, more secretive methods). Three types of support groups might be helpful: Field's psychoeducational groups for victims, which offer support and skills training; Robinson and Maines's support group (formerly called the *no-blame method*); and Sue Young's group. The latter two involve the bully and supporters of the victim in efforts to help the victim be happier in school, and the counselor talks with the victim and gets the victim's consent before proceeding with the group meeting.
- The method of shared concern is most suitable when the cyberbullying is conducted by a group. In order to ensure there is no suggestion that the victim "tattled" or "narced," the victim is not contacted before the process begins. The counselor meets with each of the bullies individually and shares his or her concerns about the victim. The bully is asked what might be done to improve the situation. When each bully has made a suggestion individually, the bullies meet with the counselor as a group to discuss progress. A meeting involving the victim may be held as well.
- Restorative justice is a more formal procedure based on a different philosophical approach. This practice aims to restore the relationships (with the victim, victim's supporters, the school, the community) that were damaged by the bullying or cyberbullying. Part of the process involves "making it right": The victim and bully discuss what is needed to correct the problem. The victim might request an apology, restitution, a publication on a website or social network acknowledging false statements and taking responsibility, and so forth. A formal agreement is signed, and follow-up meetings are held. Proponents believe this method reduces moral disengagement in addition to resolving the current problem.
- Restorative justice may be used in the workplace. In addition, employee assistance programs (EAPs) may provide counseling, and grievance procedures might provide the victim with an avenue to resolve the problem.

CHAPTER 10
Adult Cyberbullying

Although the focus of many high-profile cyberbullying cases has been on children and adolescents, one only needs to recall the Megan Meier case, in which the alleged bully was an adult, to be reminded that the practice is not restricted to youths. As with conventional bullying, the prevalence of workplace and adult cyberbullying may be underestimated, often because victims are embarrassed or afraid to report incidents. In this chapter, I focus on adults because they are not immune to victimization and may need encouragement and information from counselors when an incident occurs.

Not all cyberbullying by adults targets other adults. A recent case (Segal, 2009), disturbing on many levels, illustrates again that online anonymity is often illusory. Reminiscent of the Megan Meier scenario, this case involves a young girl's mother taking revenge on her daughter's 9-year-old schoolmate after the two girls had an argument. This time, the mother placed a suggestive ad on Craigslist.com (a well-known website for classified advertising) that directed readers to an e-mail address where they were given the first name and phone number of the 9-year-old. Fortunately, the girl's mother intercepted the more than 40 calls from men calling for sexual services. The ad and e-mail information did not mention the girl's age. The woman was identified when Craigslist was subpoenaed and provided the information. Those who are victimized by technology need to be encouraged to pursue all avenues to identify the perpetrator and, when the actions are illegal, file charges against the perpetrator.

Contexts for Adult Cyberbullying

Just as with young people, the cyberenvironments and methods for cyberbullying are varied, and the discussions earlier in the book on those environments and methods apply to adults as well. In addition, adults are joining social networks in greater numbers, where opportunities for cyberbullying abound. Most of the "residents" of Second Life are adults, engaging in simulations of daily life, including working. Although the largest percentage of online persons who use social networking sites is the 18- to 32-year age group, the use of Facebook by female users over 55 increased by 550% in a 6-month period (Sutter, 2009), making this demographic the fastest growing one on Facebook. Although these users derive many benefits from this activity (e.g., staying in contact with friends and family at a distance), they may be less familiar with and less cautious about privacy settings and friending options. Counselors could provide a valuable service to older users by training them on such options.

Twitter.com is also quite popular with adults: The demographics of visitors to this site show that the most represented age group is 18–34 years, representing approximately 45% of visitors; 24% of visitors are 35–49 years old; 14% are over 50 years of age; and only 13% are between the ages of 13 and 17, and 4% are 3–12 years old. An estimate of the number of U.S. monthly visitors by quantcast.com is between 27 and 29.2 million visitors per month, with the highest estimate given for mid-July 2009. Compared with their representation in the general population, African Americans use Twitter more than expected, Asian Americans use it somewhat less, and other groups are close to average. Many politicians, entertainers, and sports celebrities "tweet" (post Twitter messages) regularly. A member of the House of Representatives, Rep. Jason Chaffetz of Utah, believes that using social media for election campaigns and communication with constituents is a necessity in the current technological world (Chaffetz, 2009). Business schools advise businesspeople to create a personal brand online using blogs and social networking sites (Tutton, 2009).

A website that tracks numbers of followers showed that the twitterers with the most followers (on November 6, 2009) were Ashton Kutcher (with 3,932,172), Britney Spears, Ellen DeGeneres, CNN Breaking News, and Barack Obama. I, on the other hand, was ranked 1,248,146th, with 13 followers. The brevity of Twitter messages (less than 140 characters) encourages many people with smart phones to have the tweets sent to their phones as text messages rather than having to log on to the website.

LinkedIn is a networking site that is more focused on professional contacts than social interaction. It has 1.5 million users in the United States, with 46% in the 35- to 49-year age group and 34% over the age of 50. Fifty-four percent of members are men. People visit the site from both work (40%) and home, perhaps because it is used for work-related information. It is interesting to note that adults can be distressed by rejection on this and other online networks (Hare, 2009). When a woman was told that a woman she met in a discussion group on LinkedIn was not willing to join her network, she was surprised and hurt. The extent of the concern about rejection is reflected in the development of a service called Qwitter, which tells Twitter users who has stopped following them and when. Several blogs include posts from persons who have been hurt by being de-friended on a networking site, and although some responses are sympathetic, others are rather cruel. Hare quoted experts who say that online rejection can be more painful than in-person rejection because of the tendency (online disinhibition) to be less careful or polite when delivering those types of messages. Hare noted that research conducted at the University of California, Los Angeles, determined that the emotional reaction to such events, and its neurological correlates, are the same for digital and in-person rejection.

Workplace Cyberbullying

Just as schools are often the context in which cyberbullying takes place among young people, the workplace is the context for much of adult-to-adult cyber-bullying. As information and communication technologies are now pervasive in workplaces in all sectors of the economy, the tools for cyberbullying are readily available. Workplace gossip, not a new phenomenon, can now spread instantaneously to a large number of coworkers and others, and rumors that are spread electronically can have serious career consequences. Unwelcome pornography can be sent to employees, who may be concerned about job security if they complain, especially if the sender is a superior in the organization. An example is a case that occurred at a university, in which an associate dean was accused of sending unwanted pornography to an assistant professor ("New Mexico State U. Investigates," 2009). The junior faculty member complained to the dean about these messages. Shortly after that complaint, the assistant professor and his wife (also up for promotion and tenure) were denied tenure despite the unanimous support of the faculty panel. The case is still in court at the time of this writing, but the associate dean resigned.

Prevalence of Workplace Cyberbullying

Survey information on workplace cyberbullying is sparse, and the little available data are from other countries. Nevertheless, they provide some evidence of the extent of the problem. A survey in the United Kingdom of 1,072 workers found that 20% had been cyberbullied at work via e-mail and 6% by text messages (Daniloff, 2009). A study of 1,700 workers in Australia revealed that 41% of participants had experienced cyberbullying from bosses and/or management; over half had been cyberbullied by coworkers (CQR Consulting, n.d.). A survey of Australian men employed in manufacturing jobs found that almost 11% had been victimized by technological means (Privitera & Campbell, 2009). Despite the fact that this study had several important limitations (a very low response rate, male respondents only, and in an industry where constant access to technological communication is likely to be less than in many other occupations), the fact that cyberbullying was detected at all is informative. Although it is a stretch to draw any conclusions about U.S. workers from these data, there is ample anecdotal evidence that the problem exists in the United States as well.

It is clear that cyberbullying in the workplace is not an uncommon phenomenon. The increased use of technology allows the workplace bullying to extend beyond the workplace and work hours. One important finding from a U.K. survey is that adults are uncertain about the best course of action if they are the target of workplace cyberbullying (I. Williams, 2007). About 50% said they would report to senior management, 25% would go to the human resources department in the company or a union if there was one involved, 10% would do nothing, 6% would seek revenge, and 4% would resign. Although these strategies might help, in some cases it is management doing the bullying, so seeking assistance from that quarter is not an option. Seeking revenge is always dangerous, usually leading to escalating hostilities. Human resources departments or unions might be appropriate sources of help if they are prepared and knowledgeable about cyberbullying. Ignoring the cyberbullying may be effective if the bully is seeking evidence of having caused the target to be upset, but depending on the severity of the incident, it allows the cyberbully to continue the behavior with no feedback about how others are affected. It is sad to think that resignation might be the only recourse available to the target. Certainly, if workplace technology is used (computers or smart phones belonging to the company), management is more likely to take action against the offender, but cyberbullying can take place from personal computers as well.

Examples of Workplace Cyberbullying

Some examples of workplace bullying have been reported. One website gives an example of a new employee who received numerous anonymous text and e-mail messages saying, "You should know better" (Cade, 2009). The ambiguity of the content coupled with the inability to identify the sender(s) created considerable fear on the part of the employee. It turned out that the new employee had replaced a very popular worker who had been fired; the supporters of the former worker took their frustrations out on the replacement.

A single teacher I know who lived alone began to get anonymous text messages saying, "I know where you live." She was terrified and felt she was being watched at all times. She found herself so preoccupied with her safety that she was unable to sleep and had difficulty functioning at work—again, wondering if coworkers or students could be the bully. These feelings can lead to social isolation of the victim, who then is further removed from support and interpersonal connections. Although she contacted the police, they were unable to act, saying that the message was not a clear threat and that they did not have sufficient reason to attempt to identify the person sending the message.

Another example of workplace bullying recently reached the court system. An Internet forum (discussion board) that is privately operated and designed to appeal to Philadelphia police officers has had postings by White officers that include racial comments that portray African Americans very negatively (Kessler, 2009). Black officers charge that in addition to posting on the site, White officers often discuss or joke about these offensive postings in the workplace and do so when Black officers are present. The lawsuit against the department and the site's owner (a sergeant on the Philadelphia force) alleges that this situation creates a hostile work environment for the Black officers. The suit also claims that White police officers posted to or viewed this website when on duty. The case had just been filed at the time of this writing; no information was available on potential legal strategies.

When denigration occurs on the Internet, there is an additional complication for victims. This circumstance is illustrated by ongoing litigation in which plaintiffs Brittan Heller and Heidi Iravani were the targets of numerous defamatory and crude sexual comments on an online forum, AutoAdmit (Margolick, 2009). Ironically, the forum is popular with law students. When someone Googled the plaintiffs' names (as a potential date or potential employer might do), that person would find these comments at the top of the list of links the search returned. In fact, malicious posters may engage in a practice known as "google-bombing," which means posting numerous comments in order to make sure that the comments will be high on the list of sites found by a Google search (and will get the most hits or visitors to the site). Posters use pseudonyms on the site, so the two women, law students themselves, did not know the identity of the bullies. The website owner and creator, Jarret Cohen, neither a student nor a lawyer, developed the site when a similar one known as Princeton Review began to filter some posts. His goal was to have a site for law students that did not restrict postings. No filters were used, and Mr. Cohen chose not to delete comments or threads even if they were off topic and insulting. The story of this site and the women's lawsuit is long and complicated, but there are several important points to note. First, when Mr. Cohen realized that some victims were considering legal action, he stopped collecting IP addresses of posters so those addresses could not be subpoenaed. Second, the effects on the victims were extreme. A female law student at Vanderbilt was so distressed she changed schools. Heller believed the postings that came up on Google search results interfered with her ability to get a job. Iravani had significant psychological symptoms: She was unable to concentrate, was fearful of being in public, and eventually had to be hospitalized after a particularly upsetting post. Both women tried numerous strategies to have the posts removed before they resorted to litigation; no strategy was completely successful. Heller eventually was interviewed on *Good Morning America*, and after that Google (who may have seen the TV interview) notified Cohen that because the site had ads displayed alongside "adult" content, the terms of service had been violated. Cohen eventually terminated his involvement in the site, but it still existed on July 29, 2009, and described itself as "the most prestigious law school discussion board in the world." Although a scan of the discussion threads did not reveal anything salacious, there was definitely profanity.

I first learned of masquerading through a personal incident in which I was the victim. When I was studying for my psychology licensure exam in 2000, I joined an electronic mailing list that provided support, study tips, and information that was very helpful. At one point, a message was posted by a person from a place where I formerly lived and worked, and I responded to the post with an invitation to a back-channel (off-the-list) communication with that person. We exchanged a number of e-mails about the workplace and the community and what had changed since I left, and we talked about our preparation for the exam. The interaction waned, but we both continued on the electronic mailing list. One day, I received an e-mail from this person saying she was outraged that I would do "such a thing" (which at this point, I knew nothing about) and indicating she intended to inform my state licensing board that I should never receive a license to practice as a psychologist. I had no idea what she was referring to. After several pleas for an explanation, I learned that someone had sent disgusting, explicit, obscene e-mails to this individual (and several others, it turned out) that appeared to come from me. At that time, I did not possess the technical knowledge I now have, but I did contact the owner of the electronic mailing list, who was able to trace the messages to a computer in another state via the unique IP address. When the owner confronted the member who owned that computer, the individual claimed the messages had been sent by someone staying at his home and without his knowledge or consent. At the time, I settled for a formal statement from the electronic mailing list owner explaining what had happened so that I had evidence that I was not the sender of those e-mails. I now know both how to disguise one's identity in an e-mail and how to find out who actually sent an e-mail.

Stability of Victim Roles

Although there are no data yet on the stability of cyberbullying roles, researchers do know that conventional bullying roles exhibit stability beyond childhood. In a study of 4,742 adult workers in Norway, participants were surveyed about their bullying experiences in the workplace. Slightly more than 8% of participants were classified as targets of workplace bullying, 5.4% were bullies, and 2.1% were provocative victims (also known as bully–victims; Matthiesen & Einarsen, 2007). The bully–victims reported significantly more prior experience with bullying in another workplace and also reported more childhood victimization, suggesting these roles may persist into adulthood. In addition, these individuals more frequently reported being the bully in childhood. Smith, Singer, Hoel, and Cooper (2003) surveyed 5,288 adults from a variety of workplaces in the United Kingdom and found that those who were victimized in school were more likely to be victimized in the workplace. This finding applied to both genders, although women were slightly more likely to be victimized in the workplace. Those who were childhood bully–victims were at the highest risk for workplace victimization. Clearly, not every childhood victim is victimized in the workplace as an adult, but the likelihood is greater. It is certainly reasonable to think that these same vulnerable individuals might be targeted by cyberbullies.

Characteristics of Adults and Older Adults

Most adults are digital immigrants who have learned to use contemporary technology later in life. Nevertheless, many are as closely wedded to their techno-tools as are young people. Picture the businessperson with an iPhone, Blackberry, or other smart phone—which has phone, text, and Internet connectivity—checking compulsively to make sure no messages were missed. I am aware of one person who was evaluated unfavorably for a job for taking a cell phone call during the interview!

Adults of all ages are learning to use technology and finding it helpful. As of March 25, 2009, the number of Facebook.com users over the age of 35 had doubled in the previous 60 days. The fastest growing age group on Facebook was women over the age of 55. The majority of users are now over 25, with users uploading 40 million photos each day (http://www.insidefacebook.com). Cell phones may serve as a safety device for some older adults, who can contact help in an emergency when away from home. Data from a recent survey revealed that two thirds of seniors over the age of 70 used a cell phone at least weekly, and that same group is more likely to visit travel websites and almost twice as likely to visit health information websites than the average user (Warner & Hutton, 2009). One study found that Australians over the age of 55 used the Internet primarily for communication (Sum, Mathews, Hughes, & Campbell, 2008); the more time they spent on the Internet communicating with known friends and relatives, the lower the degree of social loneliness participants felt. Although the relationship is not causal, it may be that the opportunity to stay in contact with family and friends is effective at relieving social loneliness. The study also found that communicating with unknown people did not have this effect. Again, the importance of these contacts also increases the vulnerability to being victimized.

Many adults now use various matchmaking websites to meet potential romantic partners—more than 60 million adults are listed as members of the top five sites, although duplications are possible ("2009 Top Ten Internet," 2009). If one examines the terms of service for the popular site Match.com, married persons (unless separated from their spouses) are prohibited from registering; e-Harmony.com prohibits users from including any "inaccurate, misleading, or false information," and members are obligated to change any information that becomes inaccurate (Soghoian, 2008). Some critics are concerned that the e-Harmony user who does not quickly update a profile to reflect a weight gain is vulnerable to prosecution and are concerned about what could be an unmanageable deluge of legal cases for such infractions. These fears were based on the initial conviction of Lori Drew, which has since been dismissed, but they could easily resurface as the legal world wrangles with the complicated effects of the Internet's social aspects.

It is certainly possible that mean-spirited individuals could set up false profiles on online dating sites, and adults could be subjected to unwanted communication as a result. Although these sites typically have their own e-mail available, some adults will provide their regular e-mail address to someone they are interested in getting to know. This may be a dangerous practice, as the person now has a way to harass or otherwise invade one's life. Other signs of potential problems on such sites are noted in the Online Mom blog (Scully, n.d.). The author of that blog pointed out that the absence of a photo on such a site is suspicious, although photos may be misleading (taken many years earlier) as well. If marital status is not reported on a matchmaking site, that is also reason to suspect the person may not be seriously interested in a relationship. Another sign is the frequency of the person's online presence. Scully contends that a constant presence may mean the person is looking for multiple contacts rather than a serious relationship. Washington State has a useful site that offers suggestions for adults using such sites (http://www.atg. wa.gov/InternetSafety/SocializingOnline.aspx#Dating).

The Internet is widely used by adults, especially older adults, as a source of health information, and many governmental services (e.g., Social Security Administration) have made various procedures available online. This information is helpful because older adults may have limited mobility and limited finances; not having to physically go to an office means no transportation costs (gas or fare) and no need to navigate outside the home. For those who do not have Internet or computers at home, many senior citizen centers offer both computers and instruction, as do libraries. Once basic skills are acquired, some adults expand into such areas as social networking. Adults often like the ability to stay up-to-date on activities and events in the lives of family members who may be geographically widespread (Sutter, 2009). However, just as elder abuse in real life is often perpetrated by family members, older adults can be cyberbullied, and it most often is perpetrated by family members. Older adults can be the target of threats, demeaning comments, ignoring, and so forth. Because of their unfamiliarity with technology, seniors may be at a loss when such things occur.

Counselors' Tasks

Counselors who work or consult with organizations can encourage the development and publication of AUPs. Experts urge care in crafting such documents. For example, it is tempting to simplify the workplace AUP by making sweeping prohibitions: Use of any company equipment for other than official use is strictly prohibited. Such restrictions may create ill will and are likely to undermine the intent of the policy. Consider the hardworking employee who works diligently and does not leave the office at lunch. She takes a break at her desk and likes to read the news online and check her personal e-mail account for news of an ailing relative. Neither of these activities is likely to threaten the company in any way; a blanket prohibition may alienate this dedicated employee. In addition, such a universal prohibition is unrealistic and sets up an adversarial situation. To be fair, the policy might also define how the employer may use technology to reach employees outside the normal workday. If employees are subjected to mobile phone calls or text messages from the employer during personal time, it is even more offensive to those employees if their use of company computers or other equipment is rigidly restricted. Adults in the workplace should be aware that organization e-mail accounts can be inspected by the employer if the employees have been informed that this could happen (Shariff, 2005). Employees who use their company computer to cyberbully another cannot claim any rights to privacy in that situation. The counselor can urge the organization to be judicious in crafting the AUP and encourage the involvement of workers in policy development.

It is clear that many workers are uncertain about what to do when they are victimized by workplace cyberbullying. Counselors can be very helpful in these situations, such as by providing confidential assistance to employees. Especially when EAPs are available, employers and human resources offices should publicize their services so that victims of cyberbullying don't feel that the cyberbullying is something they should be able to handle without seeking help. Dr. Urs Glasser of Harvard University believes that universities (and I would extend this to include other work environments) need to counter the secrecy around cyberbullying by "mak[ing] cyberbullying an audible part of the campus conversation" (quoted in Daniloff, 2009, p. 5). He goes on to suggest that there may be a legal obligation for employers to protect employees from this type of victimization. At Boston University, the Faculty/Staff Assistance Office (a version of the EAPs available in many large organizations) is considering how best to assist victims of cyberbullying. The director of that center, Bonnie Teitleman, commented on how intense the impact of cyberbullying can be on one's personal and professional life. The center will assist employees in obtaining both legal and psychological support. This commitment is worthy of emulation by other employers.

EAPs are offered to employees in some organizations as part of the benefits for workers. Typically, services are free, although the number of sessions may be limited. Some organizations employ their own EAP counselors, whereas others contract with outside providers. The service is confidential unless informed consent documents specify otherwise. In most cases, the employers do not receive any notification that an employee is using the service. Because the cost is not a barrier to seeking services, EAPs may be an ideal first option for an employee who has been a victim of cyberbullying. The fact that the counselors are prepared to assist clients with this issue should be made clear in the literature. At the least, the employee can contact the EAP and find out if any of their counselors are familiar with this problem and prepared to assist. Workers (especially digital immigrants) may be completely unmoored by serious incidents, and knowing that help is available through the workplace could be a big relief.

Summary

- Websites that are widely used by adults include Second Life (a virtual world), in which bully behavior is not uncommon, Twitter, and LinkedIn. Adults who are rejected or targeted respond similarly to younger users but are often uncertain of how or where to get help.

- Although most adults—and certainly older adults—are digital immigrants, they are using technology in ever increasing numbers. Many enjoy the readily available information on health and other issues, and those with limited mobility appreciate being able to get information and stay in touch with family and friends from their own homes.
- Adults may be less familiar with technology than younger people, but they are far from immune from cyberbullying. Because of their lack of knowledge, adults may be more distressed by such incidents and more uncertain about how to respond. Workplace cyberbullying does occur. Adults may fear for their jobs if they report the cyberbullying, and they may experience depression and other psychological problems as a result.
- Internet dating sites can be dangerous for lonely or vulnerable adults. Counselors may help these clients by educating them about safe use of these services.
- Counselors who consult with workplaces should encourage implementation of carefully constructed AUPs, and EAP counselors should be aware of potential cybervictimization (and prepared to assist such clients) in the workplace setting.

CHAPTER 11

The Role of Counselors

Throughout this book, I have made suggestions for actions counselors might take in specific cyberbullying situations. In this chapter, I focus more generally on the broader role of counselors in addressing this problem. The roles to be discussed include advocacy, training, counseling, and ethics. By reading this book, counselors have already taken the essential first step, which is to become informed. The technology, services, and laws change so rapidly, however, that it is crucial that counselors make staying current a priority. The chapter on additional resources has some suggestions for doing so; professional associations also have a role in making sure that information is available to members.

Advocacy

The profession recognizes that advocacy is an important role for counselors. The ACA Governing Council endorsed the ACA Advocacy Competencies in 2003 (see ACA's home page at http://www.counseling.org for a link to those competencies), which identify the skills needed to be an effective advocate. This advocacy may take place at several levels: on the individual level with clients, at the community level with organizations or schools, and in the public arena with larger goals. The model suggests that counselors can "act with" clients to empower them and teach them self-advocacy skills and/or act "on behalf" of clients in advocating for them. It may be the case that existing ineffective policies or practices are barriers to reducing cyberbullying, and counselors can be an advocate for the necessary change. For example, if a counselor believes that nonpunitive counseling-based strategies could be more effective in reducing cyberbullying than present punitive strategies, he or she is likely to meet strong resistance from a system that has a punitive disciplinary policy (detention, suspension, expulsion, zero tolerance, and so forth). Nevertheless, the counselor's role incorporates advocacy as part of the profession's mission, and so the counselor would continue to present the rationale for alternative approaches, using data to make the case.

At the school and community level, collaboration is essential and can increase the impact of individual efforts. In the public domain, public information is a competency that counselors should appropriate in the service of preventing and reducing cyberbullying. In the previous chapter, I suggested some approaches to working with individuals (both cyberbullies and cybervictims) to empower them to make changes in how they use technology. If an individual school or department in an organization collaborates with others (a school district, an entire company), it can advocate at a wider level and strengthen its efforts. If a school or department develops clear and useful AUPs, for example, and gets input from all stakeholders, including the larger community, it is likely that some of those participants will see the value of AUPs and seek to expand them to other departments, schools, or organizations. Public information might be developed in an individual school or company, but expanding the influences of the information can make a difference on a larger, societal level. For example, a campaign in a school to create engaging PSAs might lead to distribution of those PSAs to other schools, districts, and venues. Community agencies (e.g., libraries, nonprofits) might sponsor programs that reach a wider audience.

The American School Counselor Association (ASCA) National Model (2005) emphasizes advocacy, including promoting systemic change in schools. In the February 2005 special issue of the *Professional School Counseling* journal, Bemak and Chung stressed the importance of the school counselor as advocate, and Trusty and Brown (2005) articulated advocacy competencies.

The targets for advocacy efforts that could reduce cyberbullying include schools and organizations, ISPs, software and cellular phone providers, organizations' information technology (IT) departments, and governmental agencies or legislators. As counselors, we know that it is axiomatic that efforts to change generate resistance, but effective counselors know how to work with that resistance and encourage movement, however small.

As part of their advocacy within schools, school counselors should take the leadership role in beginning change initiatives, such as developing and reviewing the AUP, providing informed consent to students and parents, creating reasonable and fair policies regarding cell phone use in schools, and so forth. ASCA has a position statement, revised in 2006, titled *The Professional School Counselor and Student Safety and Technology* that mentions collaborating with educators and parents to promote safe use of technology and to prevent cyberbullying. School counselors should also encourage the implementation of training for students, whether as part of the regular guidance curriculum or, at secondary schools, in a required class so that all students have current and accurate information.

At the school and organization level, counselors should advocate for both policy and programming efforts. Earlier, I discussed the importance of AUPs, and school counselors are in a position to play a leadership role in the development of such policies. Effective policies are developed with input from all stakeholders (in schools, that includes students, parents, counselors, teachers, administrators, IT personnel, community representatives), and because of their role, school counselors already have collaborative relationships with those groups. Thus, they are in an ideal position first to get administrative support for such policies and then to initiate and oversee the work of the committee that develops the policy.

I cannot help but wonder if the following serious incident of cyberbullying (and a pending lawsuit) might have been averted if there had been a clear policy and school counselor advocacy. I refer to the case of Mandi Jackson, a student at a Mississippi high school (Student Press Law Center, 2009). The suit alleges that on September 10, 2007, a cheerleading coach demanded that all cheerleaders (including Mandi) provide the coach with the password to their Facebook accounts. The password provides access not only to the public pages but to the private messages that are exchanged on the site. Many of the cheerleaders provided the password and immediately used their cell phones (with Internet access) to delete the account. Mandi did not delete the account, and the teacher–coach reviewed her messages, including a "profanity-laced" exchange with another member of the squad. The coach provided those messages to other teachers and coaches, the principal, and the district superintendent. Mandi was disciplined for the content of the messages by being prohibited from attending practice, participating in games, and participating in school events, even those for which she had previously paid required fees. In her lawsuit, Mandi also claimed she was denied an award for the previous year because the coaches opposed it, and that she was unable to take academic courses taught by the coaches because of the tension associated with the incident. Mandi's lawyer noted that there is nothing in any school policy that says that social networking site content (created and conducted off campus) is subject to scrutiny by school staff. Mandi's mother stated that she made efforts to resolve this issue with school officials for over 2 years before deciding to file a lawsuit (WAPT.com, 2009). The court documents are available from a link in the article. The student handbook is available on the school's website and makes no mention of a requirement to provide passwords to sponsors. The high school website shows that the principals and coach were still employed at the school as of November 2009.

In reading about this case, I could not help but wonder about the role of the school counselor. I wondered if the students involved had talked with the school counselor when the incident occurred and whether the counselor had advocated for the students' rights. My curiosity took me to the current school website, and there is indeed a school guidance department with three guidance counselors listed. I noticed that one of the counselors was also a coach (whom a student might perceive to be biased in favor of the coach), and another, a woman, had the same (not common) surname as the school principal, a man. I wonder how safe students would have felt to discuss this issue with counselors in that setting. The school has an anonymous reporting site that also could have been used to express concerns. I also wondered, once the incident was known, whether a counselor skilled in restorative justice might have been able to assist the parties in coming to a resolution without a lawsuit. Of course, I recognize that the student and her parents might not have felt empowered as the offenders were powerful people in the school hierarchy; in any case, I am speculating, but I found it striking that the school counselor was not mentioned in any accounts of this case.

School counselor involvement was mentioned in the tragic case of Hope Witsell (Inbar, 2009), the 13-year-old girl who committed suicide after being involved in a sexting case (discussed in Chapter 1). Given the disruption serious enough to result in disciplinary action against Hope, it is unlikely that the school counselors were unaware of what had transpired. On September 11, less than a month after the 2009–2010 school year began, Hope met with school counselors, who, according to the report, detected evidence of self-mutilation. Their response was to have Hope sign a so-called no-harm contract in which she agreed to talk to an adult before acting on any impulse to hurt herself. The counselors did not inform Hope's parents of the concern or the contract. It is beyond the scope of this book to discuss no-harm contracts at length (see Bauman, 2007, pp. 178–179, for more discussion), but it is clear that the intervention was not effective in this case. The ethical dilemma of when a counselor should violate confidentiality is the issue. On the basis of the information given in the news report, it would seem that the girl's recent history, current crisis and behavior, and her age would compel the counselors to inform the parents of their concerns.

Beyond the school or organization, counselors might want to work together, perhaps through their professional organizations, to advocate for ISPs to provide more rapid responses to requests to remove posts or sites with offensive content. Individual websites should also be lobbied to make it easier for users to report offensive content and to get information about how their report will be handled. Cell phone providers respond to marketplace concerns. For example, when texting surged in popularity and teens began to accumulate enormous charges leading parents to cancel service, cell phone providers began to offer unlimited texting at a flat rate. They can be encouraged to provide more options for parental control (such as those available on kiddie phones) on regular phones, because older children and teens will rebel at having to use phones that are obviously oriented toward small children. Options to control times of access, limit numbers that can be called, and limit download options from phones with Internet access would close some technological gaps in protecting vulnerable youths. Many of these features already exist but are not widely promoted. School counselors can inform parents about existing controls available to them. Recall the agreement in Europe that was negotiated with social networking site owners. Counselors have large and effective professional organizations that have power to wield in these situations, but individual counselors will have to raise their voices to ensure that the profession takes cyberbullying seriously and recognizes that there are actions that the technological industries can take to help.

Large professional organizations such as ACA and ASCA could be powerful voices to encourage the industry to enact some of the suggested measures. ASCA's statement of the school counselor's role is out of date and needs to be revised frequently to reflect both changes in technology and increased understanding of what is needed to curb the cyberbullying problem. The ACA magazine *Counseling Today* has published several articles dealing with cyberbullying, but there does not yet appear to be an interest network or electronic mailing list devoted to the topic. The publication of this book, however, demonstrates ACA's awareness that cyberbullying is an important issue for counselors to know about.

Schools and organizations have IT departments that can be enlisted in the service of cyberbullying prevention. Obviously, they are central in any plan that involves filters or blocks. They can be more alert to excessive use of proxy sites or anonymous texting sites at a location. They can also ensure that computers are password protected, so that outsiders cannot access the system to hide their identities. I believe that it would be helpful to remind users at any organization about the dangers of cyberbullying by having a brief reminder of the AUP on the computer (e.g., "Users of this computer agree to abide by the AUP, available at: [link]"). Random showings of PSAs not only communicate the message they are designed to impart but also convey the organization's concern about the problem. An internal PSA saying, "If you have experienced cyberbullying, see your counselor for assistance," or a similar statement of willingness and ability to assist would reinforce the organization's or school's concern.

It would be helpful for counselors to assist schools to develop rational cell phone policies. There have been several cases in which students were disciplined for talking on the phone with deployed military parents during school time (e.g., Malkin, 2005; Sinasohn, 2008). In many schools, the penalty for using a cell phone during class is to have the cell phone taken by the teacher, to be returned at the end of the school day or when the parent contacts the school. In the focus group with high school students I described earlier, the students reported that most teachers either were oblivious to the ubiquitous (and often surreptitious—under desk, in pocket) texting going on or were unwilling to confront it. A high school chemistry teacher interviewed by Hafner (2009) said, "I can't tell when it's happening and there's nothing we can do about it. And I'm not going to take the time every day to try to police it." Furthermore, 84% of parents want to be able to communicate by cell phone with the child during school hours if there are any schedule changes ("Majority of American Parents," 2006), suggesting that parents are not supportive of blanket prohibitions on cell phones at school. Having policies that are not enforced (or enforceable) serves no purpose. On the other hand, most K–12 schools do not have emergency notification systems on cell phones. These systems provide important safety messages very quickly to the entire student body. With the consent of students and parents, if such a notification system were installed, text messages could also be used to provide important reminders to students about special events, snow days, and so forth as well as to acknowledge achievements. Again, in addition to providing an important function, such activities also send a message that the organization is concerned and actively taking steps to use technology in positive ways.

Finally, school counselors (and counselors in general) should be actively engaged in influencing the content of legislation, whether they do so individually or through professional groups. Some of the legislation to date, as was noted earlier, is either too vague to be useful or too restrictive to make a difference (imposing onerous investigation requirements or not considering school disruption as a criterion). Counselors need to ensure that students' needs are met while their rights are protected.

Training–Consulting

One important role for counselors is providing information to others about how to keep safe with technology. In schools, counselors can provide in-service training to staff members and workshops to both students and parents. Community and mental health counselors can offer workshops for the public. EAP counselors can offer information workshops for employees. These are important services, both for providing information and for making it clear that counselors are prepared to help. Parent workshops are excellent ways to provide a service.

I have presented several such workshops in local schools; interest is high, and questions are very informative as well, giving clues to areas in which information is lacking. The greatest interest in such workshops has been in those attended by parents and their children. The digital divide is very apparent in those interactions. I find that these settings can provide opportunities to initiate dialogues between children and parents about the parents' responsibilities for monitoring and controlling their children's use of technological communication and children's increased need for independence and privacy as they mature. Although parents may be able to exercise tight control of the Internet or cell phone activities of younger children (up to age 9 or 10), they are likely to begin to experience resistance from older children and adolescents. Parents need reassurance that some actions are necessary even when their children protest; at the same time, parents need to understand the importance of technology in their children's lives. At one such workshop, I suggested that parents investigate their children's online activities, and I provided some specific strategies. A young man was incensed and asked me if I was really saying I approved of parents examining the computers in teenagers' rooms. When I replied that it is parents' job to ensure their children practice safe and appropriate and legal use of the Internet and that that need trumped privacy needs of youths, the teen exited the presentation. However, his friends remained for the rest of the presentation and discussion.

In another example, a colleague's teenage children had cell phones but were required to give them to their parents at a certain hour in the evening. The parents were concerned that the children were texting during the night and losing much-needed sleep. Although the children protested, the parents provided a choice: The teens could keep their cell phones and turn them in every evening, or they could relinquish their cell phones. The teens chose the former.

Parents also need to understand that standard English is not used in text and online communication. A parent may be supervising an IM session that her child is having with a friend and not notice that the session began with "POS." Although the parent would be relieved to note the absence of any disturbing content in the message, she might not realize that POS (parent over shoulder) is a way for children to alert the other party in the IM exchange that they are being observed.

ASCA's position statement on student safety and technology (ASCA, 2006) mentions collaborating with educators and parents to promote safe use of technology and to prevent cyberbullying. School counselors should also involve students—who have the most current information and expertise—in creating workshops, public lessons, PSAs, and so forth. Counselors might form a student task force, in which members would work to suggest policies or technology strategies to combat the problem of cyberbullying. The members might even conduct trainings of their own or create training videos, pages for the school website, and so forth.

An important activity for counselors, in schools and communities, is educating parents. Parents need information about what young people do online, and they also welcome guidelines on what is appropriate for children at different ages. It is important that counselors encourage parents to make rules and decisions about uses of technology based on their own knowledge of their children's needs.

Counseling Victims

Campbell (2007) pointed out that there is no evidence-based protocol for treating cyberbullying victims. I agree—and also note that for many of the mental health consequences of victimization (e.g., depression, anxiety, PTSD), there are such treatments. However, some particular practices for working with clients who have been involved in cyberbullying bear mentioning. Campbell also observed that, in addition to technological techniques that can be explained to clients and legal services that may be indicated, because bullying and cyberbullying are relationship problems, counselors need to attend to those aspects of the problem as well.

The first caveat (once the counselor is well-informed) is not to trivialize the client's concerns or experiences. Although this point seems obvious, it has long been noted in the bullying literature in general that many adults (including some counselors) still harbor beliefs that these experiences are normative and part of growing up; others believe that the questionable tactic of "just stand up to him/her/them" is all that is necessary. Taking the client's concern seriously, expressing accurate empathy, and expressing concern are absolutely necessary with victims of cyberbullying. It is also critical that counselors communicate at the outset that they recognize the importance of technology to youths and adults in today's society. Remember that youths often say they don't want to report victimization to adults because they fear that the solution will be to take their technology, which is tantamount in their world to social ostracism. As with other types of victimization, clients need to hear from the professional that they are not the cause of the other's behavior; self-blaming attributions do not promote healing but, instead, reinforce negative self-talk. Even in the case of the provocative victim who may indeed have done something to elicit an angry or hostile response on the part of the bully, the choice to cyberbully belongs to the actor, not the victim.

Campbell (2007) proposed a number of principles for counseling young victims of cyberbullying, which I summarize here. I think they apply equally well to adults.

- The first principle is to commend the client, if self-referred, on taking the step to report. Many victims do not do so; fears of retribution or being labeled are difficult to overcome, and acknowledging that the client has done so is important.
- The second principle is to ask the client what he or she is seeking from counseling. The client may want you to understand how difficult the cyberbullying situation has been but may not want you to offer solutions. Sometimes a client may be seeking information, or a client may wonder if the distress that is felt is normal or if he or she has a diagnosable disorder. It is important to tailor the counseling to the needs of the client.
- The third principle is stating and reinforcing that the client is not at fault. The message that victims are somehow responsible for their own victimization can be delivered very subtly; giving unsolicited advice about helpful strategies victims did not take may unintentionally convey that they could have prevented the incident had they only acted in some way. Because there are no clear-cut solutions, most of the advice must be tentative. For example, earlier I noted that telling the bully to stop (via e-mail or some other technological communication that can be preserved) is a first step needed for pursuing legal means. Conn (2004) observed that for many youths who took this step, the harassment increased rather than stopped.
- The fourth principle is to evaluate whether there are any preexisting or concurrent disorders that need attention. In many cases, those who are victimized in cyberspace (think of Megan Meier or Ryan Halligan, for example) were vulnerable to some degree because of existing psychological problems. It is important to focus on the presenting problem (cyberbullying) but to do so with necessary information about other disorders that may be present.

- The final principle is to assist the client in finding some positive peer relationships, whether these relationships are online or in the local context. Reducing the feelings of isolation and alienation can ameliorate some of the distress and provide a buffer against future attacks. Counselors should also inquire about the victim's social world to identify possible avenues to increasing social support.

A final note on counseling cybervictims: Group counseling may be a particularly effective milieu for cybervictims. Because of their fears about reporting, many have not told anyone; self-blaming attributions may contribute to that pattern. Having an opportunity to discuss the experience with others who have had similar experiences reduces isolation, and other benefits of group counseling also accrue. For these reasons, Evelyn Field (n.d.), an Australian authority on workplace bullying and cyberbullying, recommends that victims' groups also be offered in the workplace.

Counseling the Cyberbully

In the event that the counselor is working with the cyberbully—often a mandated or at least reluctant client—the counselor may want to develop the cyberbully's empathy. There are a variety of stories and video clips about publicized cases available, and the counselor may want to explore the client's reactions to such incidents and plan a strategy based on observations. In addition, working with cyberbullies in isolation is less likely to have an impact than when involving others (family, peers); the nonpunitive approaches discussed in Chapter 9 may be helpful here because the cyberbully is less likely to engender a defensive posture. When the counselor involves parents, it is important to help them understand that it is impossible to police computer use and cell phone use completely (e.g., students can access a friend's equipment or a public computer). Developing appropriate family rules about technology can be a topic of discussion in counseling. Campbell (2007) again pointed out that conventional wisdom might not be practical. For example, parents are often advised to keep all computers in public areas of the home. In some homes, that might be the same room in which others watch television, for example, and the sounds from the computer may interfere with others' ability to enjoy the TV. Older students often have laptops, which typically accompany them wherever they go. Some strategies for monitoring use were mentioned earlier in the book; deciding which strategies best fit the particular situation can be the focus of the counseling sessions.

Ethics

As technology has become pervasive, counselors have had to wrestle with ethical dilemmas related to their use of technology in professional capacities. Such endeavors as Internet counseling are beyond the scope of this book, but I think it is important to raise ethical issues that will eventually need to be confronted.

Given the popularity of social networking sites and the fact that counselors may choose to partake of the opportunities available on those sites, how should the counselor manage what could be ethical issues in that context? For example, Cohen (2009) responded to a reader's anonymous question about an eighth-grade teacher who was friended by many students. A dilemma arose when the teacher learned via Facebook profiles that students were drinking, using drugs, or violating school rules. In such a case, the reader asked whether the teacher was required to report what he or she had discovered on the social networking site to parents, school officials, or police. Cohen responded by saying that the teacher's first role is educator, not police, and that although when students friended the teacher they theoretically abandoned their right to privacy, that was probably not their understanding. So, he recommended that the teacher use this as a teachable moment and e-mail the students to point out the dangers of putting such material on their pages and to inform them that he or she will report in the future. I suspect the same advice would be offered to school counselors.

The bigger question here is whether interacting with clients on social networking sites is a boundary violation. How should a counselor who has a page respond to a client's invitation to be friended? The most intuitive answer is that the counselor should not friend clients. If that is the decision, I suggest making that clear at the initiation of the relationship, in the spirit of informed consent. Clients are often curious about counselors, so the invitations are likely to happen if the counselor is on a site and the client is curious. Rather than taking the chance that a client will feel rejected by the refusal, counselors might let all clients know about their practice not to friend or otherwise socialize with clients via online methods. That is the best way to avoid the dilemma described above. The importance of this dilemma was highlighted by an exchange on a counselor education electronic mailing list that took place in December 2009; some counselor educators decided to deactivate their Facebook accounts because of discomfort with the kind of personal information that could be gleaned from viewing others' posts and comments on those posts. Other members of the electronic mailing list indicated they also struggled with how to enjoy Facebook without hurting students' feelings when refusing invitations for "friendship." Some did not friend current students but did friend former students. An interesting thing that I have found is that although I have an electronic mailing list for program alumni, I get a much quicker response from most if I send a message via Facebook.

I recommend that counselors in all settings be very clear about what is acceptable. For example, clients who text routinely may choose that method to let a counselor know they will be late to an appointment or have to cancel. They are then assured that the message is delivered and don't have to wait for a machine or phone tree. Of course, to do this, they need to have the counselor's cell phone number. What keeps the client from using this to cyberbully the counselor or giving the number to others? One counselor I heard about called a parent from her cell phone (she was not in the school building and wanted to be sure to inform a parent of a concern). The student realized that the counselor's cell phone number was now stored in his mother's phone and retrieved it to use to harass the counselor.

Some counselors may want to use texting as a quick way to check on students or clients they have seen who were in distress. One way to manage these potentially problematic interactions is to keep separate accounts (Internet and cell phone) for public and private use. Many counselors and other mental health professionals have long kept unlisted personal telephone numbers while having a business number for client use. This approach is an extension of that practice. I know several school counselors who do friend students but on a separate Facebook page that is for their school counselor role only. If schools or agencies wish to use text messages or cell phones with schools or clients, those should also be separate numbers. The schooltiponline.com site mentioned earlier, for example, can text school personnel with urgent questions. If a school makes a policy of having this line of communication, then a separate device with a separate number should be available. Given that counselors sometimes deal with very troubled clients, they should not make themselves vulnerable simply in the interest of communicating availability and concern.

Summary

- A counselor's role includes that of advocacy on behalf of clients. It is hoped that counselors will advocate on behalf of students whose rights have been violated. They should also advocate for well-constructed AUPs in their school or workplace. Counselors can lobby ISPs and website owners to respond more quickly to complaints of inappropriate use and to develop agreements that make the process of reporting inappropriate use more straightforward.

- Counselors may choose to encourage cell phone providers to make more widely available the features that allow parental control of cell phones; with provider help, phones can be set to allow only certain callers, restrict times calls can be made, and limit downloads on web-accessible devices.

- Counselors in schools can be leaders in training teachers, parents, students, and administrators on the topic of cyberbullying. Counselors in the workplace and other settings can also provide informational workshops in their communities to educate the public about this problem.

- Many adults are not certain where to go for help when they are cyberbullied. EAPs and counselors in the community should publicize their interest in working with clients who have been victimized by cyberbullying.

- Counselors who provide individual and group services to victims of cyberbullying need to be careful not to trivialize the situation and should inquire about the type of help the client is seeking; they should be very careful not to suggest that the victim is at fault. Counselors also should assess for any psychological disorders, either preexisting or associated with the event, that will need to be a focus of clinical attention.

CHAPTER 12
Additional Resources

The following are websites, books, and media that may not be cited elsewhere in the book but that counselors may want to consult. I am including those with which I am well-acquainted, so the judgments about the utility of the sites are my personal ones.

Websites

http://www.bullyingnoway.com.au/talkout/spotlight/cyberbullyingmain.shtml
This is a general antibullying site maintained with government resources in Australia. Doing a search on cyberbullying at the home page leads to a number of useful resources, including research reports on online social media use and links to other sites with more resources. The site is a showcase for student-created media to prevent bullying, some of which address cyberbullying.

http://www.commonsensemedia.org
This is one of the most useful websites on the Internet for those interested in preventing cyberbullying and other problems related to misuse of media. The site includes reviews of websites, online games, and other media and has advice for parents and educators arranged by the age of the child. It is also searchable by topic. It is frequently updated and has forums in which users can participate. I frequently use its excellent short videos (particularly the ones on Club Penguin, Webkinz, and Facebook) in presentations.

http://www.cyberbully.org

This is the site of Nancy Willard, an educator and lawyer who has written several books on cyberbullying that have much useful material. The *Guide for Parents* that is available on the site is very helpful when doing workshops for parents. She posts notes for her presentations that can be helpful to counselors planning their own presentations.

http://www.cyberbully411.org

This is an excellent site for young people. It includes "Share Your Story" and "Discussion Forum" sections that can provide online support to victimized youths. The site contains quite a bit of factual information, including research findings, but is nevertheless designed to be appealing to youths. This site was created by Internet Solutions for Kids. I have great respect for that organization's work and scholarship. Users must register but may do so as a guest.

http://www.cyberbullying.org

This is the website of Bill Belsey, who is credited with coining the term *cyberbullying*. This site is valuable for all the links and resources available. In addition to the link to resources, there is a "Facts and News" link that contains many publications that are of interest to those concerned about cyberbullying. The "Talk the Talk" section has a good dictionary of acronyms and emoticons.

http://www.cyberbullying.us

This website of Justin Patchin and Sameer Hinduja includes resources, lots of research, a terrific blog, and a section where youths can share their stories of cyberbullying. Most are from victims, but the two from cyberbullies are instructive. This site is updated frequently, and one can provide an e-mail address to receive notifications of new material.

http://www.digizen.org

This is a terrific British website and is definitely one of my favorite resources. There is a video available that can be viewed online called *Let's Fight it Together* that is extremely well done and excellent for adolescents. Because the dialog is minimal, the British accent is not an obstacle for U.S. viewers. Among other positives, the site provides a downloadable teacher's guide and lesson plan. There are also short clips of each of the characters that can be shown after the video that enlighten viewers about their own thinking. There is a new (to me) interactive feature based on the film that allows viewers to make choices and see the outcome. It reinforces the lessons from the video. I have used this feature many times and find it very successful with youths and adults alike. There is an extremely valuable new booklet on supporting school staff members who may be targeted by cyberbullies.

http://www.guardingkids.com

Russell A. Sabella's website is named after his book of the same name, noted below. The resources include PowerPoint presentations on cyberbullying, and there are columns and other materials that can be used with parents, teachers, and students. The links page includes excellent sites I have not seen mentioned elsewhere. This is an outstanding site to gain general information and is particularly helpful for counselors who would like to do training programs.

http://www.isafe.org

This site describes itself as the "worldwide leader in Internet safety education . . . endorsed by the U.S. Congress." Schools need to comply with the Protecting Children in the 21st Century Act, and this site contains everything needed to demonstrate compliance—a feature users may find attractive. There are sections on the site for kids and teens, parents, educators, and law enforcement. The site has training and certification for those who complete the training, who are then eligible to "spread the word." The registration process gathers quite a lot of information.

http://www.ncpc.org

This is a national crime prevention site that includes good information on cyberbullying.

http://www.netsmartz.org

This website is another must-visit site. There are sections for parents, educators, law enforcement, teens, and kids. The educators' section includes great videos and lesson plans to accompany the videos, other safety presentations, and information in Spanish. The teen section has animated cartoons that use humor to provide instruction on such topics as "profile penalty" (how material on your profile can cause you harm). The section for kids looks like a children's game website, but the text included may be difficult for young children to read independently.

http://www.readymade.com/au/method

This website provides ordering information for a training video titled *Method of Shared Concern*. Dr. Ken Rigby narrates the video, and the two examples provide excellent modeling of the method and useful opportunities for discussion. A user's guide helps practitioners think more deeply about the approach. I use this video in training, and it is always well-received.

http://www.realjustice.org

If the reader is interested in restorative justice, this site provides links to training and a wealth of books and videos, several of which I own.

http://www.stopcyberbullying.org

This is the website of the Wired Safety Group, headed by Parry Aftab. There are descriptions of the four types of bullies proposed by this group: vengeful angel, power-hungry or revenge of the nerds, mean girls, and inadvertent cyberbully. These are interesting ideas, but there is no evidence to support the theory. There are sections of the site for children ages 7–10, 11–13, and 14–17, and there are also sections for parents, educators, and law enforcement. This site describes a teen angels program: Youths age 13–18 years are trained and then create and conduct presentations and workshops, both on- and offline.

http://www.stopbullyingnow.hrsa.gov/adults/cyber-bullying.aspx

This is a section of a more general bullying site that has some useful data and tips for dealing with and preventing cyberbullying. Some of the data cited are not the most current available.

http://www.wiredsafety.org

This is a huge site with extensive information and resources. The "KidsOnline" section has quizzes to determine if one has been cyberbullied. There are many downloadable videos and PSAs available at no cost and booklets that can be duplicated with permission. Spanish versions are available. The site also has the Megan Pledge; signing the pledge means agreeing not to cyberbully, in memory of Megan Meier.

Media

ABC News Primetime's (2006) *Cyberbullying* is an informative program hosted by Diane Sawyer. It is a good introduction to the topic for an adult audience, although teens could certainly watch it as well.

Adina's Deck (Heimowitz & Azicri [Producers & Directors], 2007, 2008) is a group of videos (three so far) that is designed as a series of mysteries related to online behaviors. Episode 1 involves a case of cyberbullying, Episode 2 focuses on online predators, and Episode 3 deals with online plagiarism. Adina is the cyberversion of Nancy Drew. Young people seem to enjoy the characters and the plot, which also provide a healthy dose of information. A teacher's guide is available on adinasdeck.com, a website devoted to the series. The developer began the project as a master's project at Stanford University.

American Teen (57th & Irving [Producer] and Burstein [Director], 2008) is an independent documentary that follows four teenagers throughout their senior year of high school. Fairly early in the film, there is an episode of cyberbullying that is shocking in the vindictiveness of the attack and the relationship between the attacker and the victim. It provides a realistic example of this phenomenon for viewers and is instructive for both adults and teens. The language includes sexual references.

Cyberbullying is part of the *Real Life Teens* series (TMW Media Group [Producer], 2008) of videos produced by TMW Media Group. It is designed for high school students (Grades 8–12), with a teacher's guide available at the TMW Media website. I do not recommend this video, but counselors may want to make their own assessment. I found the narration to be dull, with errors of pronunciation and questionable facts, and I did not find the teens' comments to be enlightening.

Inbox (National Center for Youth Issues [Producer] & Brown [Director], 2004) is a video available in VHS and DVD from Research Press that has a rather dramatic storyline that portrays the dangers of cyberbullying and relational aggression. I found it rather melodramatic, but the audiences for which it is intended (Grades 5–9) seem to respond very favorably, and there is an accompanying study guide that makes this suitable for classroom use. It demonstrates that young people often do not think of potential consequences of their electronic communication "pranks."

PBS Frontline's *Frontline: Growing Up Online* (Dretzin [Writer, Director, Producer] & Maggio [Director, Producer], 2008) is an excellent video that gives a view of the Internet world that is part of young people's lives. There are resources available on the PBS website for educators and parents, and there is also a complete lesson plan with activities.

Shredderman Rules! (Holland [Director], 2007) is a made-for-TV movie that includes cyberbullying in the storyline. It is intended for a middle school audience and is based on a book by the same name that is popular with this age group. The film includes a fair amount of slapstick, and although the film does not show cyberbullying in the usual sense, the use of technology by a victim of face-to-face bullying to retaliate against the bully is the main plot. It has a hero, a bit of romance, and an admirable teacher in the mix. The anonymity of websites is central to the story, so the film might be a way to discuss the topic with middle school students.

Books

The books in this section are not in the References, which contains only works cited in the text. These are additional titles that readers of this book might want to consult. I begin with two works of fiction that have elements of cyberbullying that are important to the plot. Then I provide a list of nonfiction works that have helpful information. The fact that they were not cited in the text is not an indication that they are not worthwhile.

Novels

The Abortionist's Daughter by Elisabeth Hyde (published in 2006 by Knopf in New York, NY) is a contemporary murder mystery that is engaging and more complex than a simple whodunit. An element of the story involves the Internet posting of compromising photos of one of the characters. Although this incident is not the book's central theme, it is important to the storyline, and it does show that cyberbullying occurs and has wide ramifications.

Destroying Avalon (by Kate McCaffrey, published in 2006 by Fremantle Arts Centre Press in Australia) is a young adult novel that focuses on cyberbullying. It is a very engaging story of a teenager who moves to a new school and is the target of a cyberbullying (and traditional bullying) campaign. Her responses—both emotional and behavioral—to the situation are very realistic, and the conclusion, while shocking, becomes a teachable moment for the characters and the reader. There apparently is some concern that the "f" word appears five times in the book (I must say I didn't even notice). For American readers, some of the Australian slang may present a problem, but that may also be part of the charm. In addition, American youths learn that this problem is not exclusively American. A teaching and learning guide can be found on the author's website, which also includes many moving comments by young readers and responses by the author (all of whom are Australian). Apparently some Australian teachers are using the book in class. One reviewer on a book reviewer's blog said that the book "gives a strong message without being preachy," and "[students] say it is the only book they have ever finished" (Miss Maxwell's Bookshelf, 2009).

Nonfiction

Brequet, T. (2007). *Cyberbullying*. New York, NY: Rosen Publishing.

This very thin volume uses color and photographs to make up for the dearth of substantive content, in my opinion. I do not recommend this book, but it is designed for the teenage reader, who may react differently. It is definitely very basic.

Chatfield, T. B. (2007). *The MySpace.com handbook: The complete guide for members and parents*. Ocala, FL: Atlantic Publishing Group.

The title is self-explanatory.

Engdahl, S. (Ed.). (2007). *Online social networking*. Farmington Hills, MI: Greenhaven Press.

Goodstein, A. (2007). *Totally wired: What teens and tweens are really doing online*. New York, NY: St. Martin's Griffin.

The information is fairly basic, but the writer includes numerous examples and speaks primarily to parents, although there is a chapter for educators as well.

High, B. (2007). *Bullycide in America*. Tri-Cities, WA: JBS Publishing.

This is a compilation of stories of young people who committed suicide after being bullied. There is one story and a supplement related to cyberbullying. This is not a source of unbiased information but, rather, is a way for those grieving the loss of a child to tell their stories.

Kelsey, C. M. (2007). *Generation MySpace: Helping your teen survive online adolescence*. New York, NY: Marlowe & Co.

This is another good resource for parents. It does a good job of demystifying this social networking site.

Magid, L., & Collier, A. (2007). *MySpace unraveled: A parent's guide to teen social networking*. Berkeley, CA: Peachpit Press.

The title is self-explanatory, but the book is printed on high-quality paper and has many color screen shots that will be very helpful to parents.

Mazzarella, S. R. (2005). *Girl wide web: Girls, the Internet, and the negotiation of identity*. New York, NY: Peter Lang.

Sabella, R. A. (2008). *GuardingKids.com*. Minneapolis, MN: Educational Media Corporation.

Shariff, S. (2008). *Cyberbullying: Issues and solutions for the school, the classroom, and the home*. New York, NY: Routledge.

This book is a collection of essays on a variety of controversial issues related to social networking. One of those issues has to do with whether schools should punish athletes who are seen in photos to be drinking or using drugs.

Vander Veer, E. A. (2008). *Facebook: The missing manual*. Sebastopol, CA: O'Reilly Media.

If you have not used Facebook and want to learn how on your own, this is the step-by-step answer. This book has very good illustrations.

Willard, N. E. (2007). *Cyberbullying and cyberthreats*. Champaign, IL: Research Press.

This is one of the first books to come out on this topic, and it is an excellent one. The author is both a teacher and a lawyer, so legal issues are covered. What counselors in schools will find particularly valuable are the appendices, which provide templates for many forms that might be useful, and also a decision tree for suggested responses to incidents of cyberbullying in the schools.

APPENDIX

Cyberbullying Research

Authors: Aricak, T., Siyahhan, S., Uzunhasanoglu, A., Saribeyoglu, S., Ciplak, S., Yilmaz, N., & Memmedov, C. (2008)
Location: Turkey
Sample: 269 secondary students (134 boys and 135 girls) in Grades 6–10 in four schools (three public) in Istanbul
Findings: Majority had personal computers (74%), 84% had personal cell phones, and 64% had both. Thirty percent of students had shared their passwords with others. Twenty-four percent had said things online they would not say face-to-face. Thirty-six percent reported only cyberbully behaviors (rates were higher in boys), and 5.9% were only cybervictims. The most prevalent form of cyberbullying reported was being insulted, followed by being threatened. Being exposed to cyberbullying behaviors online was related to being exposed to such behaviors via cell phone. Almost 50% said they expect cyberbullies to get caught, and 40% said they know who they can go to for help; however, only 1% said they would tell teachers, and 10% would tell parents.
Limitation: No psychometric data on questionnaire.

Author: Bauman, S. (2009)
Location: United States
Sample: 221 students in Grades 5–8, 54% of whom were girls. School was 54% Latino, 38% White, 6% Native American, and 3% African American. Seventy-three percent of students in the school took the survey. School was rural, with a low SES.
Findings: 1.5% were cyberbullies only, 3% were cybervictims only, and 8.6% were cyberbully–victims. The best predictor of cyberbullying was

cybervictimization and vice versa. Fifth graders were less likely to have cell phones than all other grades. No gender differences were found. Cyberbullying and cybervictimization were strongly correlated, $r = .79$. Self-blaming attributions predicted emotional distress in response to a cyberbullying scenario. Moral disengagement predicted acting-out behaviors in response to the same scenario. Fifth graders were less involved in technological communication than all other grades. Twelve percent would report cyberbullying to an adult at school, and 9% would tell parents.

Limitations: Survey was administered by school personnel, so there was no way to ensure privacy. No comparative data on students who did not take survey. Low frequency of cyberbullying meant low statistical power.

Authors: Bauman, S., & Pero, H. (2010)
Location: United States
Sample: 30 Deaf/hard of hearing students in a Deaf school and 22 hearing students on same campus matched by grade, gender, and ethnicity
Findings: Hearing students text more often and use Internet for homework more than Deaf students. Deaf students use IM more than hearing student. Cyberbullying and cybervictimization were correlated at $r = .50$. No differences between groups (Deaf or hearing) for conventional bullying were found. Larger proportions (25%) of Deaf students were victims of cyberbullying (at least two to three times) compared with 10% of hearing students. Seven percent of Deaf students reported being cyberbullied by a hearing student; no hearing student was cyberbullied by a Deaf student.
Limitations: Small sample size and low frequency of variables of interest meant low statistical power.

Authors: Beran, T., & Li, Q. (2007)
Location: Canada
Sample: 432 students in Grades 7–9
Findings: 58% of sample had been victimized by cyberbullying at least once or twice; 26% admitted cyberbullying others. No grade or gender differences were found. Victims were more likely to miss school, obtain poor grades, and have difficulty concentrating. For cyberbullies, only poor concentration was reported. Students who were cyberbullied were likely to cyberbully others and also to be victimized traditionally. Children who were cyberbullied and bullied in person were more likely to cyberbully others.
Limitations: Low response rate. Few students had camera phones when the study was conducted, so this variable was not assessed. Single-item measures of bullying and victimization.

Authors: Burgess-Proctor, A., Hinduja, S., & Patchin, J. W. (2009)
Location: Internet
Sample: 3,141 female respondents ages 8–17 years ($M = 14.6$ years); 69% were in high school; 78% were White; 75% were in the United States

Findings: 38% indicated they had been bullied online. The most frequent experiences were being ignored (46%) and being disrespected (43%). Eleven percent had been threatened online. Most victimization occurred in chat rooms, followed by text messages online and e-mail. Eighty percent of victims knew the identity of the bully, and 31% of the time it was a school friend, 36% of the time it was another student, and 28% of the time it was someone in a chat room. Many participants reported negative emotional responses, but 55% dismissed the behavior and considered the cyberbullies to be not deserving of their attention.

Limitation: Participants were recruited from websites, which may have resulted in bias.

Author: Campfield, D. C. (2008)
Location: United States
Sample: 219 students in Grades 6–8 (*M* age = 12.6 years); 43% boys; 68% White, 26% "Other/Biracial," 2% Native American, and 2% Hispanic
Findings: Sixty-eight percent were involved in cyberbullying or victimization. Girls were overrepresented as cyberbullies, cybervictims, and both. Of victims, 59% were victimized both traditionally and by cyberbullying; 46% of bullies used both methods. Best predictors of cybervictim status were total problems reported and externalizing behaviors.
Limitations: Classification system sensitivity is a problem: Classification was based on a "yes" response to even a single of the 14 questions regarding cyberbehaviors. Measurement error regarding order of response options on questionnaire is possible. Ethnic diversity was lacking in the sample.

Authors: Cross, D., Epstein, M., Clark, S., & Lester, L. (2008)
Location: Australia
Sample: 10,000 students ages 9–14 years
Findings: Cyberbullying increased slowly with age. Perpetration of cyberbullying was higher in boys, whereas victimization was higher in girls. Cyberbullying and victimization was more prevalent in nongovernment than in government schools, and it was higher in nonmetro (i.e., rural) than metro schools.
Limitation: Data are cross-sectional; longitudinal study would be valuable.

Authors: Dehue, F., Bolman, C., & Völlink, T. (2008)
Location: The Netherlands
Sample: 1,211 students in the last year of primary school or first year of secondary school and their parents
Findings: About 23% of participants had been cyberbullied, and 16% admitted to cyberbullying others. Name-calling and gossiping were the most common forms reported, and the most common context was chatting. There was a small correlation ($r = .20$) between being bullied and being victimized conventionally and electronically. In response to cyberbullying, most responded by pretending to or actually ignoring it or by retaliating

against the bully. Parents were not aware of their children's experiences as bullies or victims of cyberbullying.

Limitation: Although a definition of bullying was provided, the authors acknowledged that students may have responded to their own subjective definitions.

Authors: Gradinger, P., Strohmeier, D., & Spiel, C. (in press)
Location: Austria
Sample: 761 ethnically diverse students in Grade 9 (M age = 15.6 years) from 10 schools; 49% were boys
Findings: 7% of students had been victimized electronically, and 5% admitted to cyberbullying others. These rates were considerably lower than those for traditional forms of bullying. Higher rates of cyberbullying (but not cybervictimization) were found among boys. Very few cybervictims were also victimized conventionally. Bullies were at highest risk for externalizing problems, and victims were at highest risk for internalizing problems. Those who were victims of both conventional bullying and cyberbullying were at highest risk for both types of problems.
Limitations: Cyberbullying and cybervictimization were each measured by a single item. Indirect traditional bullying was not measured. Gender could not be included in all analyses. Causality could not be determined.

Authors: Griezel, L., Craven, R. G., Yeung, A. S., & Finger, L. R. (2008)
Location: Australia
Sample: 803 secondary school students ages 12–17 years (M = 14.03); 53% were boys; 61% were Australian, 22% were Australian + another, and 17% identified as another culture
Findings: The Revised Adolescent Peer Relations Instrument (APRI)—Bully and Target was a modification of the original APRI that was updated to include cyberbullying. The new items measure both visual and text forms of cyberbullying. Reliability of all scales was good, with alphas from .80 to .88. The researchers used confirmatory factor analysis to test the construct validity of the measure. Three traditional bullying scales were identified (physical, verbal, and social) and two cyberbully scales were identified (visual and text). Two higher order factors were also found: Traditional Bullying and Cyberbullying. Psychometrics of the measure are very strong.
Limitation: The study was conducted in one school only. Because the school was a Catholic school, the sample may not be representative of the larger population.

Authors: Hinduja, S., & Patchin, J. (2007)
Location: 75% were from the United States, and 25% were from elsewhere
Sample: 1,388 participants; 50% male; 80% White; ages 6–17 years (M = 14.7)
Findings: Victimization was reported by 32% of males and 36% of females. Most common location was chat rooms and computer text message. When cyberbullied, 30% felt angry, 34% felt frustrated, 22% reported sadness,

and 35% were not bothered. Those who were victimized were more likely to engage in offline problem behaviors (drinking, smoking marijuana, delinquent behaviors). Strain mediated the relationship between cyber-victimization and offline problem behaviors such that when both were included in an ordinary least squares regression model, cybervictimization was no longer significant.

Limitations: Participants were recruited from a website catering to adolescents. Sample included only 1,388 of the 7,000 who responded because of over-age responses and gender imbalance. No psychometric properties were given for measures. Individual behaviors were measured dichotomously.

Authors: Juvonen, J., & Gross, E. (2008)
Location: United States
Sample: 1,454 participants aged 12–17 years; 75% female; 66% White, 12% African American, 9% Mexican American, and 5% Asian
Findings: 72% of participants experienced at least one incident of cyberbullying, and 77% reported one or more incidents of conventional bullying. Of those who reported online bullying, 85% also reported offline bullying. Offline bullying was significantly more common. Only 10% reported victimization to an adult. Reasons for not reporting included believing that they must learn to deal with it alone and fearing restrictions if their parents knew. The most common type of online bullying reported was name-calling or insults, followed by password theft. In logistic regression analysis, the significant predictors of repeated victimization were repeated conventional victimization, heavy Internet use, IM use, and webcam use. Distress associated with online victimization was similar to that for offline victimization.
Limitations: Participants were recruited from a teen website. Bullying was described as "mean things." No reliability or validity data were reported for the measure of bullying experiences.

Authors: Kapatzia, A., & Sygkollitou, E. (2007)
Location: Greece
Sample: 544 students (266 in Grade 9 and 278 in Grade 11); 47% were male
Findings: 15% reported having been cyberbullied once or twice, compared with 10% reporting conventional bullying at that frequency. Three percent reported being cyberbullied two or three times a month, 1% reported being victimized once a week, and 2% were victimized several times per week. More participants reported bullying others using conventional methods than using cyber methods. Of those who had been cyberbullied, 4% told their parents, and 1% told a teacher. Duration of being victimized was 1–2 weeks for 6%, but 2% had been victimized for several years. Boys were cyberbullied by cell phone more than girls. Boys in 11th grade experienced more cyberbullying by phone than boys in 9th grade; the pattern was reversed for girls. Boys were more likely to tell a teacher when they were cyberbullied by phone, whereas girls were more likely to tell friends. More

girls than boys reported being cyberbullied on the Internet, and they also reported cyberbullying others more often than boys.

Limitation: Researchers used a short form of Smith et al.'s (2006) questionnaire, but they did not report translation procedures or testing for psychometric properties.

Authors: Katzer, C., Fetchenhauer, D., & Belschak, F. (2009)
Location: Germany
Sample: 1,700 students in Grades 5–11 from various types of schools
Findings: Chat rooms were common venues for communication, with 69% chatting regularly, for an average of 70 minutes on school days and 122 minutes on other days. The authors concluded that rates for bullying in chat rooms are similar to those in school. Twenty-eight percent of victims were victimized repeatedly by the same bullies. Chat victims were likely to also be chat bullies, which was also true for in-school bullying. Victims often reported frequenting "risky locations" (p. 32) where victimization is more likely. The new measure was found to have four factors: Major and Minor School Victimization and Major and Minor Chat Room Victimization. The distinction between major and minor victimization was determined in a confirmatory factor analysis. Significant predictors of major chat room victimization were lacking chat room popularity, visiting risky chat rooms, lying in chat rooms (the strongest predictor), and being socially manipulative in chat rooms.

Limitation: The distinction between major and minor victimization bears closer scrutiny: Minor victimization included being harassed, threatened, abused, and so forth, whereas major victimization included being excluded or avoided, being teased or slandered, or being blackmailed.

Authors: Kowalski, R., Limber, S., Scheck, A., Redfearn, M., Allen, J., Calloway, A., . . .Vernon, L. (2005); Kowalski, R., & Limber, S. (2007)
Location: United States
Sample: 3,767 students in Grades 6–8; 51% girls
Findings: 25% of girls and 11% of boys reported being electronically bullied in the previous 2 months. Thirteen percent of girls and 9% of boys acknowledged cyberbullying others. Over half of cybervictims did not know the identity of the perpetrator. The correlation between being a cyberbully and cybervictim was .43, but the correlation between traditional bullying and victimization was .22.

Limitation: No psychometric data on measures were given.

Author: Li, Q. (2006)
Location: Canada
Sample: 264 students in Grades 7–9; 75% White, 6% Asian, and 18% other minority groups
Findings: No significant differences in rates of cybervictimization by gender were reported, but boys were more likely to be cyberbullies than girls. Female cybervictims were more likely than boys to tell adults; for observ-

ing cyberbullying, 30% would tell an adult—no gender differences were detected.

Limitations: No psychometric data on survey were provided; small sample. Participants were asked about "cyberbullying," but no definition was provided and no specific behaviors were listed.

Author: Li, Q. (2007a)

Location: Canada and China

Sample: 264 seventh-grade Canadian students, 49% of whom were male and 75% of whom were White. Chinese sample included 197 seventh-grade students, 41% of whom were male.

Findings: 29% reported being cybervictimized, 18% acknowledged cyberbullying others, and 53% reported being aware of cyberbullying in others. More boys than girls were involved as both bullies and victims. Twenty-one percent reported being a bully or victim more than 10 times. Chat rooms were the most commonly reported locale for cyberbullying, followed by other or mixed, e-mail, and mobile phone. Best predictors of cybervictimization were traditional bullying, knowledge of safety strategies, and country of participant. Chinese students were victimized more than the Canadian students, but Canadian students were more likely to be cyberbullies. Best predictors of cyberbullying were being a traditional bully, being a traditional bully–victim, gender, and frequency of computer use. Boys were more likely to be cyberbullies than girls.

Limitations: No psychometric data were provided on the questionnaire. Samples were combined for most analyses.

Author: Li, Q. (2007b)

Location: Canada

Sample: 177 Grade 7 students; 70% White, 9% Asian, 20% other (Black, Hispanic, Aboriginal)

Findings: 25% had been cyberbullied, and 15% reported cyberbullying others. Regarding conventional bullying, 31% acknowledged being a bully, and 54% were bully–victims. Almost half of cybervictims had also cyberbullied others. Only 34% of victims and 35% of witnesses told adults about cyberbullying.

Limitations: No psychometric data on survey were provided; small sample. Questions were asked about "cyberbullying," but no definition was given and no specific behaviors were listed.

Authors: Lodge, J., & Frydenberg, E. (2007)

Location: Australia

Sample: 652 youths, ages 11–17 years, 58% of whom were female, from two independent and three government schools

Findings: In the sample, 21% reported being cyberbullied during the school year, compared with 91% who reported that they had experienced conventional bullying. Boys had higher means for general bullying than girls; students in independent schools had higher rates of both general and cyberbullying than students in state schools. Girls in independent schools reported more cyberbullying problems than boys in independent schools and both boys and girls in state schools. A cluster analysis on coping styles found five coping patterns. Apprehensive and avoidant girls experienced the highest level of cyberbullying. This group was less likely to seek help from a teacher or counselor. Students who were optimistic, relaxed, and active in coping styles were least likely to experience cyberbullying.

Limitations: No reliability data were given for the current sample on the ACS (Adolescent Coping Scale). Source of the Peer Victimization Scale was not given.

Author: Maher, D. (2008)

Location: Australia

Sample: One Grade 5/6 class of 22 students (ages 11 and 12) and their teacher for 1 year

Findings: Online bullying behaviors replicated offline behaviors. Boys who were targets of online bullying appeared to have good coping skills. Some boys demonstrated a desire for control and power in the online environment. The online environment generated ways to bully (e.g., "flooding" in chat rooms) that are not possible in face-to-face situations. Online bullying on the Internet was more subtle than boys' offline bullying, which was more direct. In this study, there was no cross-gender bullying.

Limitation: As in all qualitative research, generalizations beyond this classroom cannot be made.

Authors: Mishna, F., Cook, C., Gadalla, T., Daciuk, J., & Solomon, S. (in press)

Location: Canada

Sample: 2,186 students from Grades 6, 7, 10, and 11; 55% girls; 66% native Canadians

Findings: 54% of students visited social networking sites, and 52% visited online game sites. Thirty-two percent had given their password to a friend; 53% had cell phones. Twenty-one percent reported being bullied online in the previous 3 months, whereas 35% acknowledged having bullied others online, and 28% had observed cyberbullying online. Twenty-one percent of those who were victimized online also reported being victimized face-to-face, 26% of cyberbullies also bullied traditionally, and 36% of cyberbully–victims reported being both bullies and victims of face-to-face bullying. Forty-two percent of students were bullied using IM. Eleven percent did not know the identity of the perpetrator. Responses to the incident were as follows: 21% were not bothered by it, 16% were angry, 8% were embarrassed, 7% were sad, and 5% were scared. Fifty-two percent of students did nothing about the bullying, whereas 20% confronted the perpetrator, 8% told a parent, and 3% told a teacher. Students reported being victimized online because of appearance (11%), race (6%), school performance (5%), gender (3%), and sexuality (2%). Reasons given for face-to-face bullying were similar but less often endorsed. Twenty-nine percent said cyberbullying is serious, and 26% said it is not.

Limitation: Gender, grade, and ethnic differences were not reported.

Authors: Mishna, F., Saini, M., & Solomon, S. (2009)
Location: Canada
Sample: 7 focus groups; 38 students (17 boys, 21 girls) in Grades 5–8
Findings: Students emphasized the importance of technology to them and noted the young ages at which children access computers. Students perceived the anonymity of the Internet to embolden bullies and frighten victims. However, they often learned the identity of the bullies. Much of the cyberbullying happened in the context of close relationships (romantic or friendships), particularly retaliation for perceived hurt. Students said if they were confronted, they could always avoid consequences by saying someone had "hacked into their account." Students did not tell adults when they were victimized for the following reasons: Adults were "oblivious," students feared loss of access to technology, students feared that the identity of the bully could not be determined, students were afraid telling would exacerbate problem, and they thought adults would tell them to just ignore the problem.
Limitations: Qualitative findings cannot be generalized to other contexts. Also, students' personal experiences were not elicited in order to protect their confidentiality.

Author: Patchin, J., & Hinduja, S. (2006)
Location: United States and the world (via the Internet)
Sample: 384 youths under the age 18 who responded to an invitation on a popular female musician's Internet site. Seventy-six percent of respondents were female, 75% were White, and 60% lived in the United States.
Findings: 11% reported bullying others online, 29% reported being victimized online, and 47% had observed online bullying. Most commonly reported events were as follows: 60% were ignored, 50% were disrespected, 30% were called names, and 21% were threatened. Cyberbullying occurred most often in chat rooms, computer text messages, and e-mail. Among those who were victimized, 43% felt frustrated, 40% felt angry, and 27% felt sad. Thirty-two percent were affected at school, 27% were affected at home, 20% were affected with friends, and 43% were not affected. In response to the online event, 36% told the bully to stop, 32% left the online environment, 25% did nothing, 20% got offline, 56% told an online friend, and 26% told a friend. Only 20% told their parents, and 7% told an adult.
Limitations: Sample from a music site may be biased. Neither participants' identities nor the validity of responses could be checked.

Author: Pew Internet & American Life Project (reported in A. Lenhart, 2007)

Location: United States

Sample: National phone survey of 886 online teens

Findings: 32% were targets of cyberbullying, with girls more likely to be victimized than boys, and those who visited social networking sites more likely than others to have been cyberbullied. Older girls (age 15–17) had the highest rates of cybervictimization (41%). The most common experience was having something private forwarded or posted publicly. Girls more often reported having rumors about them spread online, with social network users having higher rates than nonusers. Older girls received more threats online. Teens reported that bullying happens more offline than on.

Limitations: Response rate was 46%. Race and ethnicity were not reported or analyzed. Demographics of the sample were not provided.

Authors: Raskauskas, J., & Stoltz, A. (2007)

Location: United States

Sample: 84 youths ages 13–18 years; 89% were White, 4% African American, 4% Hispanic, and 2% Asian

Findings: 49% of participants were electronic victims, and 71% were traditional victims. Twenty-one percent reported being cyberbullied, and 64% reported being bullied by traditional methods. The most common form of victimization was text messaging, next was Internet, and then camera phone. More participants identified as victims than bullies. In open-ended responses, 93% of electronic victims who responded said they were negatively affected. A significantly larger proportion of traditional victims were also electronic victims versus those who were not traditional victims. The same was true for traditional bullies and cyberbullies. There was no evidence that traditional victims were electronic bullies. In logistic regression, traditional victimization was predictive of cybervictimization. For electronic bullying, predictors were being a traditional bully and older age.

Limitations: The questionnaire was designed for this study, and no psychometric data were given. Victim classification was based on a yes/no item. The participation rate was 40%, and there was a small sample. Some classifications were based on a single item.

Authors: Ševčíková, A., & Šmahel, D. (2008)

Location: Czech Republic

Sample: 1,260 Internet users ages 12 years and older

Findings: $r = .39$ between being victimized both online and offline; $r = .47$ for aggressors being both online and offline bullies. No gender differences were detected. The most reported response to victimization was anger, then (in order) helplessness, humiliation, sadness, jeopardy, fear of being online, and desperateness. Older adolescents were most likely to be victimized only (not also be bullies), $r = .5$ between being victimized online and bullying others online; $r = .61$ between "someone abusing your pictures or personal information and forwarding them" and bullying others online. When perpetrating aggression, respondents felt (in order): desire for revenge, anger, release, impulse to irritate, desperateness, entertainment, and excitement.

Limitation: Face-to-face interviews may have led to bias in answers.

Authors: Slonje, R., & Smith, P. K. (2008)

Location: Sweden

Sample: 360 students ages 12–20 years ($M = 15.3$ years), 210 from lower secondary and 150 in sixth form

Findings: 10% said they had been bullied at school in the previous 2 months, with 6% reporting being bullied only once or twice and 4% reporting more frequent bullying. Regarding cyberbullying, 5.3% reported being victimized, and 2.8% reported being cyberbullied only once or twice. No gender differences were detected. Students rated the impact of cyberbullying highest when a picture or video clip was the method used. Girls were more likely to be victimized by e-mail than boys. When asked about specific type of cyberbullying, 11.7% of students answered "yes." Overall cybervictim rate was 17.6% in lower secondary and 3.3% in sixth form. Victimization by cyberbullying more often occurred outside of school. Of those who were cyberbullied, 50% did not tell anyone, 36% told a friend, 9% told a parent, 5% told someone else, and no one told a teacher.

Limitations: The inside versus outside school distinction may not be clear. No data were collected on the use of mobile phones or Internet.

Authors: Smith, P. K., Mahdavi, J., Carvalho, M., Fisher, S., Russell, S., & Tippett, N. (2008)

Location: United Kingdom

Sample: 533 questionnaires from five schools in the United Kingdom. Participant characteristics were as follows: 49% male; 11–16 years old; 83% White, 6% Indian, 3% mixed, and others at low rates.

Findings: Cyberbullying and victimization were less frequent than conventional experiences, with 7% saying they were cyberbullied often, 16% reporting it once or twice, and 78% saying they had never been cyberbullied. Phone and text messages were the most common forms of cyberbullying. Happy-slapping was most frequently talked about. All cyberbullying was greater outside than at school. No age effects for cyberbullying or victimization were found. Girls were more likely to be cybervictims than boys. Many cyberbullies and victims were also conventional bullies and victims. Participants reported that the most common strategy when victimized was to ignore or block the sender. Sixteen percent of victims informed their parents or guardians, and 9% informed adults at school.

Limitation: Psychometric data were not provided for the measure.

Authors: Steffgen, G., & König, A. (2009)
Location: Luxembourg
Sample: 2,070 secondary students (*M* age = 15.9 years); 46% boys; 57% in Grades 7–9
Findings: 86% were never cybervictims, 10% had been cyberbullied between one and three times per year, and 4% had been cyberbullied often. Eighty-nine percent had never cyberbullied others, 5% cyberbullied often, and 6% cyberbullied one to three times per year. Seventeen percent often witnessed cyberbullying, and 23% did so one to three times per year. Cyberbullies had less empathy for victims than nonbullies. Girls were more likely than boys to be cybervictims, but no gender difference were found for cyberbullies. Boys were more likely to be traditional bullies than girls. Traditional bullies tended to be cyberbullies, and the same was true for victims. Seventeen percent of traditional victims were cyberbullies, whereas only 8% of nonvictims were cyberbullies.
Limitations: Data were collected online. The 4-item empathy measure was new. No psychometric properties were given for other measures.

Authors: Tynes, B., Giang, M., Williams, D., & Thompson, G. (2008)
Location: United States
Sample: 264 high school students (*M* age = 16.51 years); 48% male; 51% White, 27% African American, 5% Asian, 2% Latino, 2% "Other," 10% Multiracial, and 4% unknown. For analysis, the researchers created three groups: White, African American, and Other/Multiracial.
Findings: 71% of African Americans, 71% of Whites, and 67% of Other/Multiracials had observed online racial discrimination; 29% of African Americans, 20% of Whites, and 42% of Other/Multiracials had experienced racial discrimination online themselves. This discrimination occurred most frequently via social networking sites and text message but also in chats, discussion forums, and games. Increased personal online racial discrimination was associated with increased depression and anxiety. Male students reported lower rates of depression and anxiety than females. Observing racial discrimination (vicarious experience) was not associated with any increase in psychosocial adjustment.
Limitations: Response rates were low (School A had 16% participation rate and School B had 6%). Causality cannot be inferred.

Authors: Wang, J., Iannotti, R. J., & Nansel, T. R. (2009)
Location: United States
Sample: Nationally representative sample of 7,182 students in Grades 6–10 (*M* age = 14.3 years); 49% male; 43% White, 18% African American, 26% Hispanic American, and 13% Other
Findings: 13.6% of students repeated having been bullied electronically. Boys were more often cyberbullies, and girls were more often victims. Higher parental support was associated with lower rates of all types of bullying. Having more friends was associated with less victimization by

physical, verbal, and relational bullying; however, it was not associated with less cybervictimization.

Limitations: Only two items each were used to measure cyberbullying and victimization. Participants were classified as cyberbullies or victims if they reported an experience occurring only once or twice.

Authors: Werner, N. E., Bumpus, M. F., & Rock, D. (in press)
Location: United States
Sample: 330 students in Grades 6–8 in Year 1; 150 students in Grades 7–8 in Year 2. School district from which sample was drawn was 79% White.
Findings: The authors found no differences in Internet aggression by grade or sex. Relational aggression offline (not physical or verbal) was a significant predictor of Internet aggression. Internet victimization was strongly associated with Internet aggression. Victims of Internet aggression were 385% more likely to engage in Internet and traditional aggression 1 year later. If a student approved of relational aggression, the odds of that student being an aggressor online and offline increased by 198%. The researchers found no evidence that traditional victims turn to Internet aggression.
Limitations: Sample size in Year 2 was attenuated, so statistical power was reduced. Self-report data are a limitation. No individual data on race, ethnicity, or SES were included.

Authors: Williams, K. R., & Guerra, N. G. (2007)
Location: United States
Sample: Subsample (those with both fall and spring data) from larger study of Colorado students in Grades 5, 8, and 11 from 46 schools. Sample was 46% rural and 54% urban; 55% female; 61% White, 6% African American, and 28% Latino.
Findings: Internet bullying was perpetrated by 5% of fifth graders, 13% of eighth graders, and 10% of 11th graders. No gender differences were found for Internet bullying. All three predictors (moral acceptability of bullying, school climate, and peer support) were significant for Internet bullying. When cell phone bullying items were added in Year 2, rates of Internet bullying increased. The authors concluded that precursors of cyberbullying are similar to those of conventional bullying.
Limitations: A single item was used to assess Internet bullying. There was no measure of victimization.

Authors: Wolak, J., Mitchell, K. M., & Finkelhor, D. (2007)
Location: United States
Sample: 1,500 Internet users ages 10–17 years; 51% girls; 76% White, 13% Black, and 9% Hispanic
Findings: 9% reported online harassment in the previous year, and 43% of those were harassed by known peers. Fifty-nine percent of incidents by known peers involved posting or forwarding things to others compared

with 18% for online-only contacts. More victims of known peers were female (45%) than those who were victimized by online contacts (16%). When age and high Internet use were controlled, those who were harassed by known peers were more like to use interactive Internet applications. They were also more likely to harass peers at whom they were angry than those who were not harassed. Youths with high Internet use who were harassed by known peers were less likely to be upset by the incidents.

Limitations: Online harassment was measured by two questions; any "yes" answer led to classification as a victim. The survey was not designed to collect data on cyberbullying. Analyses were based on single incident. Because of low incidents of harassment, statistical power was limited.

Authors: Ybarra, M. L., Diener-West, M., & Leaf, P. J. (2007)
Location: United States
Sample: Random contacts of Harris Poll members were invited to complete survey. Youths were ages 10–15 years; 71% were White, 13% were Black, and 18% were Hispanic.
Findings: 65% reported no online harassment, 26% reported infrequent harassment, and 8% reported frequent (monthly or more) harassment. Sixty-four percent of those harassed online were not also bullied conventionally. Victimized youths were more likely to have behavior problems and were also more likely to carry a weapon at school.
Limitation: Online survey response rate was 26%.

Authors: Ybarra, M. L., Espelage, D. L., & Mitchell, K. M. (2007)
Location: United States
Sample: 1,588 youths, ages 10–15 years, from Harris Poll Online members; 48% female; 18% Hispanic and 28% minority. Participants were classified into one of four groups by cluster analysis.
Findings: Between 2% and 3% of participants were classified as victims of Internet harassment and unwanted sexual solicitation online. One percent of participants were both victims and perpetrators. Victims were also targeted offline. Perpetrator–victims all engaged in offline aggression, including 75% reporting sexual aggression. The perpetrator–victims engaged in other high-risk behaviors involving alcohol, marijuana, inhalants, and other drugs and had poor relationships with their primary caregiver. Youths involved in unwanted sexual solicitation were also involved in Internet harassment.
Limitations: Data were cross-sectional, so causality cannot be inferred. Measure was "somewhat crude."

Authors: Ybarra, M. L., & Mitchell, K. J. (2004)
Location: United States
Sample: Youth Internet Safety Survey nationally representative sample of 1,501 Internet users ages 10–17 years; 48% were female; 47% were age 15 or older; and 75% were White

Findings: 15% of respondents were Internet harassers, 14% by making a nasty comment to someone online. Seven percent had been harassed online in the previous year. Over 33% were targeted traditionally. Online harassers were more likely to use substances, exhibit depressive symptoms, exhibit delinquent behavior, and be the target of traditional bullying. Harasser behavior was predicted in regression analysis by being a target of online harassment, visiting chat rooms as most frequent online activity, and rating self as expert on the Internet. Poor caregiver–child bond also was reported more frequently by harassers than nonharassers. No gender differences were found. White respondents were more likely to be harassers than non-Whites.

Limitations: Only two dichotomous items were used to classify respondents. Sample was from 1999–2000.

Authors: Ybarra, M. L., Mitchell, K. J., Wolak, J., & Finkelhor, D. (2006)
Location: United States
Sample: Random sample of 1,500 U.S. Internet users ages 10–17 (23% between the ages of 10 and 12); 51% female; 75% White and 9% Hispanic
Findings: 9% had been harassed online in the previous year. Of those, 32% were targeted three or more times, and 45% knew their harasser prior to the incident. Participants were more likely to be harassed online if they harassed others online, had other social problems, and were victimized elsewhere. Most were not upset by online harassment. Distress was reported by 39%; more distress was reported by those who were targeted by adults, who received requests for photos, and who also experienced offline aggression from the harasser.
Limitations: Cross-sectional sampling means that no causality can be inferred. Respondents reported on the most upsetting event only. Response rate was 45%, and minorities were not well-represented.

REFERENCES

ABC News Primetime (Producer). (2006). *Cyberbullying* [Television program available as video or DVD]. USA: AMB News.

ACLU of Pennsylvania urges court to uphold free-speech ruling in MySpace civil rights case. (2008, December 8). Retrieved from http://www.aclupa. org/pressroom/acluofpennsylvaniaurgescou.htm

American School Counselor Association. (2005). *The ASCA national model: A framework for school counseling programs* (2nd ed.). Alexandria, VA: Author.

American School Counselor Association. (2006). *The professional school counselor and student safety and technology.* Retrieved from http://asca2. timberlakepublishing.com//files/PS_Safety.pdf

Annenberg School of Communication. (2009, April 28). *Annual Internet survey by the Center for the Digital Future finds large increases in use of online newspapers.* Retrieved from http://www.digitalcenter.org/pdf/2009_ Digital_Future_Project_Release_Highlights.pdf

Appel, R. (2009). *Report of the study committee: Harassment, bullying and cyber- bullying of students in Vermont schools.* Retrieved from http://www.leg.state. vt.us/reports/2009ExternalReports/243455.pdf

Aricak, T., Siyahhan, S., Uzunhasanoglu, A., Saribeyoglu, S., Ciplak, S., Yilmaz, N., & Memmedov, C. (2008). Cyberbullying among Turkish adolescents. *CyberPsychology & Behavior, 11,* 253–261.

Armstrong, M., & Thorsborne, M. (2006). Restorative responses to bully- ing. In H. McGrath & T. Noble (Eds.), *Bullying solutions: Evidence-based approaches to bullying in Australian schools* (pp. 175–188). Frenchs Forest, NSW, Australia: Pearson.

Arrowsmith, R. (2008, March 15). Search engines—An innovative tool in tackling cyber bullying. *Workplace Violence News.* Retrieved from http:// workplaceviolencenews.com/2008/05/15/search-engines-an-innovative- tool-in-tackling-cyber-bullying/

Associated Press. (2009, December 3). *'Sexting' is more common than you might think.* Retrieved from http://www.thirdage.com/parenting/sexting- is-more-common-than-you-might-think

Attewell, P., Suazo-Garcia, B., & Battle, J. (2003). Computers and young chil- dren: Social benefit or social problem? *Social Forces, 82*(1), 277–296.

Auerbach, I. S. (2008–2009). Screening out cyberbullies: Remedies for victims on the Internet playground. *Cardozo Law Review, 30,* 1641–1675.

Bandura, A. (1973). *Aggression: A social learning analysis.* Englewood Cliffs, NJ: Prentice Hall.

Bandura, A. (1999). Moral disengagement in the perpetration of inhumanities. *Personality and Social Psychology Review, 3,* 193–209.

Bandura, A. (2001). Social cognitive theory: An agentic perspective. *Annual Review of Psychology, 52,* 1–26.

Bandura, A. (2002). Selective moral disengagement in the exercise of moral agency. *Journal of Moral Education, 31,* 101–119.

Bandura, A., Barbaranelli, C., Caprara, G. V., & Pastorelli, C. (1996). Mechanisms of moral disengagement in the exercise of moral agency. *Journal of Personality and Social Psychology, 71,* 364–374.

Barker, E. D., Boivin, M., Brendgen, M., Fontaine, N., Arseneault, L., Vitaro, F., . . . Tremblay, R. (2008). Predictive validity and early predictors of peer-victimization trajectories in preschool. *Archives of General Psychiatry, 65,* 1185–1192.

Baron, R. A., & Richardson, D. R. (2004). *Human aggression.* New York, NY: Springer.

Barton, K. B. (2003). *Restorative justice: The empowerment model.* Sydney, Australia: Hawkins Press.

Barton, K. B. (n.d.). *Theories of restorative justice.* Retrieved from http://mtsu32.mtsu.edu:11405/Restorative%20Justice.pdf

Bauman, S. (2007). *Essential topics for the helping professional.* New York, NY: Allyn & Bacon.

Bauman, S. (2008). Effects of gender, grade, and acculturation on overt and relational victimization and depression in Mexican American elementary school students. *Journal of Early Adolescence, 28,* 528–554.

Bauman, S. (2009). Cyberbullying in a rural intermediate school: An exploratory study. *Journal of Early Adolescence.* First published December 9, 2009, via Online First. doi:10.1177/0272431609350927

Bauman, S., & Pero, H. (2010). *Cyberbullying among deaf and hard of hearing students and their hearing peers.* Manuscript submitted for publication.

Bauman, S., & Summers, J. (2009). Victimization and depression in Mexican American middle school students. *Hispanic Journal for the Behavioral Sciences, 31,* 515–535.

Bauman, S., & Tatum, T. (2009). Websites for young children: Gateway to online social networking? *Professional School Counseling, 13,* 1–10.

BBC News. (2006, November 27). *Star Wars kid is top viral video.* Retrieved from http://news.bbc.co.uk/2/hi/entertainment/6187554.stm

Beckstrom, D. C. (2008). State legislation mandating school cyberbullying policies and the potential threat to students' free speech rights. *Vermont Law Review, 33,* 283–321.

Belsey, B. (2008). [Definition of cyberbullying]. Retrieved from www.cyberbullying.ca

Bemak, F., & Chung, R. (2005). Advocacy as a critical role for urban school counselors: Working toward equity and social justice. *Professional School Counseling, 8,* 196–202.

Beran, T., & Li, Q. (2007). The relationship between cyberbullying and school bullying. *Journal of Student Wellbeing, 1*(2), 15–33.

Birkinshaw, S., & Eslea, M. (1998, September). *Teachers' attitudes and actions toward boy v. girl and girl v. boy bullying.* Paper presented at the annual conference of the developmental section of the British Psychological Society, Lancaster University, England. Retrieved from http://www.uclan.ac.uk/facs/science/psychol/bully/files/birkin.htm

Björkqvist, K., Ekman, K., & Lagerspetz, K. (2008). Bullies and victims: Their ego picture, ideal ego picture and normative ego picture. *Scandinavian Journal of Psychology, 23,* 307–313.

Bosworth, M. H. (2008, October 2). *Congress passes Broadband Data Improvement Act.* Retrieved from http://www.consumeraffairs.com/news04/2008/10/congress_broadband.html

Broadband Data Improvement Act of 2008, Pub. L. No. 110–385 § 1492.

Broderick, P. C., & Blewitt, P. (2006). *The life span: Human development for helping professionals* (2nd ed.). Upper Saddle River, NJ: Pearson.

Bronfenbrenner, U. (1979). *The ecology of human development: Experiments by nature and design.* Cambridge, MA: Harvard University Press.

Buckleitner, W. (2008). *Like taking candy from a baby: Young children interact with online environments.* Retrieved from http:///consumerwebwatch.org/pdfs/kidsonline.pdf

Burgess-Proctor, A., Hinduja, S., & Patchin, J. W. (2009). *Cyberbullying research summary: Victimization of adolescent girls.* Retrieved from http://www.cyberbullying.us/cyberbullying_girls_victimization.pdf

Cade, V. (2009, January 26). *Cyber-bullying in the workplace—When bullies use technology to launch their attacks.* Retrieved from http://ezinearticles.com/?Cyber-Bullying-in-the-Workplace--When-Bullies-Use-Technology-to-Launch-Their-Attacks&id=1925602

Calvert, S. L., Rideout, V. J., Woolard, J. L., Barr, R. F., & Strouse, G. A. (2005). Age, ethnicity, and socioeconomic patterns in early computer use. *American Behavioral Scientist, 48,* 590–607.

Cameron, L., & Thorsborne, M. (1999, February). *Restorative justice and school discipline: Mutually exclusive?* Paper presented at the Reshaping Australian Institutions Conference, Canberra, Australia.

Campbell, M. (2005, October 28). *The impact of the mobile phone on young people's social life.* Paper presented at the Social Change in the 21st Century Conference, Queensland, Australia.

Campbell, M. A. (2007). *Cyber bullying and young people: Treatment principles not simplistic advice.* Retrieved from www.scientist-practitioner.com

Campfield, D. C. (2008). *Cyberbullying and victimization: Prosocial characteristics of bullies, victims, and bully/victims* (Unpublished master's thesis). University of Montana, Missoula.

Carney, A. G., & Merrell, K. W. (2001). Perspectives on understanding and preventing an international problem. *School Psychology International, 22,* 364–382.

Cashmore, P. (2009, November 4). *Twitter lists and real-time journalism.* Retrieved from http://www.cnn.com/2009/TECH/11/04/twitter.lists/

Cassidy, W., Jackson, M., & Brown, K. N. (2009). Sticks and stones can break my bones, but how can pixels hurt me? Students' experiences with cyberbullying. *School Psychology International, 30,* 383–402.

Celizic, M. (2009, March 6). *Her teen committed suicide over 'sexting.'* Retrieved from http://www.msnbc.msn.com/id/29546030/

Chaffetz, J. (2009, October 29). *Freshman rep: Social media is 21st century route to victory.* Retrieved from http://www.cnn.com/2009/POLITICS/10/29/chaffetz.social.media/index.html

Chat 101, the basics (and more) of chat . . . (n.d.). Retrieved from http://www.ker95.com/index.html

Chatfield, T. B. (2007). *The MySpace.com handbook: The complete guide for members and parents.* Ocala, FL: Atlantic.

Cheney, M. F. (2009, February 16). *Cyberbullying: The inability of current criminal and civil remedies to protect our children from a very real threat.* Unpublished note on file with Thomas Jefferson School of Law, San Diego, CA.

Child mobile phone use costs them sleep. (2009, June 8). *The Advertiser.* Retrieved from http://www.news.com.au/adelaidenow/story/0,22606,25601432-5006301,00.html

Children's Internet Protection Act (CIPA), Pub. L. No. 106-554 (2000), codified at 20 U.S.C. §§ 6801, 6777, 9134 (2003).

Children's Online Privacy Protection Act, 15 U.S.C. § 6501–6506 (1998).

Chun, S. (n.d.). *Jury deliberates case of Internet hoax that led to deadly shooting.* Retrieved from http://www.cnn.com/2007/US/law/12/20/chun.myspaceshooting/index.html

Cohen, R. (2009, July 1). A Facebook teaching moment. The ethicist. *The New York Times Magazine.* Retrieved from http://www.nytimes.com/2009/07/05/magazine/05FOB-ethicist-t.html?_r=2

Common Sense Media. (2009). *Is social networking changing childhood? A national poll.* Retrieved from http://www.commonsensemedia.org/sites/default/files/Social%20Networking%20Poll%20Summary%20Results.pdf

Communications Decency Act, 47 U.S.C. § 151 (1996).

Computer Fraud and Abuse Act, 18 U.S.C. § 1030 (1986).

Conn, K. (2004). *Bullying and harassment.* Baltimore, MD: Association for Supervision and Curriculum Development.

Cordes, C., & Miller, E. (Eds.). (2000). *Fool's gold: A critical look at computers in childhood.* College Park, MD: Alliance for Childhood.

Coughlan, S. (2007). *Cyberbullying threat to teachers.* Retrieved from http://news.bbc.co.uk/2/hi/uk_news/education/6522501.stm

CQR Consulting. (n.d.). *Workplace cyberbullying.* Retrieved from http://www.cqrconsulting.com/disconnect/Cyberbullying in the workplace.pdf

Craig, W. M. (1998). The relationship among bullying, victimization, depression, anxiety, and aggression in elementary school children. *Personality and Individual Differences, 24,* 123–130.

Craig, W., & Pepler, D. (1997). Observations of bullying and victimization in the school years. *Canadian Journal of School Psychology, 2,* 41–60.

Crick, N. R., & Dodge, K. A. (1994). A review and reformulation of social information-processing mechanisms in children's social adjustment. *Psychological Bulletin, 115,* 74–101.

Cross, D., Epstein, M., Clark, S., & Lester, L. (2008, July 16). *Cyber bullying in Australia: Trends and recommended practices.* Paper presented at the biennial conference of the International Society for the Study of Behavioural Development, Wurzburg, Germany.

Cross, D., Hall, M., Hamilton, G., Pintabona, Y., & Erceg, E. (2004). Australia: The friendly schools project. In P. K. Smith, D. Pepler, & K. Rigby (Eds.), *Bullying in schools: How successful can interventions be?* (pp. 187–210). Cambridge, England: Cambridge University Press.

Cross, J. E., & Peisner, W. (2009). RECOGNIZE: A social norms campaign to reduce rumor spreading in a junior high school. *Professional School Counseling, 12,* 365–377.

Cyberbullying: The Ryan Halligan story. (2009). Retrieved from http://www.oprah.com/media/20090501-tows-ryan-halligan

Cyberstalking. (n.d.). Retrieved from http://www.cyberguards.com/CyberStalking.html

Dake, J. A., Price, J. H., Telljohann, S. K., & Funk, J. B. (2003). Teacher perceptions and practices regarding school bullying prevention. *Journal of School Health, 73,* 347–356.

Daniloff, D. (2009, Spring). Cyberbullying goes to college. *Bostonia.* Retrieved from www.bu.edu/bostonia/spring09

Davidson, R. (2007, December 10). *The heart–brain connection: The neuroscience of social, emotional, and academic learning.* Presentation at a meeting of the Collaborative for Academic, Social, and Emotional Learning (CASEL), New York City, NY.

Dehue, F., Bolman, C., & Völlink, T. (2008). Cyberbullying: Youngsters' experiences and parental perception. *Cyberpsychology and Behavior, 11,* 217–222.

Derbyshire, D. (2009, February 24). Social websites harm children's brains: Chilling warning to parents from top neuroscientist. *Mail Online.* Retrieved from http://findarticles.com/p/articles/mi_m0EIN/is_2008_July_29/ai_n27950858

DiClemente, R. J. (1991). Predictors of HIV-preventive sexual behavior in a high-risk adolescent population: The influence of perceived peer norms and sexual communication on incarcerated adolescents' consistent use of condoms. *Journal of Adolescent Health, 12,* 385–390.

docstoc.com. (2009). *Text 2 connect with teens—Parents guide to text messaging.* Retrieved from http://www.docstoc.com/docs/5130079/Txt-2-Connect-with-Teens—Parents-Guide-to-Text-Messaging

Dodge, K. (1986). A social information processing model of social competence in children. In M. Perlmutter (Ed.), *The Minnesota Symposium on Child Psychology* (Vol. 18, pp. 77–125). Hillsdale, NJ: Erlbaum.

Dretzin, R. (Writer, Director, & Producer), & Maggio, J. (Director & Producer). (2008). Growing up online. In *PBS Frontline*. Available from http://www.pbs.org/wgbh/pages/frontline/kidsonline/etc/tapes.html

Duncan, A. (1996). The shared concern method for resolving group bullying in schools. *Educational Psychology in Practice, 12,* 94–98.

Dwyer, C. (2007). Digital relationships in the "MySpace" generation: Results from a qualitative study. *Proceedings of the 40th Hawaii International Conference on System Sciences.* Retrieved from http://csis.pace.edu/~dwyer/research/DwyerHICSS2007.pdf

Eisenberg, M. E., & Forster, J. K. (2003). Adolescent smoking behavior: Measures of social norms. *American Journal of Preventive Medicine, 25,* 122–128.

Electronic Frontiers Australia. (2000). *EFA model acceptable use policy for employee use of the Internet.* Retrieved from http://www.efa.org.au/Publish/aup.html

Epps, J., & Kendall, P. C. (1995). Hostile attribution bias in adults. *Cognitive Therapy and Research, 19,* 159–178.

Espelage, D. L., & Swearer, S. M. (2003). *Bullying in American schools: A social-ecological perspective on prevention and intervention.* Mahwah, NJ: Erlbaum.

Estroff, S. D. (2007, January 18). Online social scene clicks with younger set. *JewishJournal.com.* Retrieved from http://www.jewishjournal.com/articles/item/online_social_scene_clicks_with_younger_set_20070119/

Exploring differences in pre-teen social networking sites. (2008, March 27). Retrieved from http://www.speedofcreativity.org/2008/03/27/exploring-differences-in-preteen-social-networking-sites/

February roundup: Social networking sites for kids. (2008, February 29). Retrieved from http://www.socialmediamom.com/?s=February+roundup%2C+Social+networking+sites+for+kids

Fekkes, M., Pijpers, F. I. M., & Verloove-Vanhorick, S. P. (2004). Bullying behavior and associations with psychosomatic complaints and depression in victims. *The Journal of Pediatrics, 144,* 17–22.

Feyerick, D., & Steffen, S. (2009). *'Sexting' lands teen on sex offender list.* Retrieved from http://cnn.com/2009/CRIME/04/07/sexting.busts.index.html

Fiddle Didle. (2008, April 27). Re: KidConfidence video review for Club Penuin.com [Web log comment]. Retrieved from http://kidconfidence.com/blogs/2007/04/21/kidconfidence-video-review-for-Club-Penguin-com

Field, E. (2007). *Bully blocking* (Rev. ed.). London, England: Jessica Kingsley.

Field, E. (n.d.). *Workplace bullying.* Retrieved from http://bullying.com/au/workplace-bullying/index/php

Field, E., & Carroll, P. (2006). Effective ways to work with parents. In H. McGrath & T. Noble (Eds.), *Bullying solutions: Evidence-based approaches to bullying in Australian schools* (pp. 209–225). Frenchs Forest, NSW, Australia: Pearson.

57th & Irving (Producer), & Burstein, N. (Director). (2008). *American teen* [Documentary film]. USA: Paramount Vantage.

Franklin, C., Biever, J., Moore, K., Clemons, D., & Scamardo, M. (2001). The effectiveness of solution-focused therapy with children in a school setting. *Research on Social Work Practice, 11*, 411–434.

Fuller, S. N. (2006). *The effects of a school counseling bullying curriculum on bully behavior in an urban K–5 elementary school* (Doctoral dissertation, University of Nebraska). Available from Proquest Dissertations and Theses database.

Gini, G. (2006). Social cognition and moral cognition in bullying: What's wrong? *Aggressive Behavior, 32*, 528–539.

Glew, G. M., Fan, M., Katon, W., Rivara, F. P., & Kernic, M. A. (2005). Bullying, psychosocial adjustment, and academic performance in elementary school. *Archives of Pediatric & Adolescent Medicine, 159*, 1026–1031.

Gradinger, P., Strohmeier, D., & Spiel, C. (in press). Traditional bullying and cyberbullying: Identification of risk groups for adjustment problems. *Journal of Psychology.*

Graham, S., Bellmore, A. D., & Mize, J. (2006). Peer victimization, aggression, and their co-occurrence in middle school: Pathways to adjustment problems. *Journal of Abnormal Child Psychology, 34*, 363–378.

Graham, S., & Juvonen, J. (2001). An attributional approach to peer victimization. In J. Juvonen & S. Graham (Eds.), *Peer harassment in school: The plight of the vulnerable and victimized* (pp. 49–72). New York, NY: Guilford.

Greenfield, P. M. (2004). Developmental considerations for determining appropriate Internet use guidelines for children and adolescents. *Journal of Applied Developmental Psychology, 25*, 751–762.

Griezel, L., Craven, R. G., Yeung, A. S., & Finger, L. R. (2008, December). *The development of a multi-dimensional measure of cyber bullying.* Paper presented at the annual conference of the Australian Association for Research in Education, Brisbane, Australia.

Hafner, K. (2009, May 26). *Texting may be taking a toll.* Retrieved from http://www.nytimes.com/2009/05/26/health/26teen.html

Hanish, L. D., & Guerra, N. G. (2000). The role of ethnicity and school context in predicting children's victimization by peers. *American Journal of Community Psychology, 28*, 201–223.

Harachi, T. W., Catalano, R. F., & Hawkins, J. D. (1999). United States. In P. K. Smith, Y. Morita, J. Junger-Tas, D. Olweus, R. Catalano, & P. Slee (Eds.), *The nature of school bullying: A cross-national perspective* (pp. 279–295). London, England: Routledge.

Hare, B. (2009, October 30). *Defriending can bruise your 'digital ego.'* Retrieved from http://www.cnn.com/2009/TECH/science/10/30/online.rejection.defriending/index.html

Harris Interactive. (2008). *Cell phones key to teens' social lives, 47% can text with eyes closed.* Retrieved from http://www.marketingcharts.com/interactive/cell-phones-key-to-teens-social-lives-47-can-text-with-eyes-closed-6126

Havenstein, H. (2008, September 12). *One in five employers uses social networks in hiring process.* Retrieved from http://www.computerworld.com

Hawker, D. (1998, September). *Bullying and victims' distress: Psychological bullying hurts most.* Paper presented at the annual conference of the Developmental Section of the British Psychological Society, University of Lancaster, England. Retrieved from http://www.eclan.ac.uk/facs/science/psychol/bully/files/hawker.htm

Hawkins, D. L., Pepler, D., & Craig, W. (2001). Peer interventions in playground bullying. *Social Development, 10,* 512–527.

Hawn, C. (2007, March 23). *Time to play, money to spend.* Retrieved from http://money.cnn.com/magazines/business2/business2_archive/2007/04/01/8403359/index.htm

Heider, F. (1958). *The psychology of interpersonal relations.* New York, NY: Wiley.

Heimowitz, D., & Azicri, J. (Producers & directors). (2007, 2008). *Adina's deck* [DVD]. USA: Author.

Hinduja, S., & Patchin, J. (2007). Offline consequences of online victimization: School violence and delinquency. *Journal of School Violence, 6,* 89–112.

Hinduja, S., & Patchin, J. W. (2009). *Bullying beyond the schoolyard: Preventing and responding to cyberbullying.* Thousand Oaks, CA: Corwin Press.

Holland, S. S. (Director). (2007). *Shredderman rules!* [Cable TV program available in DVD]. USA: Sony Pictures.

Holmes, J. R., & Holmes-Lonergan, H. A. (2004). The bully in the family: Family influences on bullying. In C. E. Sanders & G. D. Phye (Eds.), *Bullying: Implications for the classroom* (pp. 111–135). Amsterdam, The Netherlands: Elsevier Press.

Holt, M. K., & Espelage, D. (2003). A cluster analytic investigation of victimization among high school students: Are profiles differentially associated with psychological symptoms and school belonging? *Journal of Applied School Psychology, 19,* 81–98.

Hostin, S. (2008, March 16). *Online campus gossips won't show their faces.* Retrieved from http://www.cnn.com/2008/CRIME/03/17/sunny.juicy/

H.R. 1966, 111th Cong. (2009). Retrieved from http://www.opencongress.org/bill/111-h1966/text and http://cnn.co.hu/2009/TECH/science/10/27/online.rejection.defriending/index.html

Huesmann, L. R., Guerra, N. G., Miller, L. S., & Zelli, A. (1992). The role of social norms in the development of aggressive behavior. In A. Fraczek & H. Zumley (Eds.), *Socialization and aggression* (pp. 139–152). Berlin, Germany: Springer-Verlag.

Hymel, S., Rocke-Henderson, N., & Bonanno, R. (2005). Moral disengagement: A framework for understanding bullying among adolescents. *Journal of Social Sciences, 8,* 1–11.

Imbee: First safe social network for kids closes. (2009, March 17). Retrieved from http://www.bluepoppy-sem.com/2009/imbee-first-safe-social-network-for-kids-closes/

Inbar, M. (2009, December 2). *'Sexting' bullying cited in teen's suicide.* Retrieved from http://www.msnbc.msn.com/id/34236377/ns/today-today_people/

Internet world stats. (2009). Retrieved from http://www.internetworldstatus.com/stats14.htm#north

Jacobsen, K., & Bauman, S. (2007). School counselors' response to school bullying scenarios. *Professional School Counseling, 11,* 1–9.

Jaeger, P. T., Bertot, J. C., & McClure, C. R. (2004). The effects of the Children's Internet Protection Act (CIPA) in public libraries and its implications for research: A statistical, policy, and legal analysis. *Journal of the American Society for Information Science and Technology, 55,* 1131–1139.

Jarvis, K. (2007, November 3). *Handling cases of bullying & the method of shared concern.* Paper presented at the National Coalition Against Bullying National Conference, Melbourne, Australia.

Jones, S., & Fox, S. (2009). *Generations online in 2009.* Retrieved from http://www.pewinternet.org/Reports/2009/Generations-Online-in-2009.aspx

Jonsson, P. (2008, February 25). Teachers strike back at students' online pranks. *Christian Science Monitor.* Retrieved from http://www.csmonitor.com/USA/2008/0225/p01s02-usgn.html

J. S. v. Bethlehem Area School District, 757 A.2d 412 (Pa. Comm. Ct. 2000). Retrieved from http://www2.bc.edu/~herbeck/cyberlaw.bethlehem.html

Juvonen, J., & Gross, E. (2008). Extending the school grounds? Bullying experiences in cyberspace. *Journal of School Health, 78,* 496–505.

Kapatzia, A., & Sygkollitou, E. (2007). *Cyberbullying in middle and high schools: Prevalence, gender, and age differences* (Master's thesis). Aristotle University, Thessaloniki, Greece.

Katzer, C., Fetchenhauer, D., & Belschak, F. (2009). Cyberbullying: Who are the victims? A comparison of victimization in Internet chatrooms and victimization in school. *Journal of Media Psychology, 21*(1), 25–36.

Kelley, H. H. (1967). Attribution theory in social psychology. In D. Levine (Ed.), *Nebraska Symposium on Motivation* (Vol. 15, pp. 192–238). Lincoln: University of Nebraska Press.

Kerkhof, E. (2009). Myspace, yourspace, ourspace: Student cyberspeech, bullying and their impact on school discipline. *University of Illinois Law Review, 2009,* 1623–1654.

Kessler, J. (2009). *Black Philadelphia police sue over message board, say it's racist.* Retrieved from http://www.cnn.com/2009/CRIME/07/17/police.racism.lawsuit/index.html

Kidswirl. (2009, March 11). *Facebook for kids.* Retrieved from http://www.anewmorning.com/2009/03/11/kidswirl-facebook-for-kids/

Kim, V. (2009, December 14). *Judge backs student's First Amendment rights.* Retrieved from http://www.boston.com/news/nation/articles/2009/12/14/judge_rules_students_cruel_remarks_online_are_not_unconstitutional/

Kingsbury, W., & Espelage, D. (2008). Attribution style and coping along the bully–victim continuum. *Scientia Paedogogica Experimentalis, 44,* 71–102.

Kochenderfer-Ladd, B. (2003). Identification of aggressive and asocial victims and the stability of their peer victimization. *Merrill-Palmer Quarterly, 49,* 401–425.

Kowalski, R., & Limber, S. (2007). Electronic bullying among middle school students. *Journal of Adolescent Health, 41,* S22–S30.

Kowalski, R., Limber, S., & Agatston, P. W. (2008). *Cyberbullying*. Malden, MA: Blackwell.

Kowalski, R., Limber, S., Scheck, A., Redfearn, M., Allen, J., Calloway, A., . . . Vernon, L. (2005, August). *Electronic bullying among school-aged children and youth.* Paper presented at the 113th Annual Convention of the American Psychological Association, Washington, DC.

Kraft, E. (2006). Cyberbullying: A worldwide trend of misusing technology to harass others. *WIT Transactions on Information and Communication Technologies, 36,* 155–166.

Leff, S. S., Power, T. J., & Goldstein, A. B. (2004). Outcome measures to assess the effectiveness of bullying-prevention programs in the school. In D. L. Espelage & S. M. Swearer (Eds.), *Bullying in American schools: A social–ecological perspective on prevention and intervention* (pp. 1–12). Mahwah, NJ: Erlbaum.

Leishman, J. (2005, March). Cyber-bullying. *CBC News Online.* Retrieved from http://www.cbc.ca/nationa/news/cyberbullying/

Lenhart, A. (2007, June 27). *Data memo.* Washington, DC: Pew Internet and American Life Project.

Lenhart, A. (2009, May). *Cyberbullying: What the research is telling us.* Paper presented at the National Association of Attorneys General Year of the Child Conference, Philadelphia, PA.

Li, Q. (2006). Cyberbullying in schools: A research of gender difference. *School Psychology International, 27,* 157–170.

Li, Q. (2007a). Bullying in the new playground: Research into cyberbullying and cybervictimization. *Australian Journal of Educational Technology, 23,* 436–454.

Li, Q. (2007b). New bottle but old wine: A research of cyberbullying in schools. *Computers in Human Behavior, 23,* 1777–1791.

Limber, S. (2002, May 13). *Addressing youth bullying behavior.* Paper presented at the Educational Forum on Adolescent Health, American Medical Association, Chicago, IL. Available at http://www.ama-assn.org/ama1/pub/upload/mm/39/youthbullying.pdf

Livingstone, S. (2008). Taking risky opportunities in youthful content creation: Teenagers' use of social networking sites for intimacy, privacy, and self-expression. *New Media & Society, 10,* 393–411.

Lodge, J., & Frydenberg, E. (2007). Cyberbullying in Australian schools: Profiles of adolescent coping and insights for school practitioners. *The Australian Educational and Developmental Psychologist, 24,* 45–58.

Ma, L., Phelps, E., Lerner, J. V., & Lerner, R. M. (2009). Academic competence for adolescents who bully and are bullied: Findings from the 4-H study of positive youth development. *Journal of Early Adolescence, 29,* 862–897.

Ma, X. (2004). Who are the victims? In C. E. Sanders & G. D. Phye (Eds.), *Bullying: Implications for the classroom* (pp. 20–34). Amsterdam, The Netherlands: Elsevier Press.

MacBrayer, E. K., Milich, R., & Hundley, M. (2003). Attributional biases in aggressive children and their mothers. *Journal of Abnormal Psychology, 112*, 698–708.

Maher, D. (2008). Cyberbullying: An ethnographic case study of one Australian upper primary school class. *Youth Studies Australia, 27*(4), 50–57.

Majority of American parents reject school cell phone bans. (2006, August 29). *Cellular-News*. Retrieved from http://www.cellular-news.com/story/19044.php

Malik, O. (2007, August 23). *All Americans to have mobile phones by 2013*. Retrieved from http://gigaom.com/2007/08/23/all-americans-to-have-mobile-phones-by-2013/

Malkin, M. (2005, May 6). *School to soldier's son: No "conversating" allowed!* Retrieved from http://michellemalkin.com/2005/05/06/school-to-soldiers-son-no-conversating-allowed/

Margolick, D. (2009, March). *Slimed online*. Retrieved from http://www.portfolio.com/news-markets/national-news/portfolio/2009

Marsh, H. W., Parada, R. H., Craven, R. G., & Finger, L. (2004). In the looking glass: A reciprocal effects model elucidating the complex nature of bullying, psychological determinants and the central role of self-concept. In C. S. Sanders & G. D. Phye (Eds.), *Bullying: Implications for the classroom* (pp. 63–106). Amsterdam, The Netherlands: Elsevier Academic Press.

Matthiesen, S. B., & Einarsen, S. (2007). Perpetrators and targets of bullying at work: Role stress and individual differences. *Violence and Victims, 22*, 735–753.

Mazzarella, S. (Ed.). (2005). *Girl wide web: Girls, the Internet, and the negotiation of identity*. New York, NY: Peter Lang.

McKay, S., Thurlow, C., & Zimmerman, H. T. (2005). Wired whizzes or technoslaves? Young people and their emergent communication technologies. In A. Williams & C. Thurlow (Eds.), *Talking adolescence: Perspectives on communication in the teenage years* (pp. 185–203). New York, NY: Peter Lang.

Media General News Service. (2008, August 19). *Kids getting first cell phones at young age*. Retrieved from http://www2.mcdowellnews.com/content/2008/aug/19/kids-getting-first-cell-phones-young-age/

Menesini, E., Sanchez, V., Fonzi, A., Ortega, R., Costabile, A., & Lo Feudo, G. (2003). Moral emotions and bullying: A cross-national comparison of differences between bullies, victims, and outsiders. *Aggressive Behavior, 29*, 515–530.

Mirsky, L. (2009, June 22). Restorative practices and the transformation at West Philadelphia High School. *Restorative Practices E-Forum*. Retrieved from http://www.safersanerschools.org/media/wph.pdf

Mishna, F., Cook, C., Gadalla, T., Daciuk, J., & Solomon, S. (in press). Cyber bullying behaviors among middle and high school students. *American Journal of Orthopsychiatry*.

Mishna, F., Saini, M., & Solomon, S. (2009). Ongoing and online: Children and youth's perceptions of cyber bullying. *Children and Youth Services Review, 31*, 1222–1228.

Miss Maxwell's Bookshelf. (2009, February 3). *Destroying Avalon, Kate McCaffrey* [Review of the book *Destroying Avalon,* by K. McCaffrey]. Retrieved from http://missmaxwellsbookshelf.blogspot.com/2009/02/destroying-avalon-kate-mccaffrey.html

Mitchell, K. J., Finkelhor, D., & Wolak, J. (2005). Protecting youth online: Family use of filtering and blocking software. *Child Abuse and Neglect, 29,* 753–765.

Morrison, B. (2007). *Restoring safe school communities.* Sydney, Australia: Federation Press.

Morrison, B., Blood, P., & Thorsborne, M. (2006). Practicing restorative justice in school communities: The challenge of culture change. *Public Organization Review: A Global Journal, 5,* 335–357.

Mynard, H., Joseph, S., & Alexander, J. (2000). Peer-victimisation and posttraumatic stress in adolescents. *Personality and Individual Differences, 29,* 815–821.

Naish, J. (2009, June 23). *Mobile phones for children: A boon or a peril?* Retrieved from http://women.timesonline.co.uk/tol/life_and_style/women/families/article6556283.ece

Nansel, T., Overpeck, M., Pilla, R., Ruan, W., Simons-Morton, B., & Scheidt, P. (2001). Bullying behaviors among U.S. youth: Prevalence and association with psychosocial adjustment. *Journal of the American Medical Association, 285,* 2094–2100.

Nasby, W., Hayden, B., & DePaulo, B. M. (1980). Attributional bias among aggressive boys to interpret unambiguous social stimuli as displays of hostility. *Journal of Abnormal Psychology, 89,* 459–468.

National Campaign to Prevent Teen and Unplanned Pregnancy. (2009). *Sex and tech: Results from a survey of teens and young adults.* Retrieved from http://www.thenationalcampaign.org/sextech/PDF/SexTech_Summary.pdf

National Center for Youth Issues (Producer), & Brown, T. (Director). (2004). *Inbox* [Educational video]. USA: Research Press.

National Conference of State Legislatures. (2009). *State electronic harassment or "cyberstalking" laws.* Retrieved from http://www.ncsl.org/default.aspx?tabid=13495

National Crime Prevention Council. (2007). *Teens and cyberbullying: Executive summary of a report on research conducted for NCPC.* Available at http://www.ncpc.org/resources/files/pdf/bullying/Teens%20and%20Cyberbullying%20Research%20Study.pdf

National Science Board. (1998). *Science and engineering indicators. 1998.* Arlington, VA: National Science Foundation (NSB98-1).

New Mexico State U. investigates pornography charges in couple's tenure case. (2009, March 13). *The Chronicle of Higher Education.* Retrieved from http://chronicle.com/article/New-Mexico-State-U/40638/

News Staff. (2007, May 31). *Second Life or same life? Bullying continues online.* Retrieved from http://www.scientificblogging.com/news/second_life_or_same_life_bullying_continues_online

O'Connell, P., Pepler, D., & Craig, W. (1999). Peer involvement in bullying: Insights and challenges for intervention. *Journal of Adolescence, 22,* 437–452.

O'Connell, R. (2001). *Be somebody else but be yourself at all times: Degrees of identity deception in chatrooms.* Retrieved July 20, 2002, from http://www.theonceproject.net

O'Connell, T., Wachtel, B., & Wachtel, T. (1999). *Conferencing handbook: The new real justice training manual.* Pipersville, PA: Piper's Press.

Olweus, D. (1978). *Aggression in the schools: Bullies and whipping boys.* Washington, DC: Hemisphere.

Olweus, D. (1993). *Bullying at school: What we know and what we can do.* Cambridge, MA: Blackwell.

O'Neill, M. (1995, March 8). The lure and addiction of life online. *New York Times.* Retrieved from http://find.galegroup.com/gtx/retrieve.do?contentSet=IAC-Documents&resultListType=RESULT_LIST&qrySerId=Locale(en%2CUS%2C)%3AFQE%3D(JN%2CNone%2C16)%22New+York+Times%22%3AAnd%3ALQE%3D(DA%2CNone%2C8)19950308%24&sgHitCountType=None&inPS=true&sort=DateDescend&searchType=PublicationSearchForm&tabID=T004&prodId=AONE&searchId=R1&currentPosition=9&userGroupName=uarizona_main&docId=A155497543&docType=IAC

PA gym killer George Sodini's blog [archived]. (2009, August 5). Retrieved from http://www.shabooty.com/2009/08/05/pa-gym-killer-george-sodinis-blog-archived.php

Parr, B. (2009, November 6). *WOW: Facebook adding half a million new users every day.* Retrieved from http://mashable.com/2009/11/06/facebook-325-million-users/

Patchin, J., & Hinduja, S. (2006). Bullies move beyond the schoolyard: Preliminary look at cyberbullying. *Youth Violence and Juvenile Justice, 4,* 148–169.

Payne, A. A., & Gottfredson, D. C. (2004). Schools and bullying: School factors related to bullying and school-based bullying interventions. In C. E. Sanders & G. D. Phye (Eds.), *Bullying: Implications for the classroom* (pp. 159–176). Amsterdam, The Netherlands: Elsevier.

Pellegrini, A. (2004). Bullying during the middle school years. In C. E. Sanders & G. D. Phye (Eds.), *Bullying: Implications for the classroom* (pp. 177–202). Amsterdam, The Netherlands: Elsevier Press.

Pellegrini, A. D., & Long, J. D. (2002). A longitudinal study of bullying, dominance, and victimization during the transition from primary school through secondary school. *British Journal of Developmental Psychology, 20,* 259–281.

Pepler, D., Jiang, D., Craig, W., & Connolly, J. (2008). Developmental trajectories of bullying and associated factors. *Child Development, 79,* 325–338.

Perle, L. (2009). *What is this "bathroom wall" feature on Facebook?* Retrieved from http://www.commonsensemedia.org/what-bathroom-wall-feature-facebook

Perren, S., & Alsaker, F. D. (2006). Social behavior and peer relationships of victims, bully–victims, and bullies in kindergarten. *Journal of Child Psychology and Psychiatry, 47,* 45–57.

Pikas, A. (1989). The common concern method for the treatment of mobbing. In E. Roland & E. Munthe (Eds.), *Bullying: An international perspective* (pp. 91–104). London, England: David Fulton.

Pikas, A. (2002). New developments of shared concern method. *School Psychology International, 23,* 307–326.

Police: Gym shooter 'had a lot of hatred' for women, society. (2009, August 5). Retrieved from http://www.cnn.com/2009/CRIME/08/05/pennsylvania.gym.shooting/index.html

POS: Parents over shoulder. (2009). Retrieved from http://www.wgal.com/slideshow/family/13415032/detail.html

Prensky, M. (2001). Digital natives, digital immigrants part 1. *On the Horizon, 9*(5), 1–6.

Privitera, C., & Campbell, M. (2009). Cyberbullying: The new face of workplace bullying? *Cyberpsychology & Behavior, 12,* 395–400.

Raskauskas, J., & Stoltz, A. (2007). Involvement in traditional and electronic bullying among adolescents. *Developmental Psychology, 43,* 564–575.

Reardon, M. (2008, May 20). U.S. cell phone sales take a dip [Web log post]. Retrieved from http://news.cnet.com/8301-10784_3-9948424-7.html

Reid, P., Monsen, J., & Rivers, I. (2004). Psychology's contribution to understanding and managing bullying within schools. *Educational Psychology in Practice, 20,* 241–258.

Remembering Ryan Halligan video [Online video]. (2009). Retrieved from http://www.oprah.com/media/20090501-tows-ryan-halligan

Rideout, V., & Hamel, E. (2006). *The media family: Electronic media in the lives of infants, toddlers, preschoolers and their parents.* Menlo Park, CA: Kaiser Family Foundation.

Rigby, K. (2004). Addressing bullying in schools: Theoretical perspectives and their implications. *School Psychology International, 25,* 287–300.

Rigby, K. (2005). The method of shared concern as an intervention technique to address bullying in schools: An overview and appraisal. *Australian Journal of Guidance and Counselling, 15,* 27–34.

Rigby, K., & Johnson, B. (2006). Expressed readiness of Australian schoolchildren to act as bystanders in support of children who are being bullied. *Educational Psychology, 26,* 425–440.

Robinson, G., & Maines, B. (2008). *A complete guide to the support group method.* Los Angeles, CA: Sage.

Ross, D. M. (1996). *Childhood bullying and teasing: What school personnel, other professionals, and parents can do.* Alexandria, VA: American Counseling Association.

Safer social networking principles for the EU. (2009, February 10). Retrieved from http://ec.europa.eu/information_society/activities/social_networking/docs/sn_principles.pdf

Salmivalli, C. (1999). Participant role approach to school bullying: Implications for interventions. *Journal of Adolescence, 22,* 453–459.

Salmivalli, C., Lappalainen, M., & Lagerspetz, K. M. J. (1998). Stability and change of behavior in connection with bullying in schools: A two-year follow up. *Aggressive Behavior, 24,* 205–218.

San Miguel, R. (2008, November 20). *MySpace suicide case exposes legal gap.* Retrieved from http://ecommercetimes.com/story/MySpace-Suicide-Case-Exposes-Legal-Gap-65232.html?wlc=1256412814

Schäfer, M., Korn, S., Brodbeck, F. C., Wolke, D., & Schulz, H. (2003). *Bullying roles in changing context: The stability of victim and bully roles from primary to secondary school* (Research Report No. 165). Munich, Germany: Ludwig-Maximilians-University, Department of Psychology, Institute for Educational Psychology.

Scholte, R. H. J., Engels, T. C. M. E., Overbeek, G., de Kemp, R. A. T., & Haselager, G. J. T. (2007). Stability in bullying and victimization and its association with social adjustment in childhood and adolescence. *Journal of Abnormal Child Psychology, 35,* 217–228.

School sued in online photo controversy. (2009, October 30). Retrieved from http://news.aol.com/article/aclu-sues-churubusco-high-school-for/745429

Scully, A. (n.d.). Online dating: Tips for success part I. *The Online Mom* [Blog]. Retrieved from http://www.theonlinemom.com/secondary.asp?id=550

Seals, D., & Young, J. (2003). Bullying and victimization: Prevalence and relationship to gender, grade level, ethnicity, self-esteem, and depression. *Adolescence, 38,* 735–748.

Segal, L. (2009, July 3). *Woman accused of targeting girl, 9, with Craigslist ad.* Retrieved from http://www.cnn.com/9009/CRIME/07/03/craigslist.girl/index.html

Ševčíková, A., & Šmahel, D. (2008). *Cyberbullying among Czech Internet users: Preliminary results.* Paper presented at the Cyberspace Conference, Brno, Czech Republic. Retrieved from http://ivdmr.fss.muni.cz/english/storage/Sevcikova_Smahel_Cyberbullying_among_Czech_Internet_users.pdf

Shariff, S. (2005). Cyber-dilemmas in the new millennium: School obligations to provide student safety in a virtual environment. *McGill Journal of Education, 40,* 467–487.

Shariff, S., & Gouin, R. (2006). Cyber-dilemmas: Gendered hierarchies, new technologies and cyber-safety in schools. *Atlantis—A Women's Studies Journal, 31*(1), 26–36.

Sharp, S. (1995). How much does bullying hurt? The effects of bullying on the personal wellbeing and educational progress of secondary aged students. *Educational and Child Psychology, 12,* 81–88.

Shellenbarger, S. (2006, October 23). When is a child too young to join MySpace? *The Wall Street Journal.* Retrieved from http://students.cgps.org/studentssite/grammar/subpages/When%20is%20a%20child%20too%20young%20to%20join%20MySpace.pdf

Sinasohn, R. (2008, April 16). *Dad calls from Iraq, son gets suspended.* Retrieved from http://www.parentdish.com/2008/04/16/dad-calls-from-iraq-son-gets-suspended/

Slonje, R., & Smith, P. K. (2008). Cyberbullying: Another main type of bullying? *Scandinavian Journal of Psychology, 49,* 147–154.

Smith, P. K. (2007). Why has aggression been thought of as maladaptive? In P. H. Hawley, T. D. Little, & P. C. Rodkin (Eds.), *Aggression and adaptation: The bright side to bad behavior* (pp. 65–83). Mahwah, NJ: Erlbaum.

Smith, P. K., Mahdavi, J., Carvalho, M., Fisher, S., Russell, S., & Tippett, N. (2008). Cyberbullying: Its nature and impact in secondary school pupils. *Journal of Child Psychology and Psychiatry, 49,* 376–385.

Smith, P. K., Mahdavi, J., Carvalho, M., & Tippett, N. (2006). *An investigation into cyberbullying, its forms, awareness and impact, and the relationship between age and gender in cyberbullying: A report to the Anti Bullying Alliance* (Brief No. RBX03-06). Available at http://www.dcsf.gov.uk/research/data/uploadfiles/RBX03-06.pdf

Smith, P. K., & Sharp, S. (Eds.). (1994). *School bullying: Insights and perspectives.* London, England: Routledge.

Smith, P. K., & Shu, S. (2000). What good schools can do about bullying: Findings from a survey in English schools after a decade of research and action. *Childhood, 7,* 193–212.

Smith, P. K., Shu, S., & Madsen, K. (2001). Characteristics of victims of school bullying. In J. Juvonen & S. Graham (Eds.), *Peer harassment in school: The plight of the vulnerable and victimized* (pp. 332–352). New York, NY: Guilford.

Smith, P. K., Singer, M., Hoel, H., & Cooper, C. L. (2003). Victimization in the school and the workplace: Are there any links? *British Journal of Psychology, 94,* 175–188.

Smith, P. K., Talamelli, L., Cowie, H., Naylor, P., & Chuahan, P. (2004). Profiles of non-victims, escaped victims, continuing victims, and new victims of school bullying. *British Journal of Educational Psychology, 74,* 565–581.

Smokowski, P. R., & Kopasz, K. H. (2005). Bullying in school: An overview of types, effects, family characteristics, and intervention strategies. *Children & Schools, 27,* 101–110.

Soghoian, C. (2008, December 1). *MySpace ruling could lead to jail time for online daters.* Retrieved from http://news.cnet.com/myspace-ruling-could-lead-to-jail-for-lying-online-daters/

Star Wars kid files lawsuit. (2003). Retrieved from http://www.wired.com/culture/lifestyle/news/2003/07/59757

State action on cyberbullying. (2008, February 6). *USA Today.* Retrieved from http://www.usatoday.com/news/nation/2008-02-06-cyber-bullying-list_N.htm

Steffgen, G., & König, A. (2009). Cyberbullying: The role of traditional bullying and empathy. In B. Sapeo, L. Haddon, E. Mante-Meijer, L. Fortunati, T. Turk, & E. Loos (Eds.), *The good, the bad and the challenging* [Conference Proceedings] (Vol. 2, pp. 1041–1047). Brussells, Belgium: Cost Office.

Stein, N. (2003). Bullying or sexual harassment? The missing discourse of rights in an era of zero tolerance. *Arizona Law Review, 45,* 783.

Storch, E. A., Nock, M. K., Masia-Warner, C., & Barlas, M. E. (2003). Peer victimization and social–psychological adjustment in Hispanic and African American children. *Journal of Child and Family Studies, 12,* 439–452.

Student Press Law Center. (2009, July 22). *Student files lawsuit after coach distributed private Facebook content.* Retrieved from http://www.splc.org/newsflash.asp?id=1938

Students to be punished for MySpace postings. (2007, August 16). Retrieved from http://www.wlky.com/news/13897653/detail.html

Stutsky, G. (2006). *Cyber bullying information.* Retrieved from http://www.ippsr.msu.edu/Documents/Forums/2006_Mar_CYBER_BULLYING_INFORMATION_2006%20-%20Provided%20by%20Mr.%20Glenn%20Stutzky.pdf

Suler, J. (2004). The online disinhibition effect. *CyberPsychology & Behavior, 7,* 321–326.

Sum, S., Mathews, M., Hughes, I., & Campbell, A. (2008). Internet use and loneliness in older adults. *Cyberpsychology and Behavior, 11,* 208–211.

Sutter, J. D. (2009, April 13). *All in the Facebook family: Older generations join social networks.* Retrieved from http://www.cnn.com/2009/TECH/04/13/social.network.older/index.html

Swearer, S. M., & Doll, B. (2001). Bullying in schools: An ecological framework. *Journal of Emotional Abuse, 2*(2-3), 7–23.

Swearer, S. M., & Espelage, D. L. (2004). Introduction: A social ecological framework of bullying among youth. In D. L. Espelage & S. M. Swearer (Eds.), *Bullying in American schools: A social–ecological perspective on prevention and intervention* (pp. 1–12). Mahwah, NJ: Erlbaum.

Swearer, S. M., Espelage, D. L., & Napolitano, S. A. (2009). *Bullying prevention and intervention: Realistic strategies for schools.* New York, NY: Guilford.

Sydell, L. (2009, October 21). *Facebook, MySpace divide along social lines.* Retrieved from http://npr.org/templates/story/story.php?storyID=113974893

Tanneeru, M. (2009, November 17). *Can the law keep up with technology?* Retrieved from http://edition.cnn.com/2009/TECH/11/17/law.technology/

Teen beaten with chair in videotaped attack. (2008, April 15). Retrieved from http://www.kpho.com/news/15887677/detail.html

Thomas, S. C., & Johnson, M. H. (2008). New advances in understanding sensitive periods in brain development. *Current Directions in Psychological Science, 17,* 1–5.

TMW Media Group (Producer). (2008). *Real life teens: Cyberbullying* [Educational video]. USA: Author.

Too old for Webkinz; To young for Facebook. (2008, July 29). *Businesswire.* Retrieved from http://findarticles.com/p/articles/mi_m0EIN/is_2008_July_29/ai_n27950858

Top ten reviews. (n.d.). *Internet filter software review.* Retrieved from http://www.internet-filter-review.toptenreviews.com/

Treyvaud, R. (2007, August 28). *Don't ask, don't tell: Why Internet safety policy is cracked.* Retrieved from http://www.abc.net.au/news/stories/2007/08/28/2017058.htm

Trusty, J., & Brown, D. (2005). Advocacy competencies for professional school counselors. *Professional School Counseling, 8,* 259–265.

Turkle, S. (1995). *Life on the screen: Identity in the age of the Internet.* New York, NY: Touchstone Books.

Tutton, M. (2009, November 10). *Me 2.0: Branding yourself online.* Retrieved from http://www.cnn.com/2009/BUSINESS/10/29/personal.brand.internet/index.html

2009 top ten Internet dating sites reviewed. (2009). Retrieved from http://datingonlinesitereview.com/online-dating-sites/hello-world/

Tynes, B., Giang, M., Williams, D., & Thompson, G. (2008). Online racial discrimination and psychological adjustment among adolescents. *Journal of Adolescent Health, 43,* 565–569.

United States v. Drew. (2008). Retrieved from http://www.citmedialaw.org/threats/united-states-v-drew

University of Delaware Police. (n.d.). *How to view email headers.* Retrieved from http://128.175.24.251/headers.htm

U.S. Department of Justice. (2005). *Indicators of school crime and safety.* Washington, DC: National Center for Education Statistics, Bureau of Justice Statistics.

U.S. Department of Justice. (n.d.) *Model acceptable use policy: Information technology resources in the schools.* Retrieved from http://www.justice.gov/criminal/cybercrime/rules/acceptableUsePolicy.htm

Valkenburg, P. M., & Peter, J. (2007). Preadolescents' and adolescents' online communication and their closeness to friends. *Developmental Psychology, 43,* 267–277.

van der Wal, M. F., de Wit, C. A. M., & Hirasing, R. A. (2003). Psychosocial health among young victims and offenders of direct and indirect bullying. *Pediatrics, 111,* 1312–1317.

Vander Veer, E. (2008). *Facebook: The missing manual.* Sebastopol, CA: O'Reilly Media.

Varjas, K., Henrich, C. C., & Meyers, J. (2009). Urban middle school students' perceptions of bullying, cyberbullying, and school safety. *Journal of School Violence, 8,* 159–176.

Veenstra, R., Lindenberg, S., Oldehinkel, A. J., DeWinter, A. F., Verhulst, F. C., & Ormel, J. (2005). Bullying and victimization in elementary schools: A comparison of bullies, victims, bully/victims, and uninvolved preadolescents. *Developmental Psychology, 41,* 672–682.

Violence Against Women and Department of Justice Reauthorization Act of 2005, Pub. L. No. 109–162, 119 Stat. 2960 (2006).

Virginia Department of Education. (n.d.). *Acceptable use policies: A handbook.* Retrieved from http://www.doe.virginia.gov/VDOE/Technology/AUP/home.shtml

Vlingo. (2009). *More than one in four mobile phone users drive while texting.* Retrieved from http://www.vlingo.com/pdf/Vlingo%20DWT%20FINAL.pdf

Walsh, D. (2004). *WHY do they act that way? A survival guide to the adolescent brain for you and your teen.* New York, NY: Free Press.

Wang, J., Iannotti, R. J., & Nansel, T. R. (2009). School bullying among adolescents in the United States: Physical, verbal, relational, and cyber. *Journal of Adolescent Health, 45,* 368–375.

WAPT.com. (2009, July 29). *Cheerleader sues school for $100M over Facebook message.* Retrieved from http://www.wapt.com/news/20208919/detail.html

Warner, E., & Hutton, T. (2009, February 5*). Greying gadgets: How older Americans view consumer electronics* [Webinar]. Retrieved from http://www.scribd.com/doc/12183604/CEA-Webinar-Slides-Greying-Gadgets-How-Older-Americans-Shop-for-and-Use-Consumer-Electronics

Wechsler, H., Nelson, T. F., Lee, J. E., Siebring, M., Lewis, C., & Keeling, R. P. (2003). Norms marketing interventions to reduce college students' heavy alcohol use. *Journal of Studies on Alcohol, 54,* 484–494.

Weinberger, D. R., Elvevåg, B., & Giedd, J. N. (2005). *The adolescent brain: A work in progress* (A report of the National Campaign to Prevent Teen Pregnancy). Available at http://www.thenationalcampaign.org/resources/pdf/BRAIN.pdf

Weiner, B. (1986). Attribution, emotion, and action. In R. M. Sorrentino & E. T. Higgins (Eds.), *Motivation & cognition: Foundations of social behavior* (pp. 281–310). New York, NY: Guilford.

Weiner, B. (1992). *Human motivation: Metaphors, theories, and research.* New York, NY: Guilford.

Werner, N. E., Bumpus, M. F., & Rock, D. (in press). Involvement in Internet aggression during early adolescence. *Journal of Youth and Adolescence.*

West, A., & Salmon, G. (2000). Bullying and depression: A case report. *International Journal of Psychiatry in Clinical Practice, 4,* 73–75.

Willard, N. E. (2007a). The authority and responsibility of school officials in responding to cyberbullying. *Journal of Adolescent Health, 41,* S64–S65.

Willard, N. E. (2007b). *Cyberbullying and cyberthreats.* Champaign, IL: Research Press.

Williams, I. (2007, July 24). *Cyberbullying rife in UK business.* Retrieved from http://www.v3.co.uk/vnunet/news/2194824/cyber-bullying-rife-uk-business

Williams, K. R., & Guerra, N. G. (2007). Prevalence and predictors of Internet bullying. *Journal of Adolescent Health, 41,* S14–S21.

Wilson, J. (2008). *What to know before buying your kid a cell phone.* Retrieved from http://www.cnn.com/2008/TECH/ptech/08/11/cellphones.kids/index.html

Wireless quick facts. (2009). Retrieved from http://www.ctia.org/advocacy/research/index.cfm/AID/10323

Wolak, J., Mitchell, K. M., & Finkelhor, D. (2007). Does online harassment constitute bullying? An exploration of online harassment by known peers and online-only contacts. *Journal of Adolescent Health, 41,* S51–S58.

Yalom, I. (1995). *Theory and practice of group psychotherapy* (4th ed.). New York, NY: Basic Books.

Ybarra, M. L., Diener-West, M., & Leaf, P. J. (2007). Examining the overlap in Internet harassment and school bullying: Implications for school intervention. *Journal of Adolescent Health, 41,* S42–S50.

Ybarra, M. L., Espelage, D. L., & Mitchell, K. M. (2007). The co-occurrence of Internet harassment and unwanted sexual solicitation victimization and perpetration: Associations with psychosocial indicators. *Journal of Adolescent Health, 41,* S31–S41.

Ybarra, M. L., & Mitchell, K. J. (2004). Online aggressor/targets, aggressors, and targets: A comparison of associated youth characteristics. *Journal of Child Psychology and Psychiatry, 45,* 1308–1316.

Ybarra, M. L., Mitchell, K. J., Wolak, J., & Finkelhor, D. (2006). Examining characteristics and associated distress related to Internet harassment: Findings from the second Youth Internet Safety Survey. *Pediatrics, 118,* 1169–1177.

Yoon, J. S., & Kerber, K. (2003). Bullying: Elementary teachers' attitudes and intervention strategies. *Research in Education, 69,* 27–34.

Young, S. (1998). The support group approach to bullying in schools. *Educational Psychology in Practice, 14,* 32–39.

Young, S. (2002). *Solutions to bullying.* Stoke-on-Trent, United Kingdom: NASEN.

Young, S., & Holdorf, G. (2003). Using solution-focused brief therapy in individual referrals for bullying. *Educational Psychology in Practice, 19,* 271–282.

Yurgelun-Todd, D. (2002). *Inside the teenage brain* [*Frontline* interview]. Retrieved from http://www.pbs.org/wgbh/pages/frontline/shows/teen-brain/interviews/todd.html

Zdanowicz, C. (2009, December 10). *Social media brings bullying to light.* Retrieved from http://www.cnn.com/2009/CRIME/12/10/social.media.bullying/index.html

INDEX

Figures and tables are indicated by "f" and "t" following page numbers.

(continued)

I

J

K

L

M

P